D1689727

Creole Houses

Creole Houses
TRADITIONAL HOMES OF OLD LOUISIANA

PHOTOGRAPHS BY STEVE GROSS AND SUE DALEY

COMMENTARY BY JOHN H. LAWRENCE

FOREWORD BY JAMES CONAWAY

ABRAMS, NEW YORK

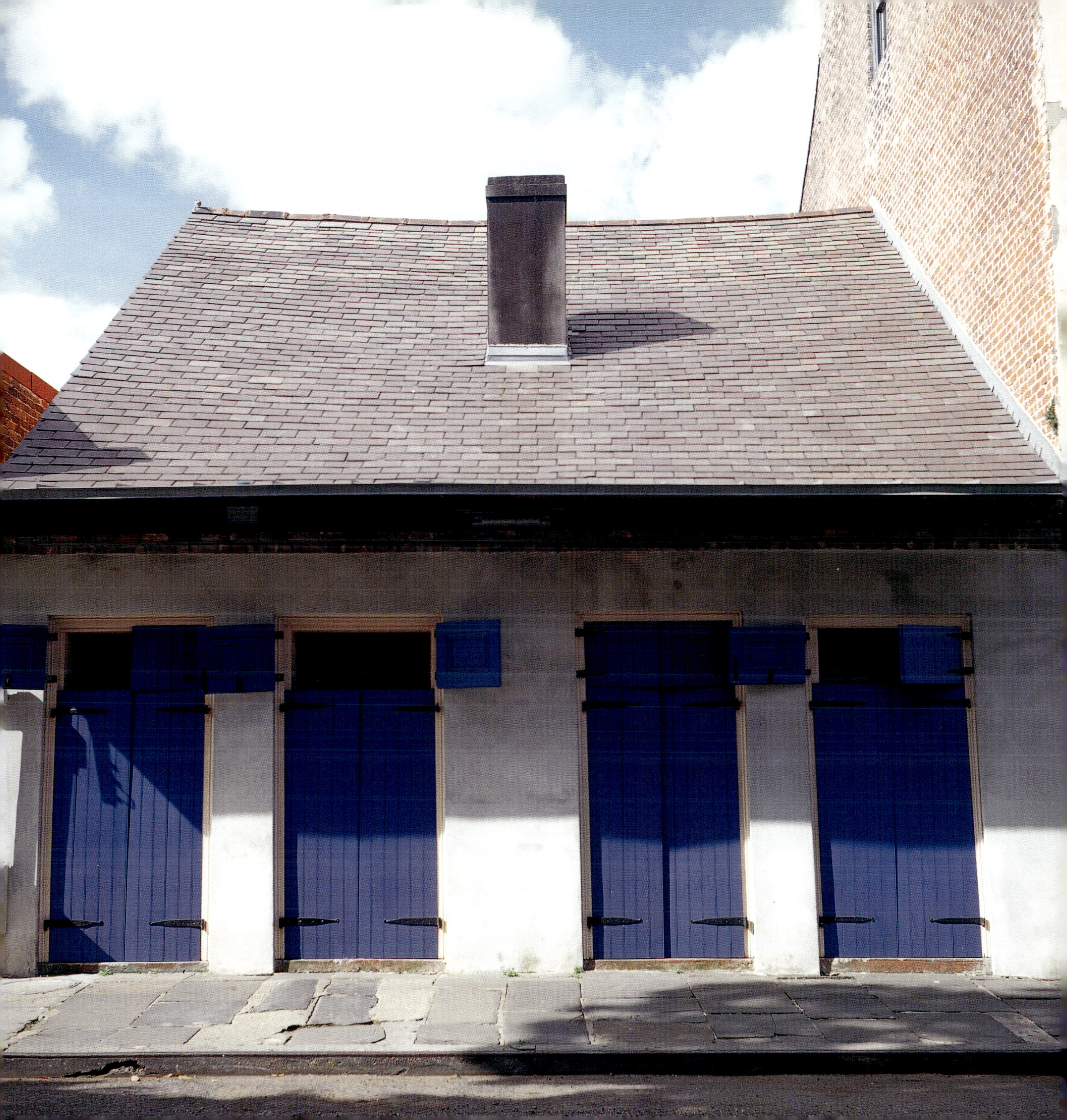

Table of Contents

6 ACKNOWLEDGMENTS

8 FOREWORD: Still Standing, Still Inspiring
    by James Conaway

20 A Note on Louisiana's Creole Culture

24 NEW ORLEANS
- 26 Pitot House
- 34 Bourgoyne House
- 44 Cooper-Thomann House
- 52 Patout Cottage
- 60 The Pontalba Buildings
- 66 O'Brien Cottage

72 RIVER ROAD
- 74 Laura Plantation
- 82 Chêne Vert
- 90 Magnolia Mound

98 POINTE COUPÉE
- 100 Austerlitz Plantation
- 108 Maison Chenal
- 116 Parlange Plantation
- 126 Lacour House
- 132 Jaques Dupre House

138 THE BAYOU COUNTRY
- 140 Couret Plantation
- 148 Acadian Village
- 154 Hilaire Lancon House
- 162 Dumesnil House

168 NATCHITOCHES AND CANE RIVER
- 170 Tante Huppé House
- 176 Wells House
- 182 Cherokee Plantation

190 SUGGESTED READING

PAGE 1: Family portraits, like the ones displayed at Laura Plantation in Vacherie, are fundamental elements of Creole decor.

PAGE 3: Perrin-Ransdell House, on Saint Philip Street in New Orleans's Vieux Carré, is a classic early-1800s Creole cottage.

OPPOSITE: The "rolling pin" on headboards like this one from Abbeville could be detached and used to smooth out lumps in the mattress.

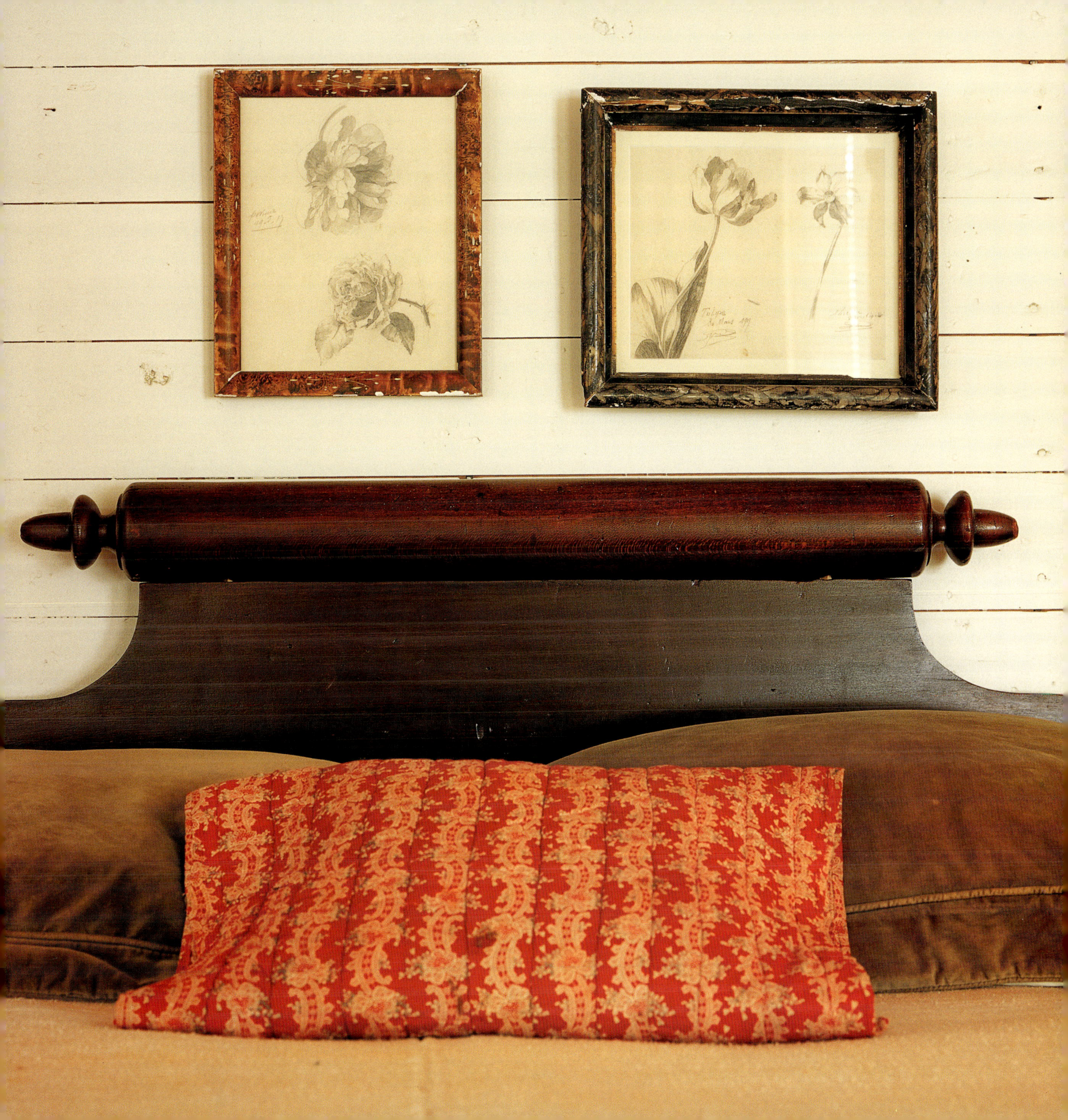

THIS BOOK IS DEDICATED TO THE PEOPLE OF LOUISIANA, WHOSE RICH CULTURE AND TENACITY ARE INSPIRATIONS TO US ALL.

Acknowledgments

We would like to thank all the homeowners and museum curators who gave us their time, let us photograph, and so helpfully shared the stories of their houses. Special thanks to Pat and Jack Holden and also to Peter Patout for their advice and generous hospitality. Steve and Sue Stirling and the parishioners of Saint Mary's Church in Franklin most graciously let us stay at the Trowbridge House. Thanks to Bobby DeBlieux, who helped spark the idea for this book more than twenty years ago. He has been an invaluable guide to many amazing houses.

Many others were very encouraging along the way: Gene Cizek, Lloyd Sensat, Beth and Joe Rougon, Danny Ackers, Gladys Stephens, Jay Bourgoyne, Jay Tyburski, Albert Belton, Amanda Chenault, Paul Fitch, Anton J. Warr Sr., Bonnie Mabry, Betty Herzog, Michel Delsol, Mabel Ginsburg, Andy Reaux, and especially Wade Lege, who saved the day. Apologies to the other wonderful Creole houses that we couldn't include due to lack of space.

Thanks to Leigh McGowan for bluebonnets and boudin, and thanks to Mary Cooper and Tomio Thomann for the memorable dinners. A special thanks to Edith, Ernie, and Nick for all their help.

We are most grateful to John H. Lawrence for his eloquent and informative text and to James Conaway for his thoughtful foreword. Finally, we thank our editors, Eric Himmel and Nancy Cohen, and everyone at Harry N. Abrams for their enthusiastic support and the tremendous care they took with this book, and Bob McKee for his exceptionally beautiful design.

STEVE GROSS AND SUE DALEY

The information gathered here comes from many sources and individuals. The owners of the homes in this volume graciously allowed me to invade their lives and elicit their properties' lively histories. All were hospitable beyond compare and eager to assist my work in any way. I wish to especially acknowledge invaluable assistance from Mary Cooper and Tomio Thomann, Peter Patout, Pat and Jack Holden, Wayne and Cheryl Stromeyer, Meg Lousteau (former director of Pitot House), Steve and Suzanne Stirling, Beth and Joe Rougon, Bobby DeBlieux, Sis Hollensworth, Sand and Norman Marmillion, Lucy and Walter Parlange, Terry Cox (director of Magnolia Mound), Pat O'Brien, Jay Bourgoyne, Jay Tyburski, and Carol Wells.

For answering specific questions on Louisiana's furniture history, Peter Patout, the Holdens, and H. Parrott Bacot have both my admiration for their knowledge and my gratitude for sharing it with me. I am deeply in debt to the authors listed in the Suggested Reading for their often pioneering and always careful research on the subjects that encompass Louisiana's Creole history, architecture, and culture.

Finally, sincere thanks to my wife, Priscilla Lawrence, whose encouragement, support, and good cheer have been indispensable to the successful completion of this project.

JOHN H. LAWRENCE

The primary entrance to a Creole town house is the porte cochere, or covered passage. Leading from a gateway at the sidewalk to a rear courtyard or garden, it provides a sheltered transition from the public realm to the private one.

The interior of the Napoleon House, with its atmospheric lighting, conveys a timeworn gentility. This town house in New Orleans's Vieux Carré, built at the turn of the nineteenth century, has been owned and operated as a bar and restaurant by one family since 1914.

Foreword: Still Standing, Still Inspiring

The link between romance and menace in New Orleans is, for me, left over from the 1960s. The port city's exuberant friction made my opportunities as a young newspaper reporter and marked me forever with its peculiar sensibilities. Here the beautiful and decrepit—cast-iron balconies holding up tottering facades along Royal and Chartres streets, crumbling bougainvillea-wrapped columns in the Garden District—contrasted wildly with the bump-and-grind garishness of Bourbon Street and the low-rent commerce in the hot light of Magazine Street in those days before regentrification. The city's particular scent blended coffee roasting in the Irish Channel, deep-fried oysters and garlic surging from restaurant exhaust fans, the acrid electric flash from the cable above the trolley car, funereal magnolias, rain-washed patios, the distinctive perfume of marijuana drifting from an alley, a rich undercurrent of rotting fruit, and the earthiness of the roiling Mississippi River. Everywhere the closeness of moist air abetted appetite and desire.

I arrived in 1965, the same day as Hurricane Betsy, and consumed too much Dixie beer with a friend. I woke the next morning to the sight of wind-felled trees in the streets and made my way to the *Times-Picayune,* the first person to arrive. I sat for an hour reading old editions of the newspaper before the city editor came in, gazed through the grimy panes, and told me to go out and write a story about the effects of the storm.

Cheers!
The Esquire Guide to the 100 Best Bars in America
A Toast
NAPOLEON HOUSE
CHEERS

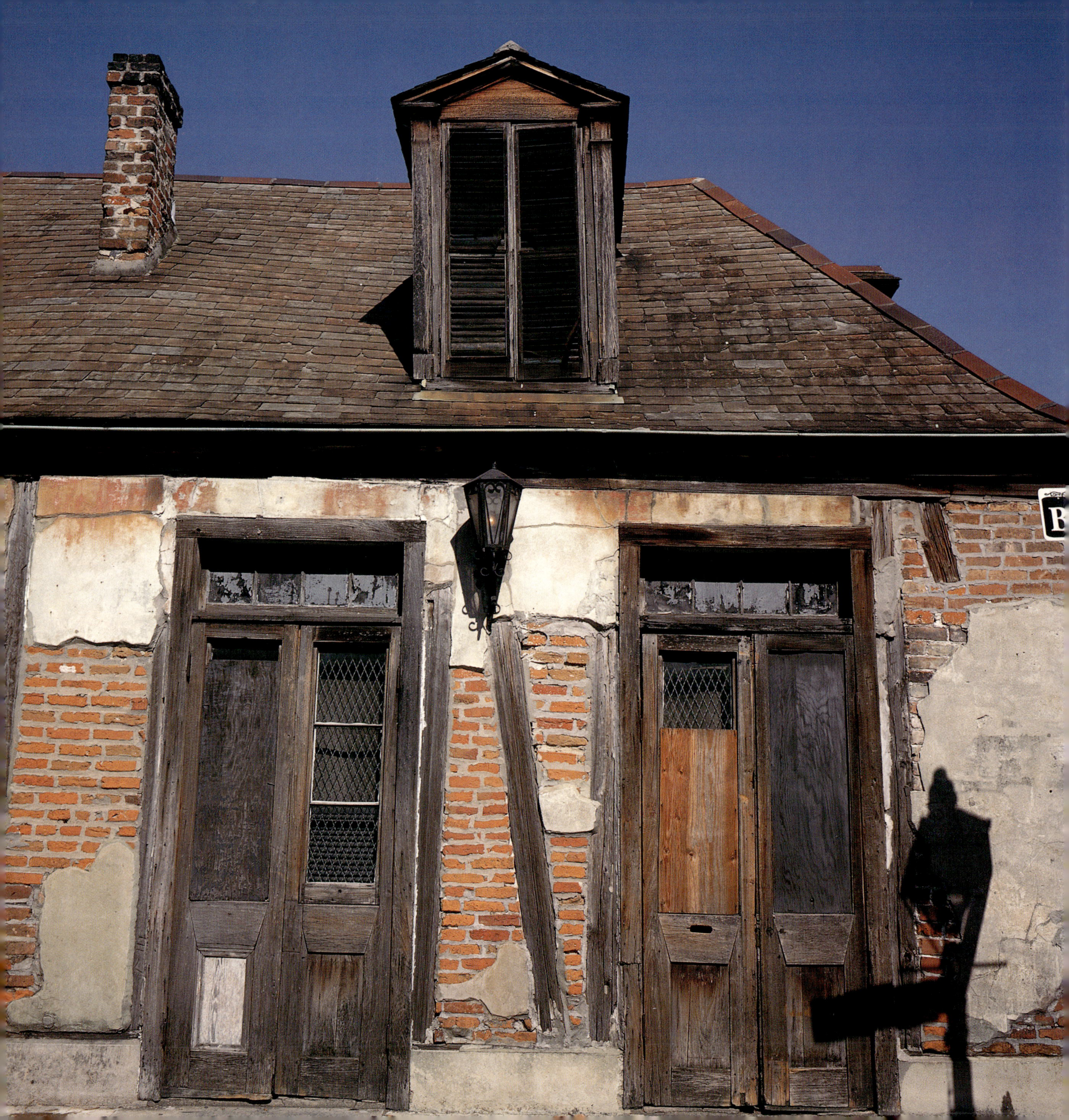

Lafitte's Blacksmith Shop, built in the late 1700s, stands on Bourbon Street in the French Quarter. The hipped-roof Creole cottage now serves as a tavern. Its brick-between-posts construction is clearly displayed; only patches remain of the stucco that once weatherproofed the understructure of soft brick and timber.

I knew nothing about New Orleans but quickly learned about human suffering at and just above sea level. I had never taken a journalism course or written a newspaper article, but since I was the only reporter available—everyone else was tending to home and family—my story appeared on the front page with a byline. So indelible were the images that they reappeared in my first novel, *The Big Easy*, a few years later: "There were so many drowned and bloated bodies that he could smell the morgue from two blocks away; the city was crippled, with hundreds of old shotgun houses shoved off the foundations, the streets of the Ninth Ward covered with ooze, left by receding floodwaters. He could still hear the supernatural keening of the killer wind, the pop of windows sucked outward in the fury."

That storm brought unprecedented misery to the most accepting city in America. Betsy caused at least seventy deaths and was the first hurricane to wreak more than a billion dollars of damage. The destruction spurred the Army Corps of Engineers to build a new ring of levees—the very levees that would fail New Orleans during Hurricane Katrina in 2005. The same disasters recurred that year—though on an exponentially worse scale. Many of the same lessons were taught. Perhaps they were learned this time.

My own education, over the course of my first year in New Orleans, included some of its incredibly diverse, chaotic past ("colorful" is an inadequate description). It was a history lesson full of po'boys, crawfish étouffé, and oysters in various incarnations—one preparation named for Jean-Baptiste Le Moyne, sieur de Bienville, who founded New Orleans in 1718. It took in Cajuns and characters like Andrew Jackson, Benjamin "Spoons" Butler, the Union major general who ruled the city briefly during the Union occupation, and Huey Long, Louisiana's flamboyant governor and a nationally known populist who was gunned down in 1935. And through it all ran streets with names like Terpsichore, Elysian Fields, Desire—avenues of myth, literature, and seduction.

My wife, Penny, our infant son, Brennan, and I moved into a house on Pleasant Street, in the Garden District, two blocks from Prytania Street, where F. Scott Fitzgerald supposedly corrected proofs of *The Great Gatsby*. Nearby was an old cemetery, full of stone crosses and moldering crypts that held the remains of earlier citizens—Confederate generals, yellow fever victims, and immigrant laborers alike. Here in "uptown" New Orleans, west of Canal Street, the city shed its commercial and roustabout elements and took on an antebellum somnolence, with columned porches, dense shrubbery obscuring glossy white facades, towering ceilings, overhead fans, and second-story galleries where families once sat of an evening.

Our house was long and narrow, a variety of a shotgun house. I had never heard that term before moving to New Orleans: It meant that a shot could be fired through the front door and travel the length of the interior—in theory, of course—hitting nothing before sailing out the back door. The rooms opened directly into each other, without any hallways, and the doorways lined up in a row. Our second-floor digs had both a side gallery over the landlady's profuse garden and a front balcony overlooking other quaint shotgun cottages across the street. They were built on narrow lots; New Orleanians generally lived in close proximity to each other, often without regard for class and race.

Perhaps that attitude stemmed from New Orleanians' broadly spread roots, which reached from Europe to the Caribbean and Africa to create a uniquely Creole city. The notion of "Creole" is essential to understanding New Orleans and other parts of Louisiana—the people as well as the architecture. The word literally means "of the place," or homegrown, and is a designation claimed with pride by descendants of Louisiana's original French and Spanish settlers, although the category is sometimes stretched to include early immigrants from other countries—even Ireland. (Creoles of color are those whose lineage includes African and/or Native American as well as European ancestry.) The word's broader meaning—often misunderstood outside Louisiana—is more cultural than racial and derives from the non–Anglo-Saxon life-style that flourished before 1803, when Louisiana became part of the United States. Creoles were concerned with social status and avoided ostentation—although, as is always the case in New Orleans, there were exceptions of the most flamboyant kind, like Mardi Gras and jazz funerals. They were far from puritans, and they liked to party—clear holdovers in today's Big Easy and its surrounds.

And they loved fabulous food, another lasting Creole legacy. The cuisine draws from many cultures—French, Spanish, West Indian, and African among them—generally adapting European technique to local foods to produce a rich, creamy tradition all its own. Many recipes begin with a roux, flour browned slowly in butter or oil on top of the stove, which becomes a binding and base for a panoply of ingredients. True Creole taste is harder to find in restaurants these days, muted by the demands of tourists and the depravations imposed by nouvelle cuisine, although takeoffs on traditional Louisiana cooking do produce some wonderful modern-day adaptations: crawfish-and-andouille cheesecake, for instance, or crispy smoked quail salad with pears and bourbon molasses dressing. As a friend and longtime New Orleanian puts it, "New Orleans no longer has five hundred restaurants and five recipes"—gumbo, jambalaya, shrimp remoulade, red beans and rice, and anything deep-fried—but many exciting variations on a Creole theme.

Creoles combined practicality with a love of both life and beauty. As the wonderful photographs in this book show, they applied this gentle harmony to their architecture as well, creating houses of simple, understated good looks and essential utility. Evidence of the latter lives on in the abodes of a wide variety of sizes and styles that have proved equal to the subtropical elements, including floods and high winds, further testament to the genius of their builders. Their keen understanding of their environment and their willingness to accommodate its realities serve as good—and often ignored—examples for contemporary society.

The origins of the architectural style remain a bit of a mystery, like many things in this terrain; the cultures it draws from are as varied as France, the West Indies, and Canada, from which the French-speaking Acadians, or Cajuns, began arriving in the 1760s. Even the Italians may have gotten in on the act, contributing a double loggia they had exported to the Caribbean. West Indians brought a variation of that loggia to Louisiana, where it was transformed into an expanded gallery.

New Orleans sits in a big-bellied loop of the river that at one point flows northeast. It is a densely packed city, with overlapping neighborhoods resonant of its past. Canal Street begins at the river and runs more or less north, neatly dividing the French Quarter—the Vieux Carré, the historic heart of New Orleans—from the commercial district to its west. Canal Street originally partitioned the Creole residents of the Vieux Carré from the Americans—generally wealthy businessmen of British extraction—who arrived in waves after the Louisiana Purchase, swelling the city's population. The Americans established their own jurisdiction west of Canal—and the Creoles were happy to maintain a separation from the newcomers. They proudly defended their languid,

At the north end of Jackson Square stands the imposing Saint Louis Cathedral, established on this site in the Vieux Carré in the 1720s. The present structure dates from a mid-1800s expansion and rebuilding. To the left is the Spanish-era Cabildo, or town hall, constructed in 1799 and modified in 1847 with the addition of a French-style mansard roof. Jackson Square (so named in 1851) has been New Orleans's gathering place since the city was laid out in 1721.

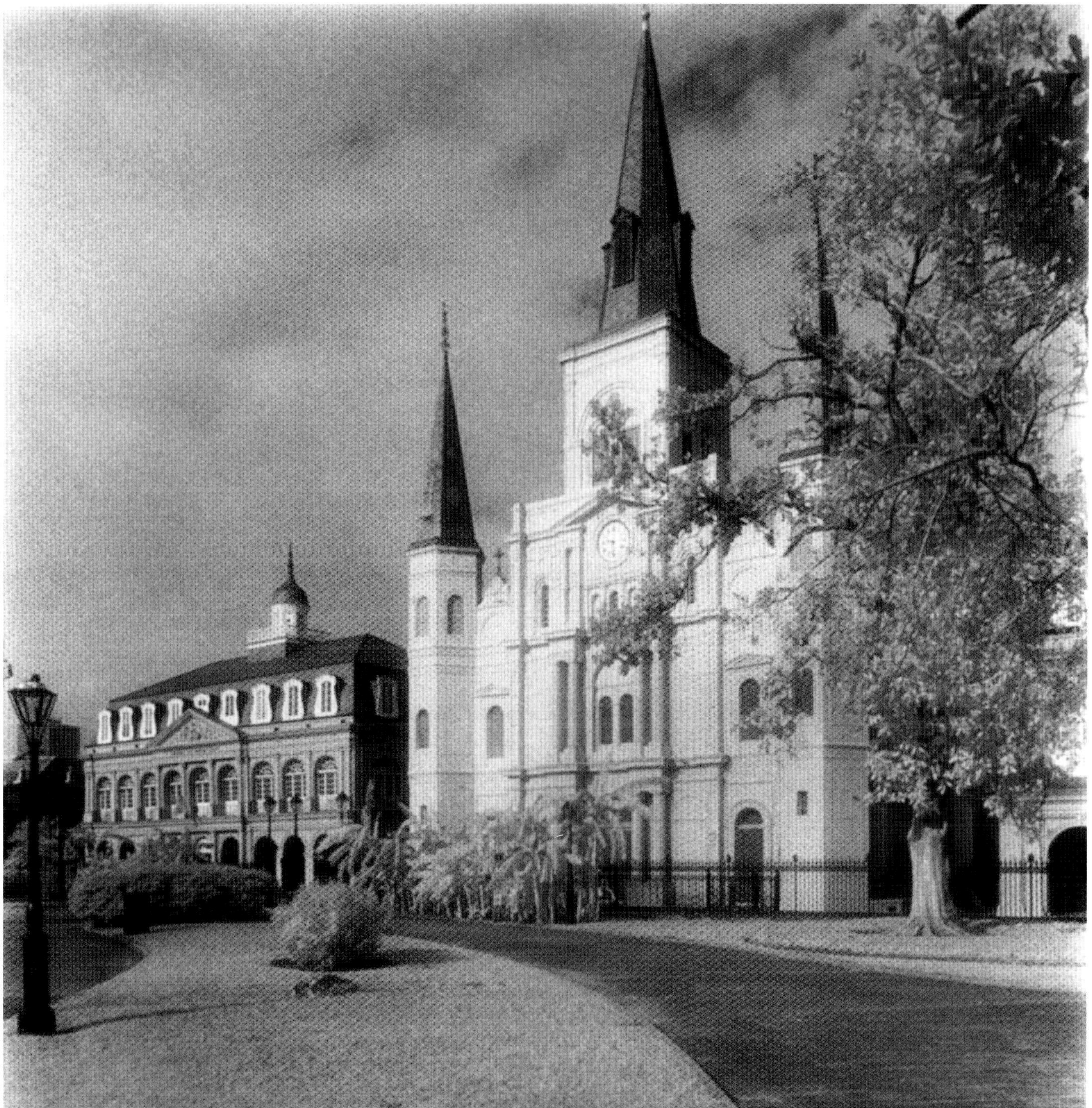

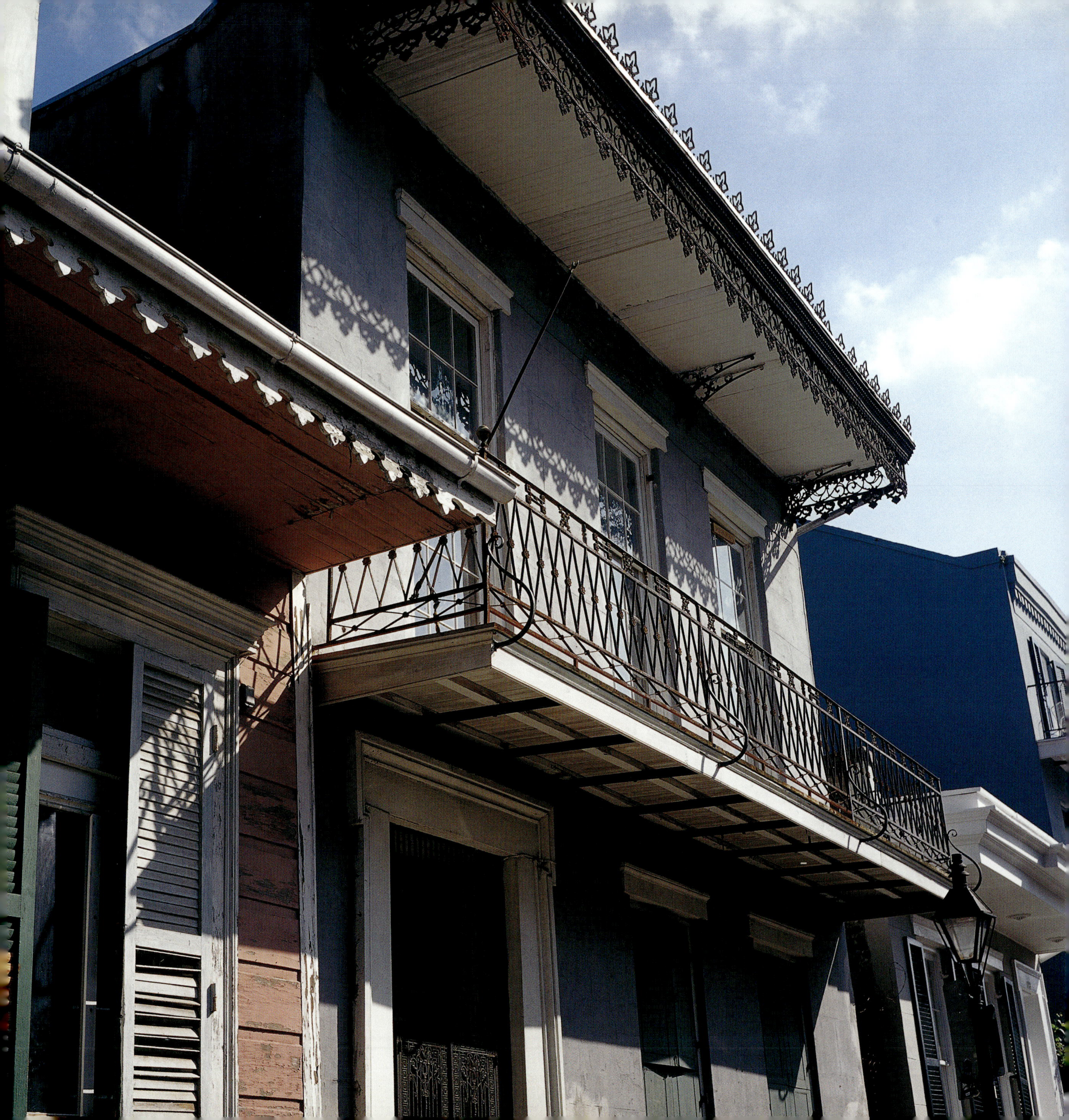

OPPOSITE

Frances Benjamin Johnston, a pioneering photographer, lived in this mid-1800s Bourbon Street town house from 1945 until her death, at age eighty-eight, in 1952. West Virginia–born, she chose to retire in the French Quarter, which she found bohemian and romantic.

RIGHT

This stuccoed brick French Quarter town house was built in 1836; the cast-iron galleries were added later. In contrast to many multistory residences in the Quarter, Gardette-Lepretre House did not devote the ground floor to commercial space but was used entirely as a home—a reflection of its owner's wealth. It was constructed by a prosperous dentist, Joseph Coulon Gardette, who sold it several years later to Jean Baptiste Lepretre, a banker and planter.

continental-style culture (and their French language) against the American incursion, even after the state's admission to the Union in 1812. But over time, national and ethnic squabbles were obscured by the city's ongoing, relentless mixing.

Trade expanded, the city prospered, and the French Quarter, today virtually synonymous with hedonistic pastimes and the colorful satisfaction of various appetites, became "downtown." It was the Quarter that charmed every visitor—as it still does—with its narrow streets and iron-balconied Creole houses built flush to the pavement. Many of the buildings had—or still have—shops at ground level and living quarters above, opening onto secluded gardens at the rear.

Perhaps the most famous examples of Creole architecture in the Quarter are the Pontalba residences that rise three full stories on opposite sides of Jackson Square. Considered some of the oldest apartment buildings in America, they were built as row houses by Micaela Almonester de Pontalba, the daughter of the man who financed the construction of Saint Louis Cathedral, the Cabildo, and the Presbytere on the north side of the square. The Pontalba Buildings are accurately described in *The Smithsonian's Guide to Historic America* as "Neoclassical in a casual Creole way," a description that applies to many structures in New Orleans. The relatively elegant residences on the upper levels have attracted artists and creative types since their completion in 1850. Sherwood Anderson, the famed author of short stories, lived there in the early twentieth century.

The expansive red-brick Pontalba Buildings struck me on first viewing as the most romantic vision of life in the American subtropics, close to both God (the cathedral) and sybaritic Decatur Street. So inspired was I by the stacked balconies, the wide floorboards, and the high ceilings that years later I moved the protagonist of my second novel, *World's End,* into an apartment on the top floor of the western building. His name was Michael Duran and in the evening he liked to have a drink overlooking the square, the French Market, and the promenade beyond. "The street lights had come on, and the coolness of the rain lingered. The oven of summer was contracting, bringing the threat of hurricane. Lovers strolled on the levee, and downstream a powerful light blazed . . . flickering in the distance, beckoning."

Another of my favorite Creole buildings is the Napoleon House at the corner of Chartres and Orleans, built in 1798. Originally a six-bay Spanish colonial town house that was home to the city's mayor, it was expanded to three stories with cupola, supposedly to serve as Napoléon's retreat after his escape from exile. But Bonaparte never made it to the Louisiana he had so unceremoniously sold to Thomas Jefferson and the United States, and his eponymous dwelling was consigned to being simply the best bar anywhere, with peeling walls, inner double doors typical of Creole dwellings, a phonograph, and stacks of records any customer can play. I remember a scratchy but apt version of the 1812 Overture, which Tchaikovsky wrote to commemorate the Napoleonic defeat in Russia.

Penny, Brennan, and I would leave the city on weekends and travel west into the countryside, often by way of River Road, the route along the Mississippi that is lined with Creole houses. Some rural Creole houses have a beautiful simplicity; others are opulent—grand pillared plantation houses amid spreading live oaks hung with Spanish moss. All hearken back to the sensible art of builders who designed for the probable: not just for ease and convenience, but also in anticipation of unwelcome visitations by the river, rising damp, and ravenous insects. It is no surprise that the raised plantation houses for the most part survived Hurricane Katrina.

Their main living areas rest atop brick pillars and walls of what are essentially aboveground basements that allow air to circulate beneath the house proper, expose the upper floors to breezes, and keep the living quarters above water during floods. This ground floor was sometimes partitioned to provide discrete spaces for dining rooms, warming kitchens, and storage of food, wine, and carriages. The porches had deep eaves and sometimes encircled the house, shielding it from rain and sun. Stairs on the outside of the house connected the first- and second-story galleries. Lovely hipped roofs helped alleviate the heat.

Longleaf pine was one popular building material, but virgin cypress abounded in southern Louisiana and proved to be ideal since it was also strong and flexible—a near-miraculous medium that defied the considerable environmental challenges and was attractive as well. Cypress also was used for hand-crafted furniture, including the armoires that took

OPPOSITE
This building on Bayou Saint John is popularly known as the Spanish Custom House, although history offers no credible evidence that it ever served as such. It is likely a reconstruction or remodeling done about 1807 of a house dating from 1780, when the site was a working plantation. In classic Creole style, the two-story house has a double gallery across the front, brick columns along the lower level, and lighter wooden colonnettes above.

LEFT
Beyond the garden statuary—a recurring feature of the Creole landscape—stands the magnificent Shadows on the Teche, in New Iberia. This white-columned brick plantation house, constructed in 1831–34, is set amid lush greenery and towering live oak trees.

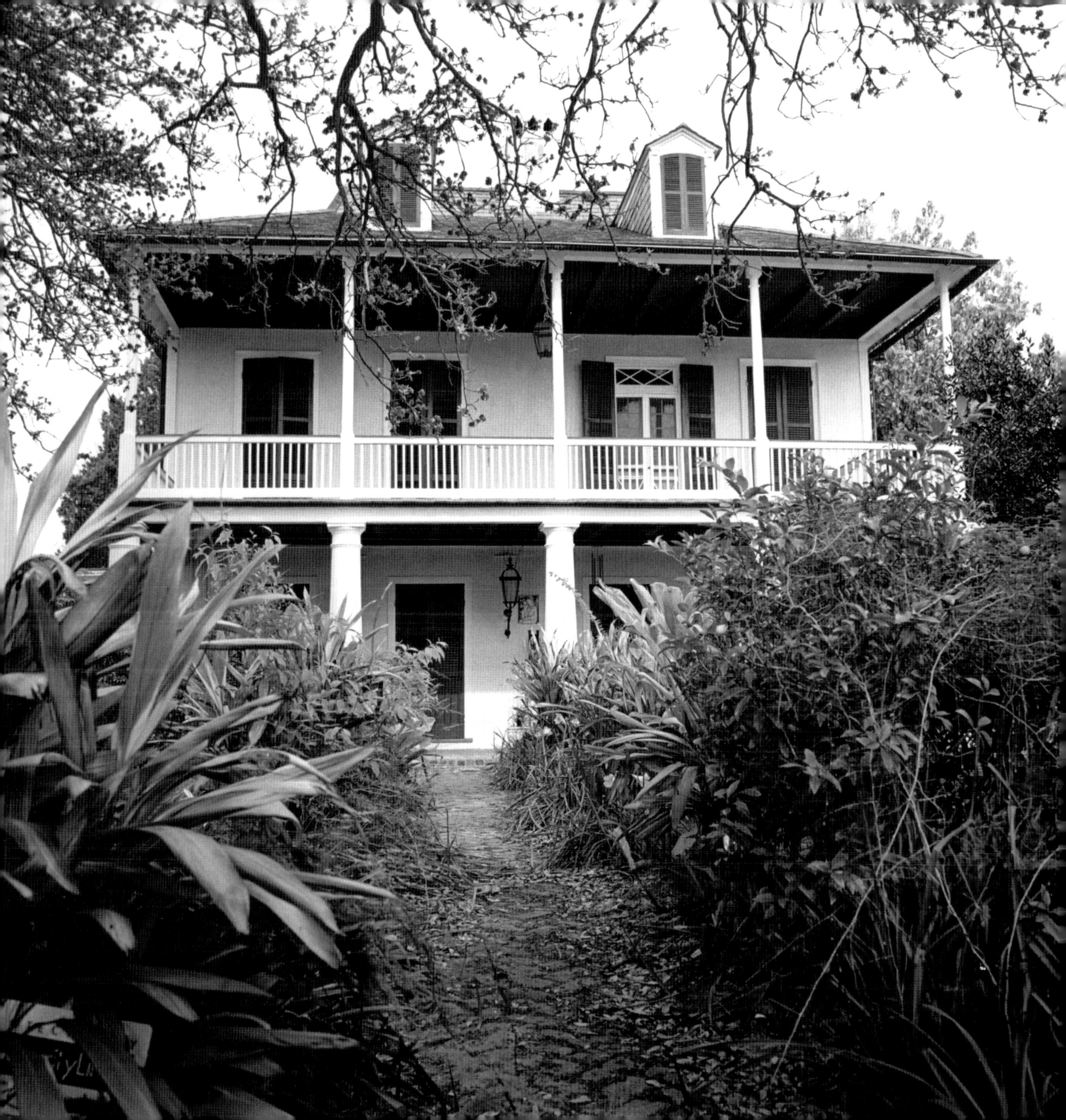

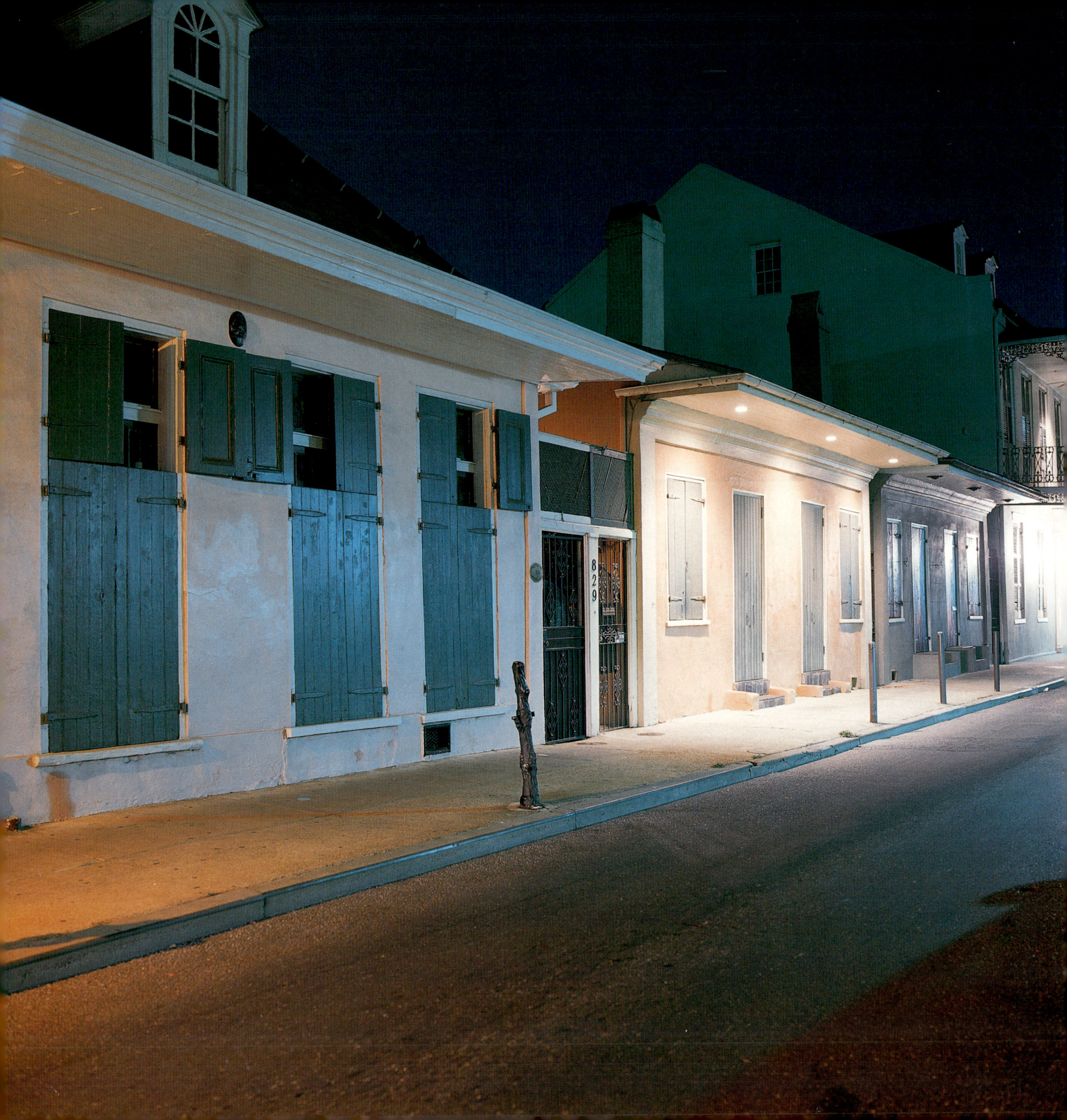
829

Though now illuminated by electricity rather than gaslight or oil lamps, this block of Creole cottages and town houses in the Vieux Carré looks much as it did in the mid-nineteenth century. These archetypal cottages each exhibits the protective overhang called an abat-vent and four symmetrically arranged, shuttered openings (two doors and two windows).

the place of closets in Creole country. So plentiful and resistant to the elements was Louisiana cypress that it found its way to the West Indies to be used for the same purposes; exporting cypress lumber was one of the state's first successful mercantile enterprises.

In many Creole houses, both urban and rural, timber was used just for the frames. The walls were constructed of an infill, either brick or *bousillage*—a medley of earth, animal hair, Spanish moss, and sometimes burned oyster shells—affordable, widely available, and effective insulation. (The residue of Louisiana's protean oyster appetite appears in some of the most original recycling anywhere. Driveways and back roads are often made of crushed shells left over from the state's favorite pastime, dining.)

New Orleans today includes twenty distinct neighborhoods on the National Register of Historic Places, a record for American cities of its size. Of the historic structures left, many are Creole in origin, although just how many is unclear; competition in the numbers game comes from Greek Revival houses, bungalows, and simple shacks raised a few feet above the ground. But Creole planning and construction techniques inform many a house, and it is these that either survived Katrina intact or could be repaired. Many, in the French Quarter and elsewhere, were sited on ground high enough to escape the floodwaters.

As time passes since Katrina's landfall, fewer and fewer houses are covered with blue tarpaulins, the hieroglyphics of disaster when viewed from above and the saviors of many a historic interior. The collective efforts of local and national preservationists have salvaged many Creole and other structures that have inspired—as they will again—not just historians and tourists but also students of the specialties of this enigmatic, fascinating land. Among the unheralded benefits of Katrina is a renewed appreciation of Louisiana's unique architecture. From that has evolved the realization that all could—and still can—be lost without adequate protection from levees and natural barriers in an era of increasingly violent storms.

The strength and resilience of so many of the houses that survived depended, as they always have, on native wood, sound construction, good siting, and that difficult-to-quantify characteristic summed up by the idea of "homegrown" and the pride taken in it.

JAMES CONAWAY

A Note on Louisiana's Creole Culture

France first laid claim to Louisiana—a vast territory stretching from the Gulf of Mexico to Canada, and from the Appalachian Mountains past the Rockies—in 1682. But it did not establish New Orleans, the colony's most celebrated city, until 1718. Four years later New Orleans became capital of La Louisiane, a recognition of the importance of its site near the mouth of the Mississippi River.

Throughout its tenure in North America, France vied with Britain for control of the interior, a struggle that culminated in the French and Indian War. In 1762, as British victory loomed, a treaty transferred to Spain ownership of Louisiana west of the Mississippi River, including New Orleans; the eastern territory went to England in 1763.

During Spain's forty-year reign, the influx of Spanish settlers, including two thousand Canary Islanders, was greatly outnumbered by a surge in French speakers: Acadians driven from Nova Scotia, aristocrats fleeing the French Revolution, and planters escaping West Indian slave rebellions. Louisiana's population also included Native Americans, free blacks, African slaves, and people of German, Irish, and Anglo-American extraction. The colony's richly diverse mix of inhabitants and customs gave rise to a unique Creole culture—one with an aristocratic, European flavor and a markedly French accent.

Even the United States' acquisition of the territory through the Louisiana Purchase in 1803 did not shake the Creoles' French orientation. The population remained largely French in language, culture, and disposition—a proclivity reinforced by the arrival of nearly ten thousand former residents of Saint Domingue after 1804, when the French West Indian colony won its independence as the nation of Haiti.

The Roque House, built about 1780, is located on the Cane River in Natchitoches. It has a characteristically Creole central chimney and wood-shingled hipped roof (with four sides sloping up toward the peak), supported at its edges by cypress posts driven directly into the ground—an early technique that gave way to columns on moisture-resistant blocks or piers.

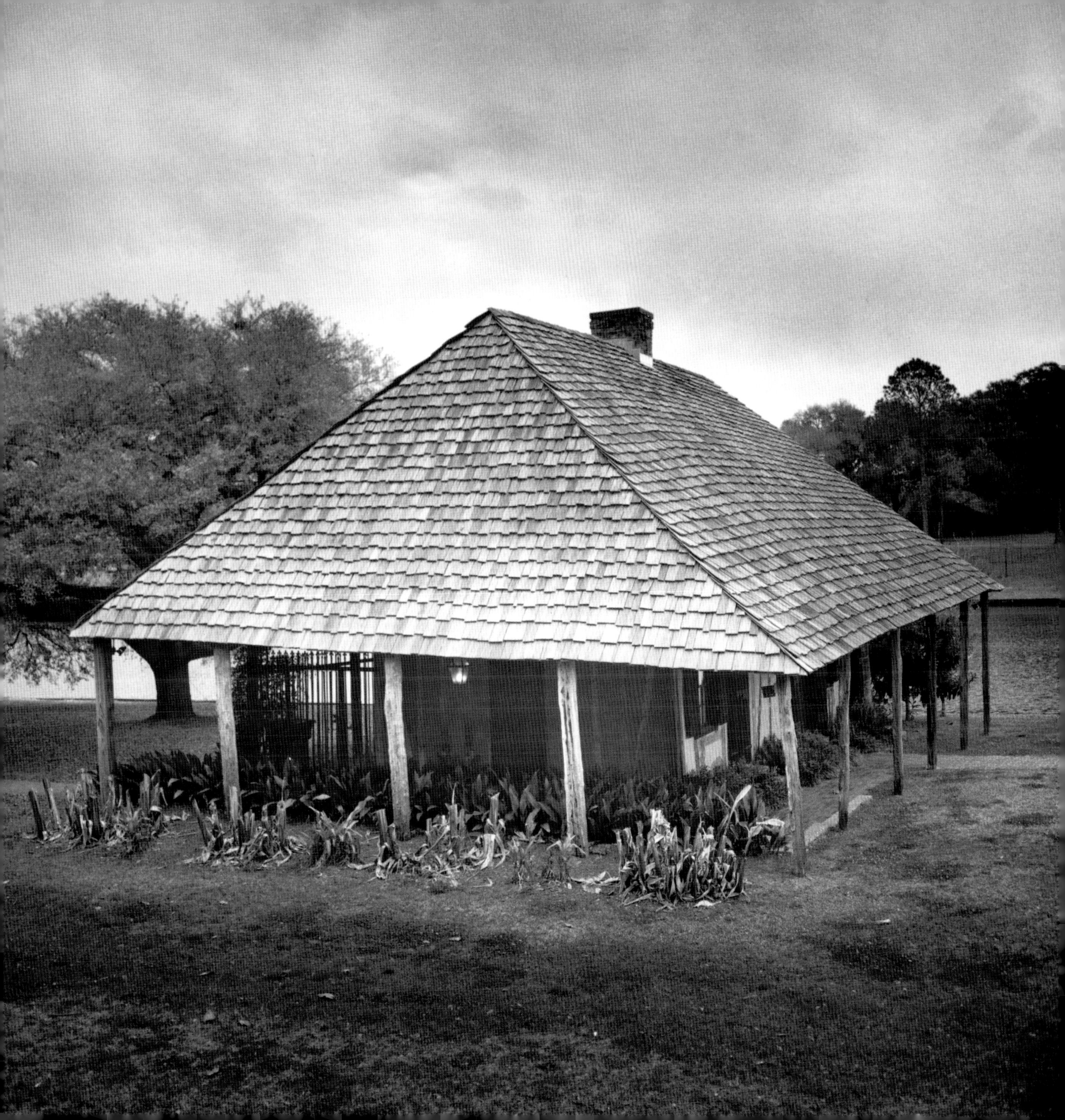

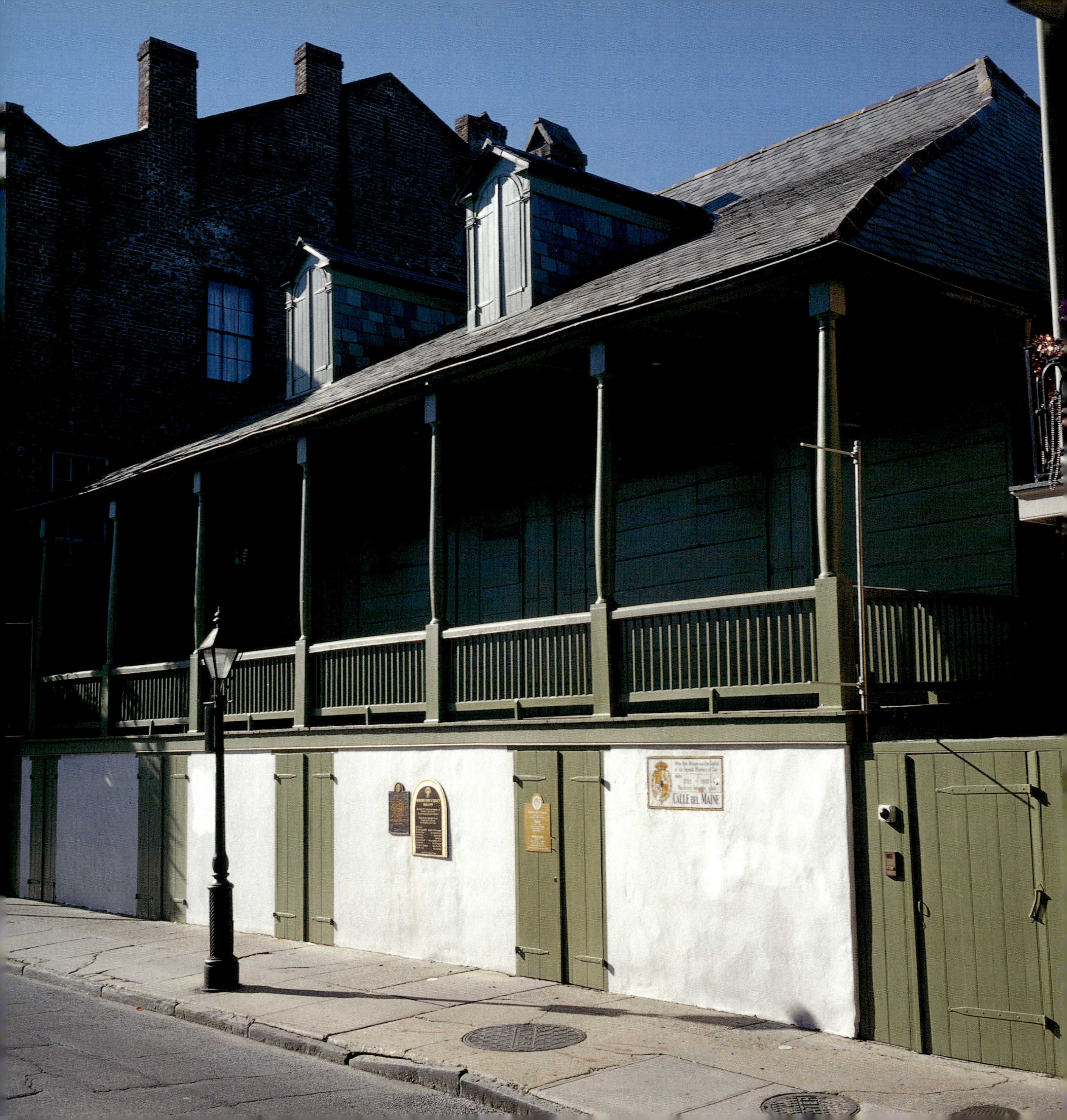
CALLE del MAINE

OPPOSITE
Madame John's Legacy, in the French Quarter, dates from about 1789. (The name springs from a short story by George Washington Cable, in which a woman named Madame John inherits the property.) The double-pitch hipped roof, small dormers, and deep gallery are typical of Louisiana's colonial-era homes. The ground floor, constructed of brick and used for storage, elevated the upper-level living quarters above damp earth.

RIGHT
Yucca House was built about 1796 as the original main residence at what is now called Melrose Plantation, near Natchitoches. The hand-hewn beams are made of local cypress and the thick walls are constructed of *bousillage*, mud mixed with deer hair and Spanish moss. The sturdy, solid shutters provided good security.

So it was a vibrantly French Creole Louisiana that joined the Union as the eighteenth state in 1812. And despite their American citizenship, Creoles proudly viewed themselves as a group apart into the mid-1800s: *Les Américains* were their English-speaking neighbors.

The Creoles' houses primarily drew upon French and Spanish styles and construction techniques, adapting them to the local materials and environment to create a distinctive regional architecture. Characteristic Louisiana buildings—modest cottages, grand town houses, raised cottages in rural locales, and narrow shotgun houses—all share plans, materials, and features meant to foster comfort and ventilation in a hot, humid climate: high ceilings, a lack of interior halls, shallow building depths, overhanging roofs, galleries, shutters, French doors and casement windows, and foundations set well above wet earth and potential floods.

The furnishings reflected the occupants' heritage, wealth, and refined tastes, which were informed by Europe. The Creoles maintained close ties to the Old World through travel and business, and many sent their children to be educated in Paris. Their homes were filled with imported goods and family heirlooms—Louis XVI armchairs, Napoleonic memorabilia, Old Paris porcelains, European textiles, and ancestral portraits. Other signature elements of Creole interiors, such as armoires of native cypress and low-slung *butaca* chairs, were expertly crafted in New Orleans workshops by free men of color and artisans from France. On Creole plantations, slaves skilled in woodworking made furniture as well. Local designs tended to echo French proportions and trends, often modified for greater simplicity.

And all types of goods from around the globe flowed into Louisiana through the port of New Orleans, including silver, cabinetry, and other furnishings produced in cities along the Atlantic seaboard. Well-stocked shops in the Vieux Carré allowed Creole sophisticates to stay current with the latest decorative fashions. Combining the new with pieces that had been in their families for generations, they created a harmonious stylistic language with many dialects.

New Orleans

New Orleans, founded by the French in 1718, was essentially a European city on the banks of the Mississippi. It was designed, like other French cities of the era, with a densely built grid of streets and a central square forming the historic core—the Vieux Carré, today's French Quarter—where buildings were set close to the street and to each other on narrow lots. The arches, ironwork balconies, covered passageways, and secluded gardens that characterize many of the historic structures in the French Quarter today are products of both the French colonial presence and the forty years of Spanish control that succeeded France's rule. However, much of the surviving colonial architecture dates from the Spanish era, as disastrous blazes in 1788 and 1794 destroyed many earlier structures, leading to the adoption of stricter building codes and the use of fire-resistant brick and roofing materials.

As capital of Louisiana, and as a major port near the mouth of the Mississippi River, New Orleans was the most heavily settled area of the vast colony. The French, Spanish, and ultimately the English actively traded there, attracting other immigrants to seek their fortunes in an increasingly prosperous and diverse city.

The city limits steadily expanded over the years to accommodate the swelling population—including the Americans who streamed in after Louisiana joined the Union in 1812, establishing their own sector to the west of the French Quarter. The plantations surrounding the city, divided into building lots, became faubourgs, or suburbs. Consequently, New Orleans today offers fine examples of country-style homes, such as Creole plantation houses, as well as urban forms like town houses and Creole cottages.

Pirate's Alley, in the French Quarter, is lined with ironwork-bedecked houses. It runs a single block, alongside Saint Louis Cathedral, to Jackson Square.

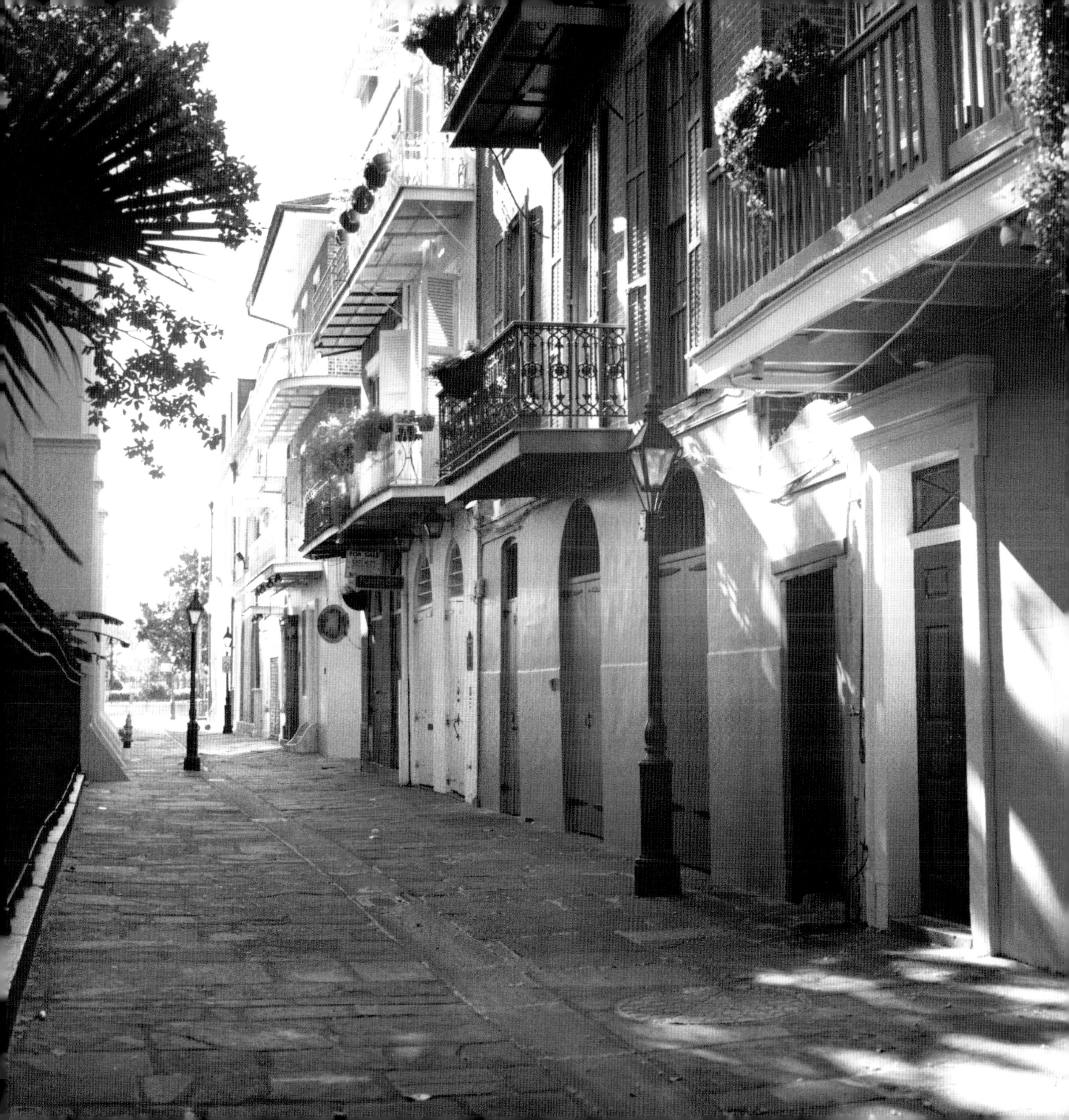

Pitot House

Viewed from across Bayou Saint John, its reflection shimmering in the still water, Pitot House evokes its original appearance at the dawn of the nineteenth century. It is still graced by the traditional front parterre with its beds of flowering plants and fruit trees, which sets it back from the bayou. But extensive lands under cultivation stretched behind it once, and it would have had a rear kitchen garden and numerous outbuildings (including barn, kitchen, and workshops), all of which gave way long ago to an expanding New Orleans. As a result, Pitot House today offers a visual paradox: a plantation manor house of rural character nestled in a city setting.

With its deep gallery, or veranda; massive, plastered brick columns rising from ground level; and imposing roof, Pitot is a quintessential Creole house, with something of a West Indian feeling. Its grandeur makes it seem larger than its actual size. Each of its two levels has only three main rooms, as well as small rooms called "cabinets" projecting at each rear corner, with a loggia between them.

Turned wooden colonnettes, which lend a sense of lightness to the upper floor, support the edges of the roof, but most of the support is provided invisibly by a substantial Norman truss in the attic. This heavy timber framing, fastened by pegged mortise-and-tenon joints, was widely used in France and its colonies for buildings large and small.

Like many historic homes, Pitot House bears the name of neither its original occupant nor its most recent; it is named for the period when the owner, the house, and the history of its location came together most meaningfully. It was built in 1799, during the Spanish colonial era, but the Louisiana Landmarks Society—which saved the house (moving it about two hundred feet in the mid-1960s to prevent its demolition for the construction of a school) and is headquartered there—focused its restoration on

ABOVE
Louvers span the full width of the rear loggia at the top of the winding stairway, providing ventilation and light control. Loggias and galleries were used to expand the house's living space. Commonly used as sleeping porches, as well as for dining, bathing, and other purposes, they were often furnished with pieces that could be moved easily as needed. The chairs here are Louisiana ladder-backs with cowhide seats.

OPPOSITE
When built in 1799, Pitot House was not in New Orleans proper but in the country, some two-and-a-half miles from the Vieux Carré. The house faces Bayou Saint John, which was once a bustling commercial waterway. Paved paths were essential to avoid walking in the soft, wet earth; they also were defining features of parterres, used to set off the formal gardens' geometric beds.

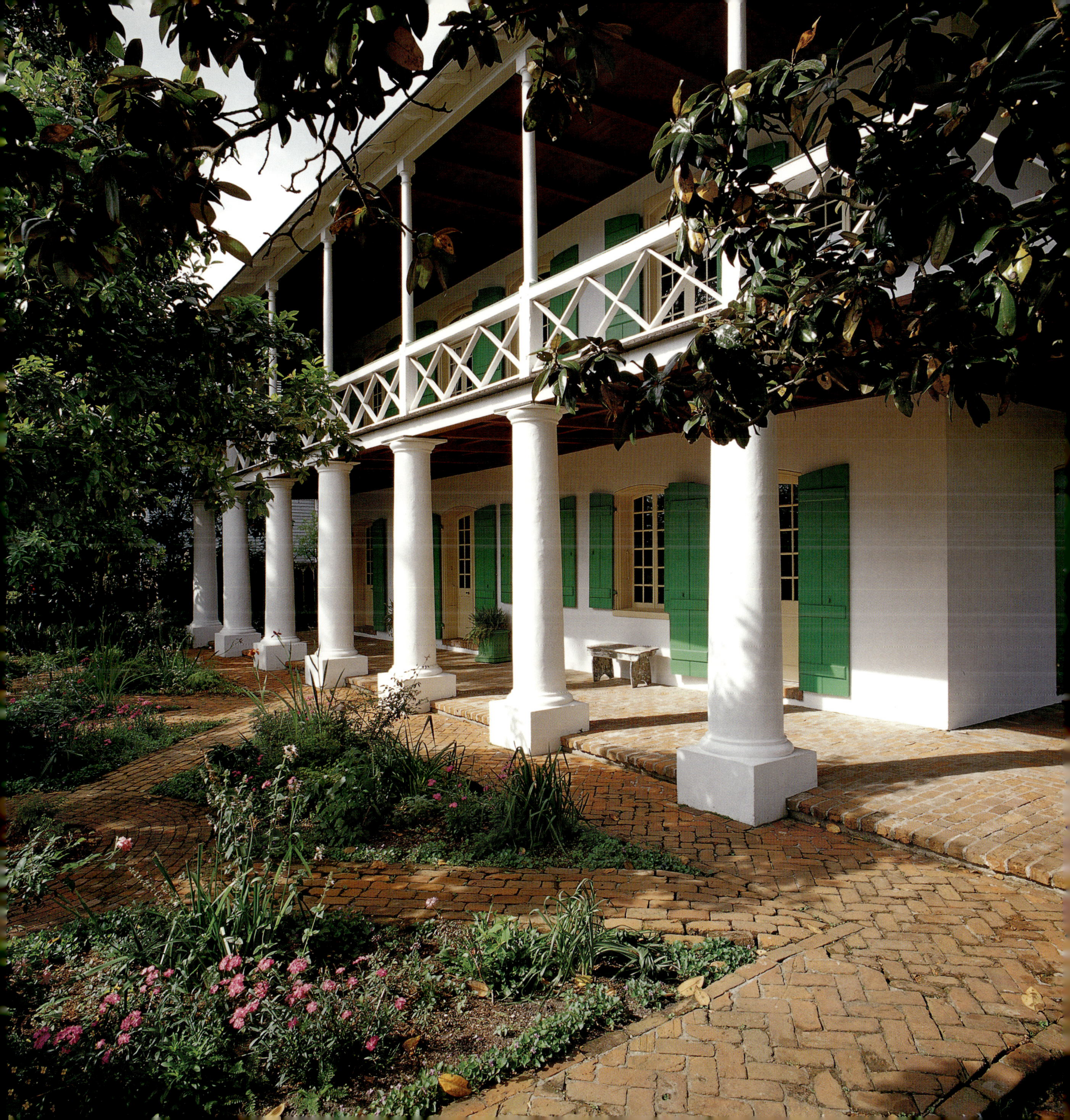

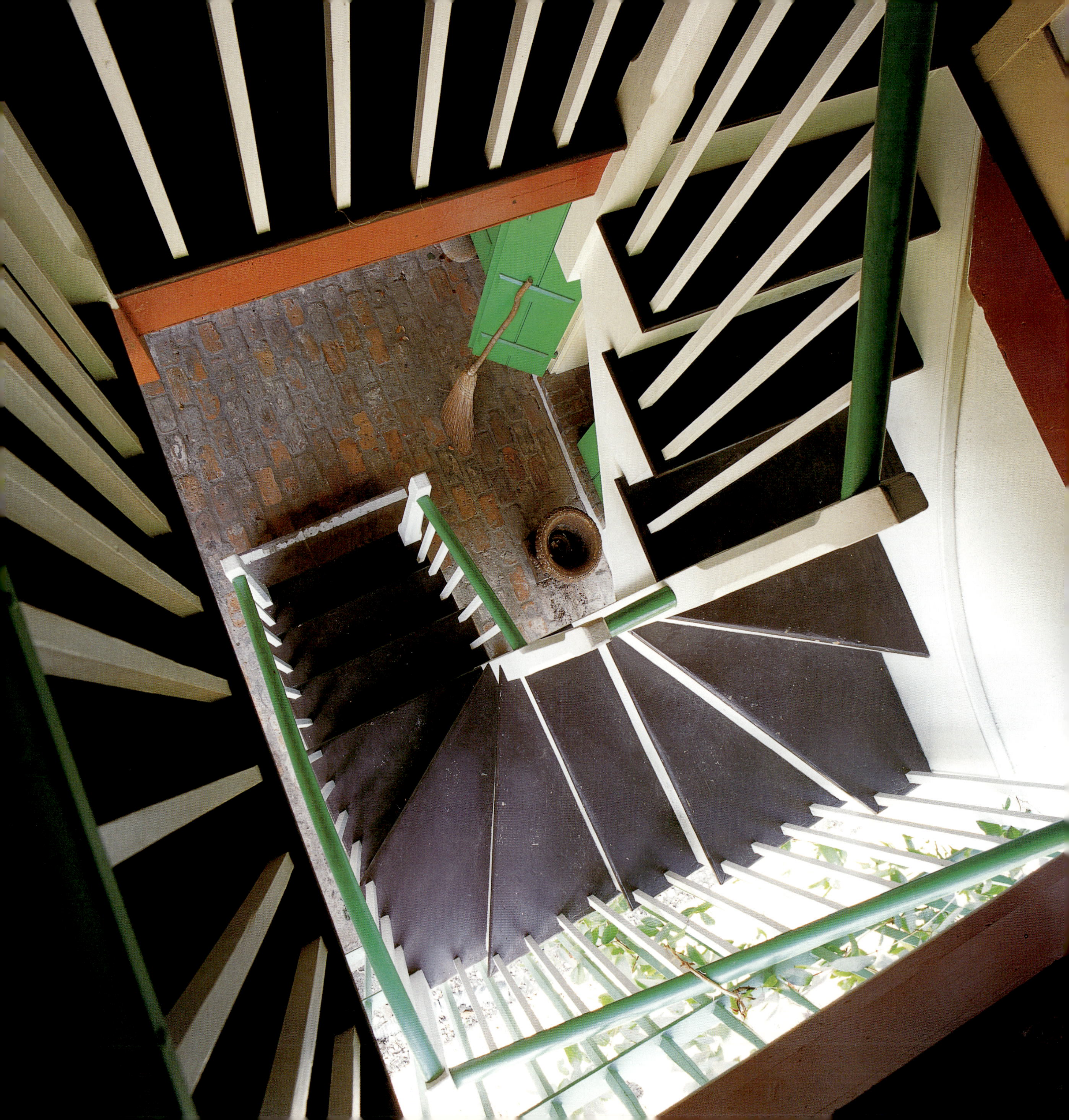

OPPOSITE
Creole houses eschewed space-consuming interior stairways; this winding exterior stair ascends from the brick-paved ground floor to the second-story loggia. Like every wooden element remaining from the original construction, including the green batten shutters visible at its base, the stair is made of cypress.

ABOVE
The mango-colored walls of the second-floor salon and the paint treatments throughout the house are based on colors typical of the period. Although many Creole houses were as chromatically vibrant as this one, others were restrained, with whitewashed walls and gray or green moldings. An R. Havell edition print of John James Audubon's *Reddish Egret* hangs above a pianoforte made in Boston about 1840.

1810–19. At that time it was occupied by Jacques-François (or James Francis) Pitot, a successful import-export merchant who was its fourth owner.

Pitot had left his native France some years earlier to seek his fortune in that country's richest colony, Saint Domingue. Revolution was stirring there; it would lead Saint Domingue to independence as the nation of Haiti in 1804. The unrest caused Pitot to return briefly to France, which, in the aftermath of its own revolution, was also unsettled. Pitot then sought refuge in Philadelphia, where he became a citizen of the United States. He went to New Orleans in 1796, during the waning years of Louisiana's Spanish government, and in 1802 authored a lengthy text on the subject of Louisiana and its economic prospects. Pitot became the second mayor of the American city of New Orleans and was later a parish (or county) judge.

Though European born, and therefore not a Creole (that is, someone born in the colonies), Pitot shared the cosmopolitan taste of his Creole contemporaries. The Pitot House collections suggest how he might have furnished his home, with locally made items as well as pieces imported from Europe and the eastern seaboard of the still-young United States.

TOP LEFT
The blue bedroom opens directly onto the salon, which opens onto a yellow bedroom. There are no interior halls—a defining characteristic of Creole style. Instead, galleries connect the rooms along the exterior. The hall-less plan likely derived from residential architecture in Europe's Caribbean colonies and aided the circulation of air, equally important in Louisiana as in the West Indies. Except where the two cabinets protrude, the house is only one room deep, allowing light and air to stream in from at least two exposures.

BOTTOM LEFT
Mantels and overmantels were important focal points of Creole homes, and much attention was paid to their decoration; overmantels were generally reserved for the most prominent room, the salon. This salon's ornate mantelpiece bears carved details—a sailing ship, crossed flags, and lions' heads—recalling the Spanish naval career of Bartholomé Bosque, who built the house in the waning days of Spain's colonial rule. The overmantel's cruciform panel is embellished with a painted floral design.

OPPOSITE
The salon's wide plank floors also serve as the ceiling of the room below, just as the floor of the attic above—supported by exposed, beaded joists—forms the salon's ceiling. This ceiling type, associated with high-style sixteenth-century French construction, persisted in buildings grand and modest throughout southern Louisiana until the mid-1800s; then, plastering or other smooth finishes began lending ceilings a more formal appearance. The muntins on the transoms repeat the X motif seen on the gallery railing.

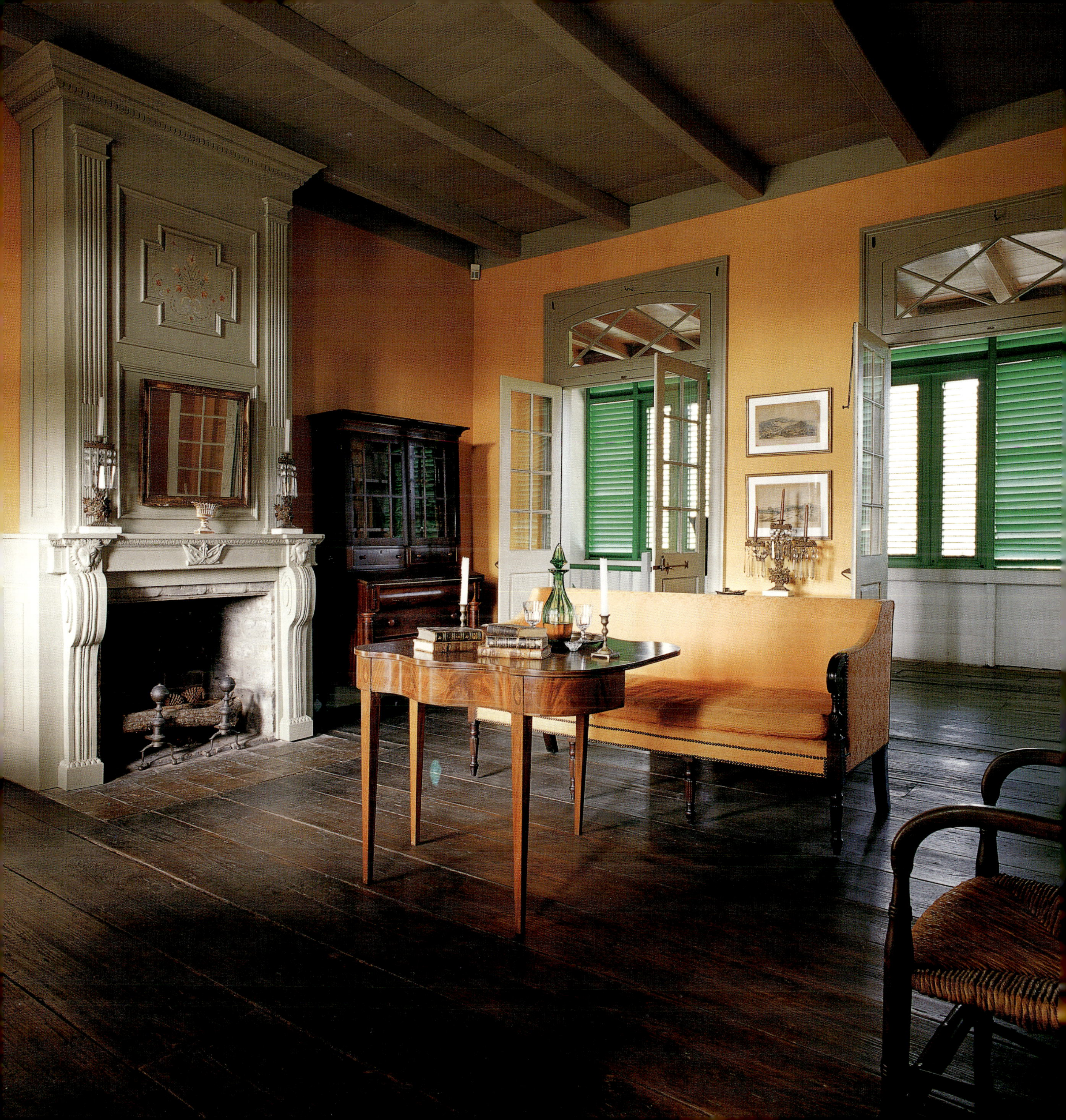

LEFT
This bedroom appears in summer dress, with bare wooden floors instead of rugs or carpets and the bed pulled from the wall to encourage air circulation. The four-poster tiger maple bed is from the Northeast, but its distinctive melon-shaped headboard of cypress is undoubtedly a local replacement. The high, arched melon design was popular in Louisiana, and it was practical: It kept the mosquito netting from collapsing over the sleeper's head.

OPPOSITE
Pitot House's windows are the casement type seen in this cabinet, reflecting the French influence and a lasting Creole preference for windows that could be fully opened. Cabinets, small rooms projecting from the rear corners of the house, were not always used for extra bedrooms, as here, but for various purposes, including office and storage space. Chests, trunks, and armoires (the one here is Louisiana-made of walnut) provided storage for clothing, bed linens, and other items in Creole houses; built-in closets were not yet in use.

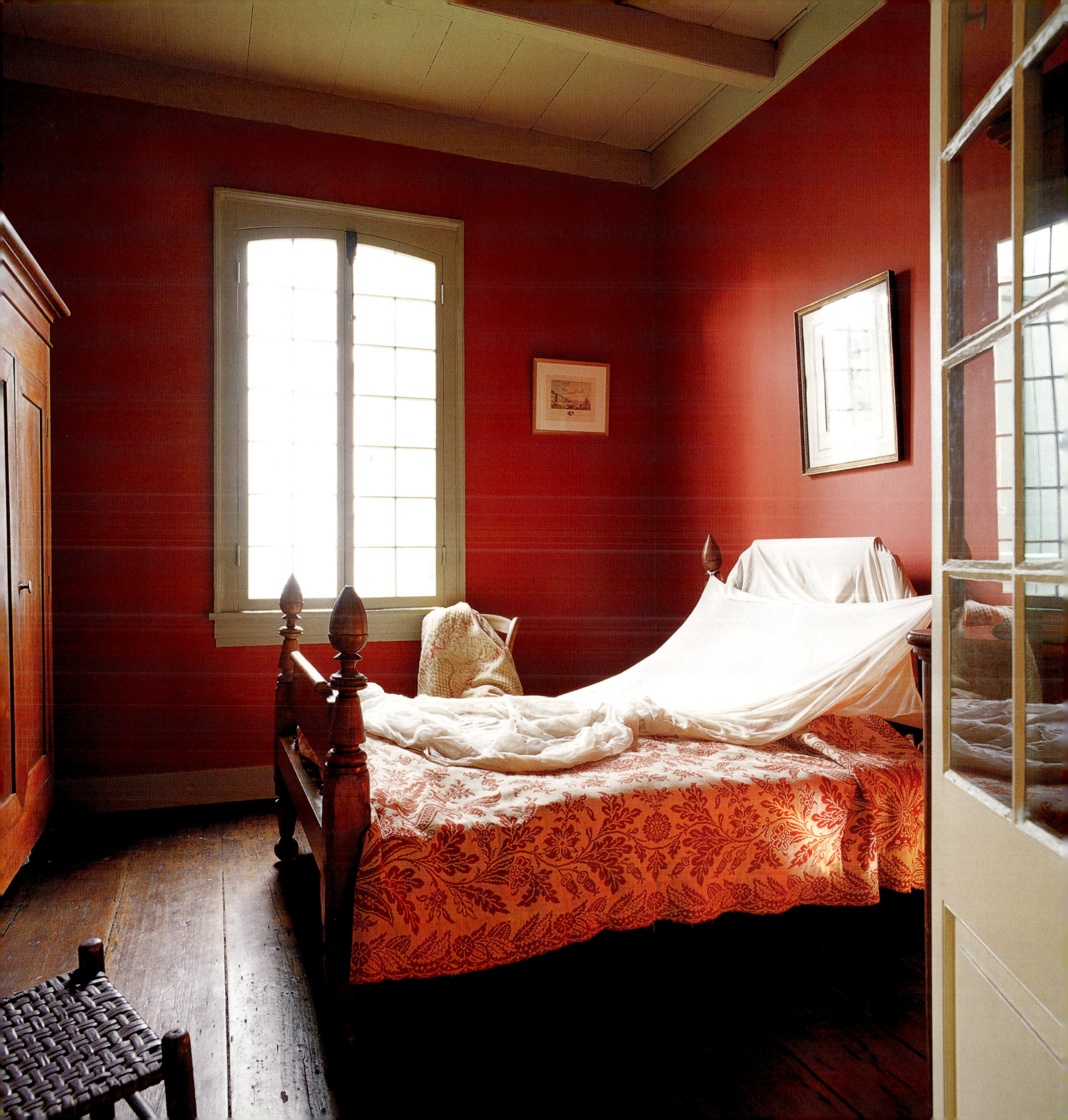

Bourgoyne House

The Bourgoyne House stands amid a cluster of similar town houses on the 800 block of Bourbon Street, in New Orleans's French Quarter. Those who know Bourbon Street only as a mawkish carnival where strong drink and weak character go hand in hand might be surprised by the quiet, residential character of the thoroughfare's lower, or downriver, stretch. It was a fashionable address more than a century and a half ago and remains a splendid place to live.

An elegant Creole town house, sharing walls with neighboring buildings and made of brick, Bourgoyne represents one of the classic building types in the Quarter. Town houses were often home to merchants and other businessmen, whose shops and offices occupied the street level; they also served as city homes for wealthy planters whose primary residence was in the country.

The Bourgoyne House dates from the mid-1830s, well into New Orleans's American era. Yet the building's architectural and design elements hearken to an earlier taste, a Creole taste, with a porte cochere, or covered passageway, leading to the rear of the property; the ground-floor loggia sheltering an exterior stairway to the upper floors; and an enclosed courtyard with a two-story service building containing the kitchen and the bedroom for servants or slaves. Rooms at the back, facing away from Bourbon Street, are designed to engage with the outdoors. A ground-floor *salle à manger* (dining room) opens onto the deep and shaded loggia and enjoys views of the courtyard.

J. E. Bourgoyne, who resides here with Jay Tyburski, has dwelt in Bourgoyne House for more than thirty years. They have filled their home with many furnishings consonant with the period of its construction. Numerous items have ties to Bourgoyne's family, which was established in Louisiana in the late eighteenth century. The Bourgoyne House serves as both a vehicle for its occupants' present interests and a direct connection to an ancestral epoch.

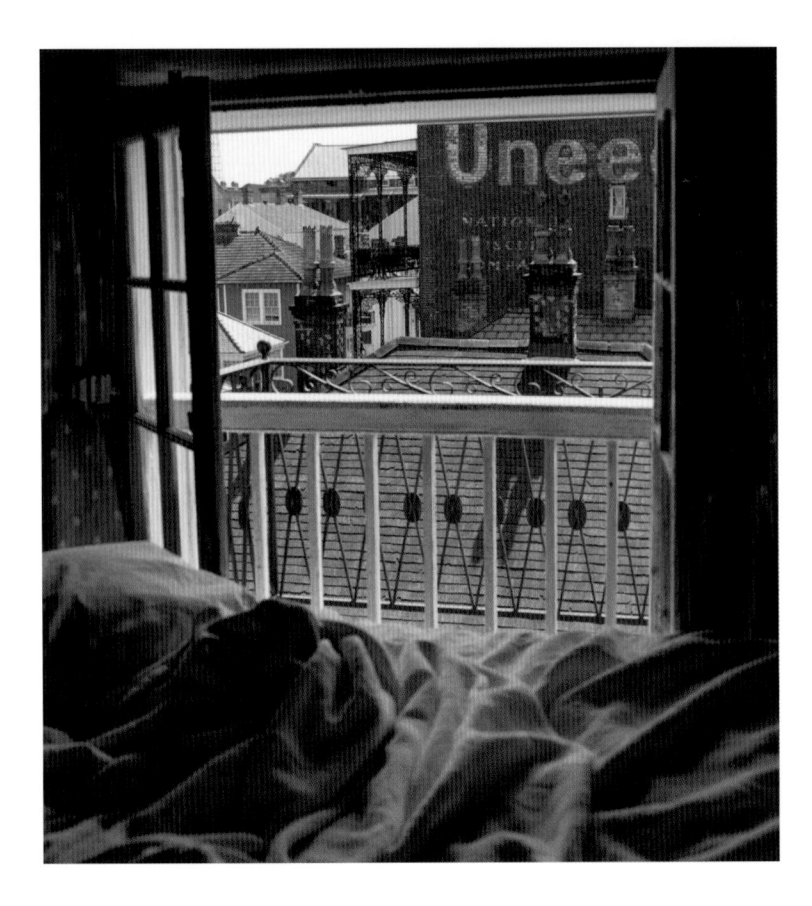

ABOVE
A third-floor bedroom, casement windows open, overlooks Bourbon Street and the rooftops and galleries beyond. Prominent in the view is an early-twentieth-century painted wall advertisement, one of several still visible on French Quarter buildings.

OPPOSITE
The Bourgoyne House (the gray and green building, center) shares the block with other town houses, as well as businesses suited to a residential neighborhood—laundromats, restaurants, art galleries, and shops. Typical of a Creole town house, its primary entrance is the arched door of the porte cochere at the side, which leads to the rear courtyard. That feature distinguishes it from its American counterpart, which always has a formal entrance on the street; so too does the characteristically Creole absence of interior halls and stairways.

Bon Maison
Guest House
835
839
The WASHING WELL
LAUNDRYTERIA
SHIRTS

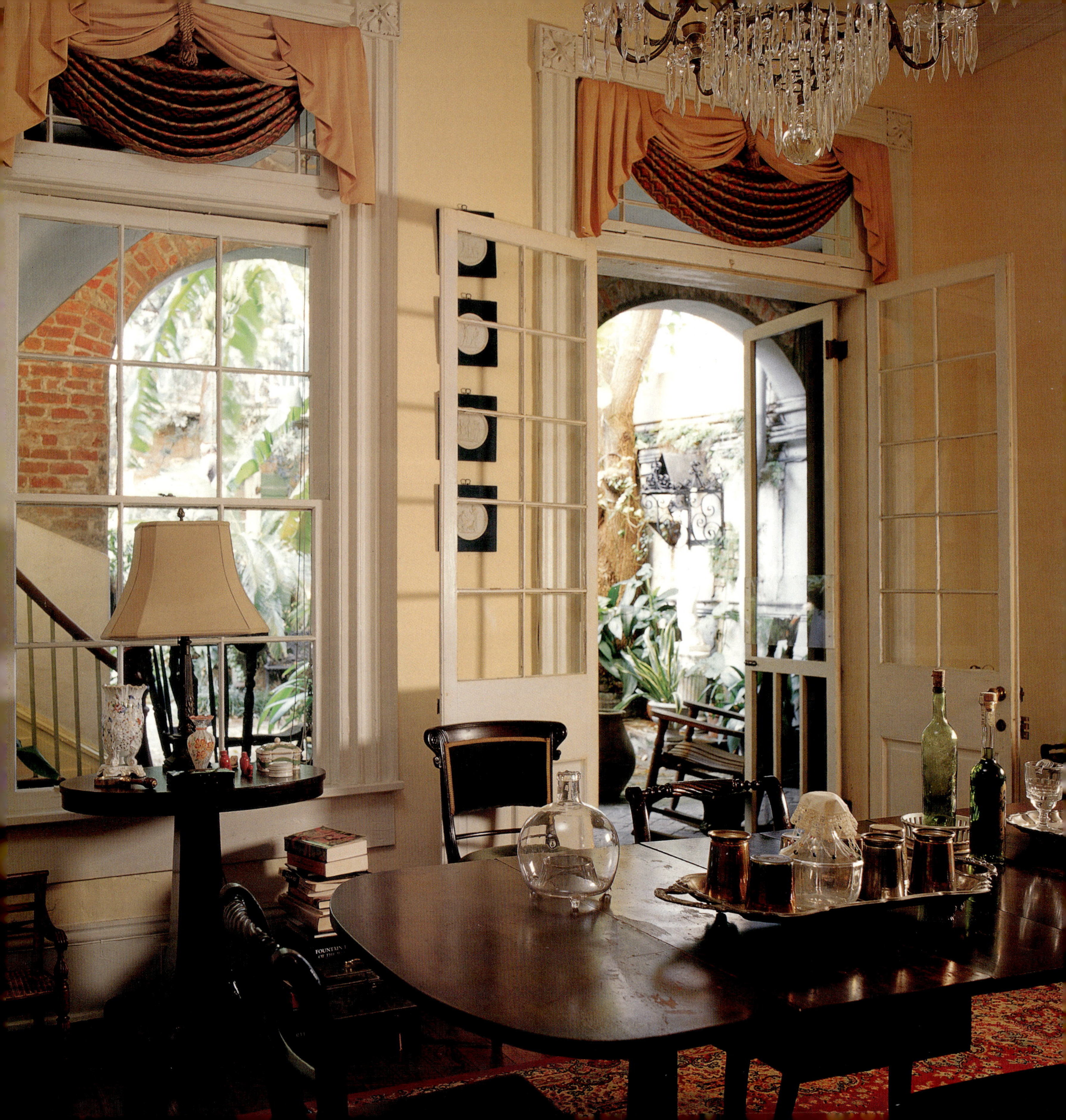
FOUNTAIN

OPPOSITE

The dining room looks out past the covered loggia to the lushly planted courtyard. Four Italian marble bas-relief plaques with scenes from classical mythology occupy the narrow space on the wall between the window and the door. Gracing the dining table are a silver tray with silver tumblers and a glass flycatcher, which would lure insects through the open bottom with syrup, honey, or sugar water poured inside.

TOP RIGHT

Referencing New Orleans's history of dueling—used to settle points of honor well into the latter half of the nineteenth century—two Spanish fencing swords are mounted above an oval looking glass. The ancestral portraits flanking the mirror are of the duc and duchesse de Bourgogne, an earlier spelling of the name of the house's current owner.

BOTTOM RIGHT

A tray with the accoutrements for preparing absinthe sits on the dining table. The slightly bitter green liqueur was traditionally served sweetened and diluted: Water was poured through cubed sugar resting on pierced silver spoons into the liqueur-filled glasses below. Absinthe, popular in the nineteenth century, was banned by many countries, including the United States in 1912, as it was thought to induce madness and delirium. It is once again being distilled in parts of Europe.

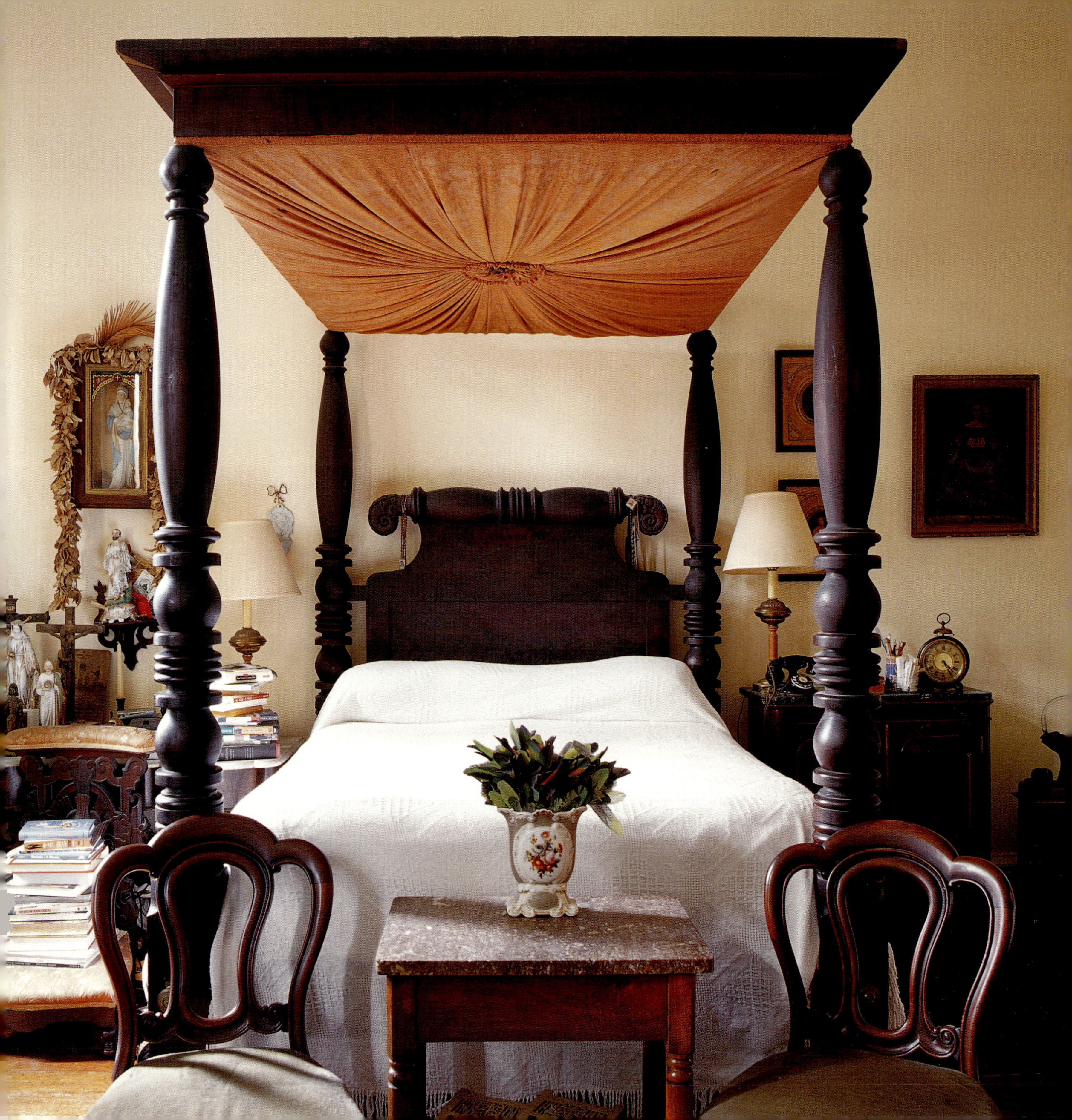

OPPOSITE
An array of crucifixes is displayed on the bedside table beneath a framed Madonna and Child. Tucked behind the artwork is a piece of blessed palm from a long-past Palm Sunday service. At the foot of the bed, on a Louisiana-made cherry table topped with marble, is an Old Paris vase containing feathers from Harry, the resident parrot.

RIGHT
The carved ram's horn detail on the headboard of this 1830s mahogany bed, thought to be of Louisiana origin, holds mementos of Creole religious practice. The rosary and cloth scapulars are devotional artifacts and reminders of New Orleans's strong Catholic heritage.

TOP LEFT
The second-floor loggia and stair landing, semienclosed by a wall of casement windows with arched fanlights, functions as a summertime dining room. The tea service on the table pays homage to the brief residence at 839 Bourbon of Broadway composer Vincent Youmans, who wrote the musical *No, No, Nanette* and its hit song "Tea for Two." The hanging liturgical light fixture is from a now-demolished church in the Faubourg Marigny.

BOTTOM LEFT
Bourgoyne House's courtyard is filled with plants, including a camphor tree, a species introduced to New Orleans from China in the first quarter of the nineteenth century. On the wall above the statue is a wrought-iron bell, which would be rung to alert neighbors in the event of fire or other disaster.

OPPOSITE
The covered loggia is paved in brick laid in a herringbone pattern. Tucked beneath the gracefully winding stair, with its mahogany handrail, is a *cave*, or outdoor pantry, whose masonry walls and shaded site kept foodstuffs cool. The door still has its original wooden grillwork, which provides ventilation, and hand-forged iron strap hinges.

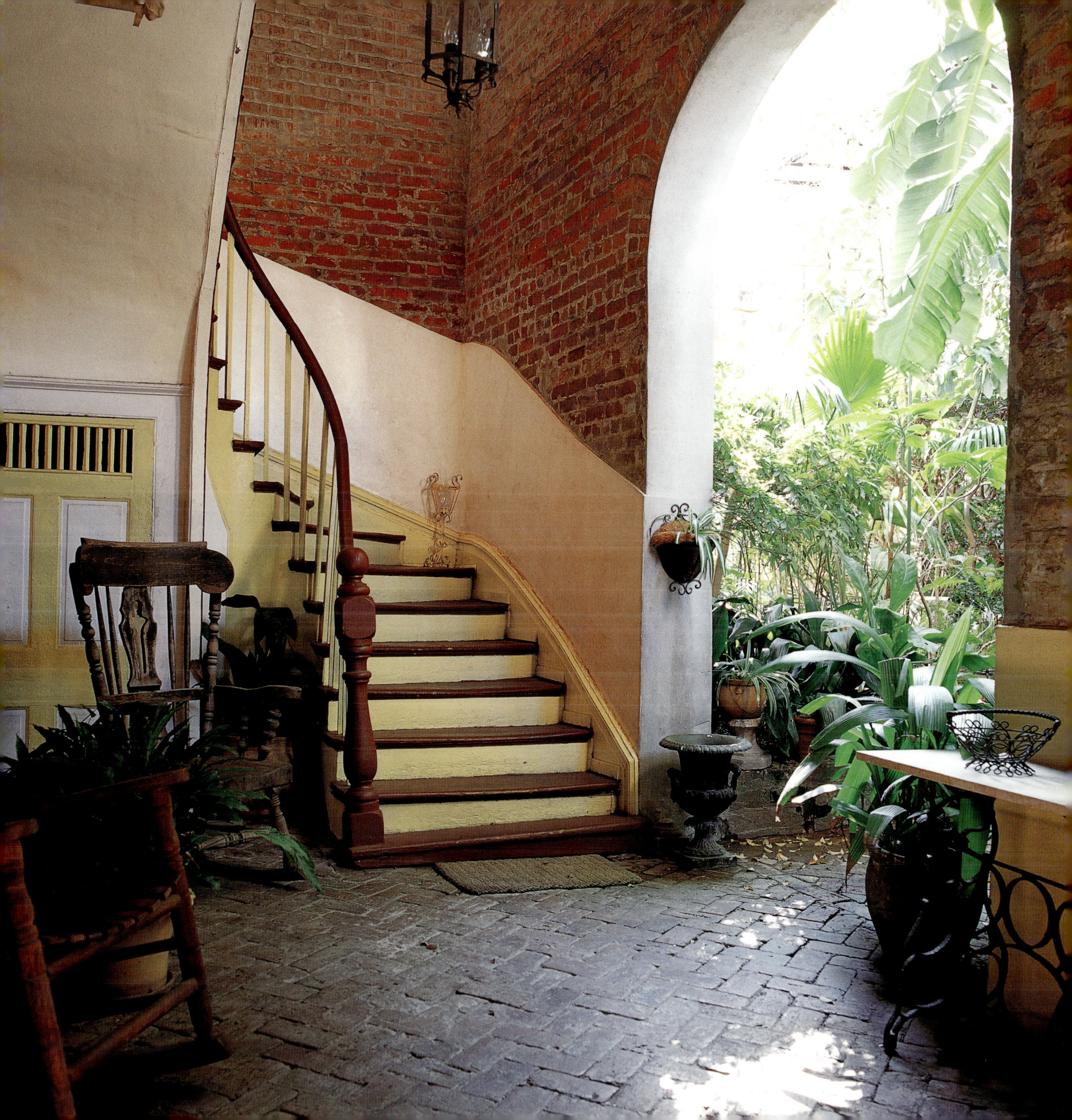

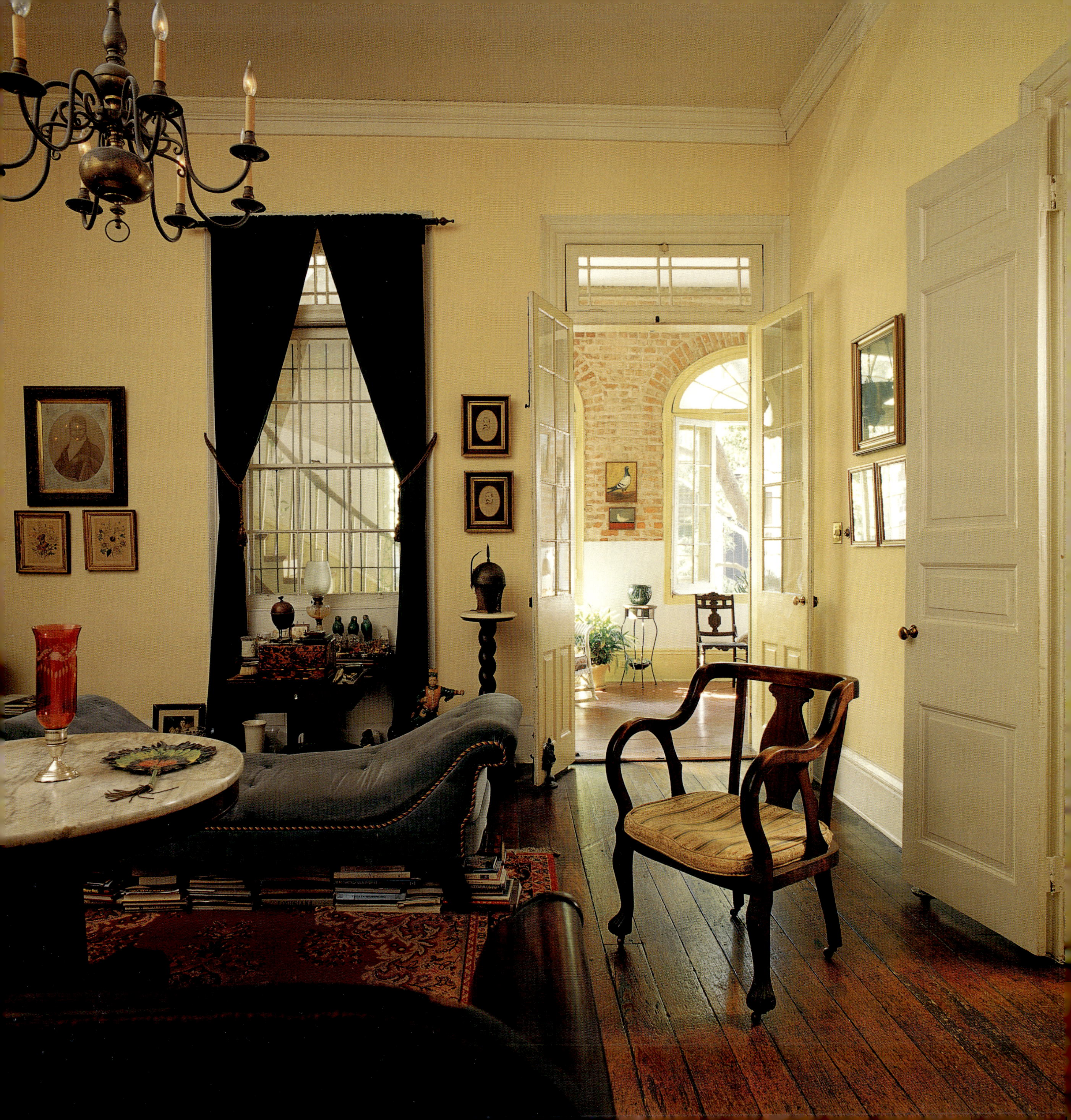

OPPOSITE
A second-floor salon contains a marble-topped table, a recamier, or backless couch, and a sixteenth-century Persian helmet displayed on a stand. The portrait on the wall to the left is of Bourgoyne's great-great-grandfather Balmio Dumas, who contracted rabies and, in what was considered a humane solution, was smothered to death by two of his sons. Light fills the room via the adjacent loggia, which overlooks the courtyard.

RIGHT
The dining room is illuminated by a crystal chandelier and mid-nineteenth-century girandoles in the Sultana motif (with a richly dressed Middle Eastern female figure forming each base). Above the simple mantel, *Young Dimiter,* a portrait by Dutch artist Johannes Engel Masurel (1826–1915), hangs by a ribbon in front of the mirror, as if surveying the diners.

Cooper-Thomann House

The sophisticated color scheme of citron, Spanish brown, blue gray, silver, and black sported by Mary Cooper and Tomio Thomann's New Orleans home makes a striking first impression. Although vibrant and singularly expressive, the house integrates well within Bywater, an architecturally rich neighborhood hard by the Mississippi River.

Bywater—almost two miles east of the French Quarter—began forming as a suburb when former plantation lands were subdivided into building lots to accommodate the population expansion that occurred in the wake of the Louisiana Purchase (1803). As was typical in early New Orleans neighborhoods, most houses here were built abutting the sidewalk, providing open space at the property's rear, away from the noise and bustle of the street. The neighborhood's prevalent building form was the relatively modest Creole cottage.

Cooper and Thomann's house, which they date to about 1840, is a two-story Creole town house of wood construction, with a wooden balcony. It is simply constructed and detailed, set close to the street, and squarish, with four rooms per floor, a hall-less floor plan, and shuttered, symmetrical facade openings.

It was utterly decrepit when Cooper and Thomann undertook an extensive, yearslong restoration, seeing possibilities where others saw none. Inside, they removed previous renovations, revealing and reestablishing the original room plan. They also improved upon the long-ago annexation of a kitchen building to the main house by enclosing the connecting breezeway at one end with French doors and at the other with a double-hung sash, creating a dining area. Framed vistas from one room to the next through doorways and windows that are now openings in interior walls lend the house a sense of spaciousness.

ABOVE
The one-story kitchen building (now abutting the main two-story house) has a characteristic Creole plan, with a recessed loggia flanked by two small rooms, or cabinets. In the backyard, herbs and flowering plants crowd around the flagstones. In New Orleans, carefully selected plants, trees, and shrubs will grow luxuriantly and, if unchecked, out of control. Bowling balls covered with fragments of nineteenth-century ceramics discovered in the garden add a touch of history and whimsy to the site.

OPPOSITE
In a neighborhood of many brightly painted homes, this one stands out for the sophistication of its color combination. Cooper and Thomann sought to give the exterior a Caribbean feel; New Orleans and the West Indies share not only a French colonial past, but a taste for lively palettes.

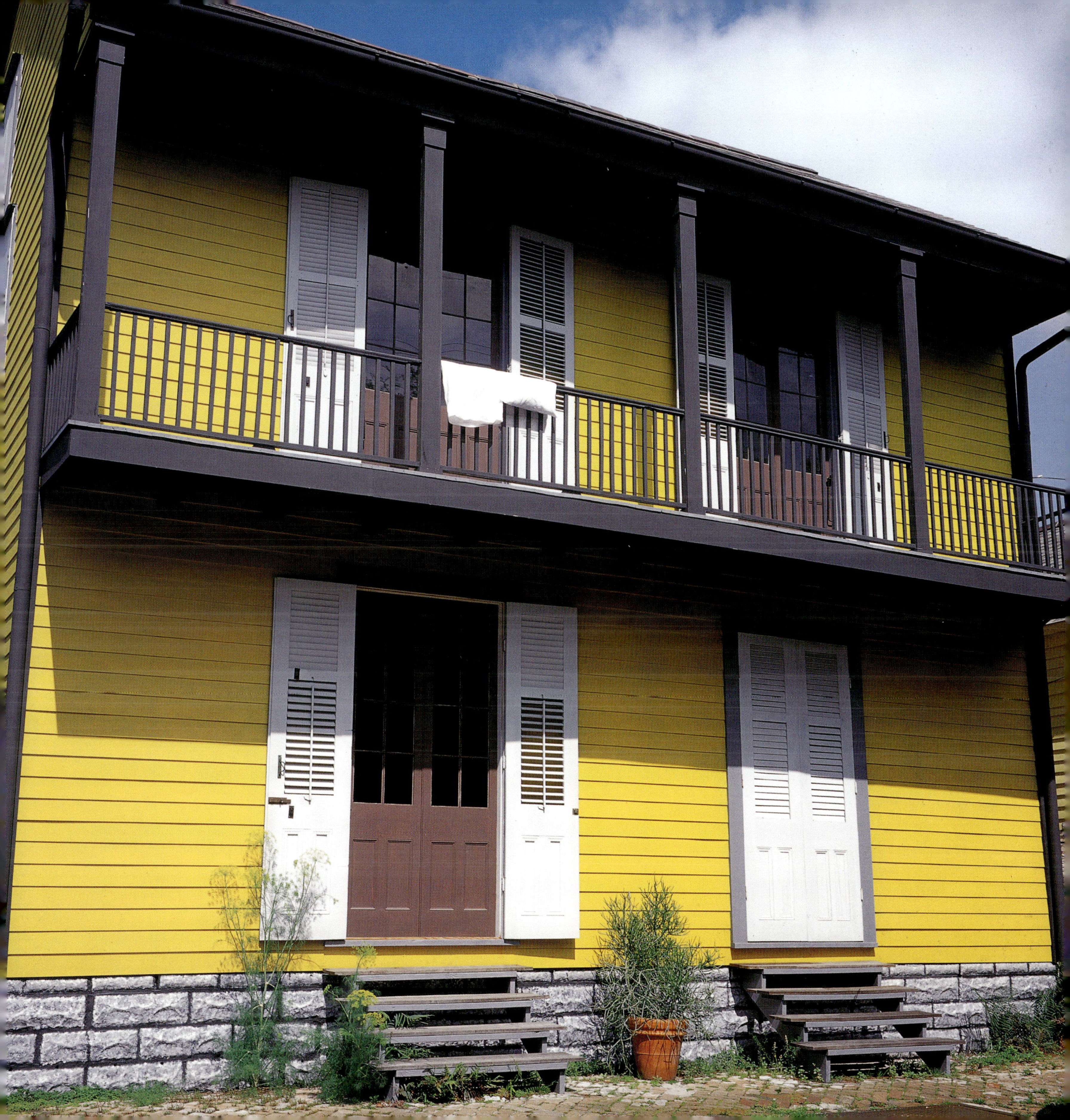

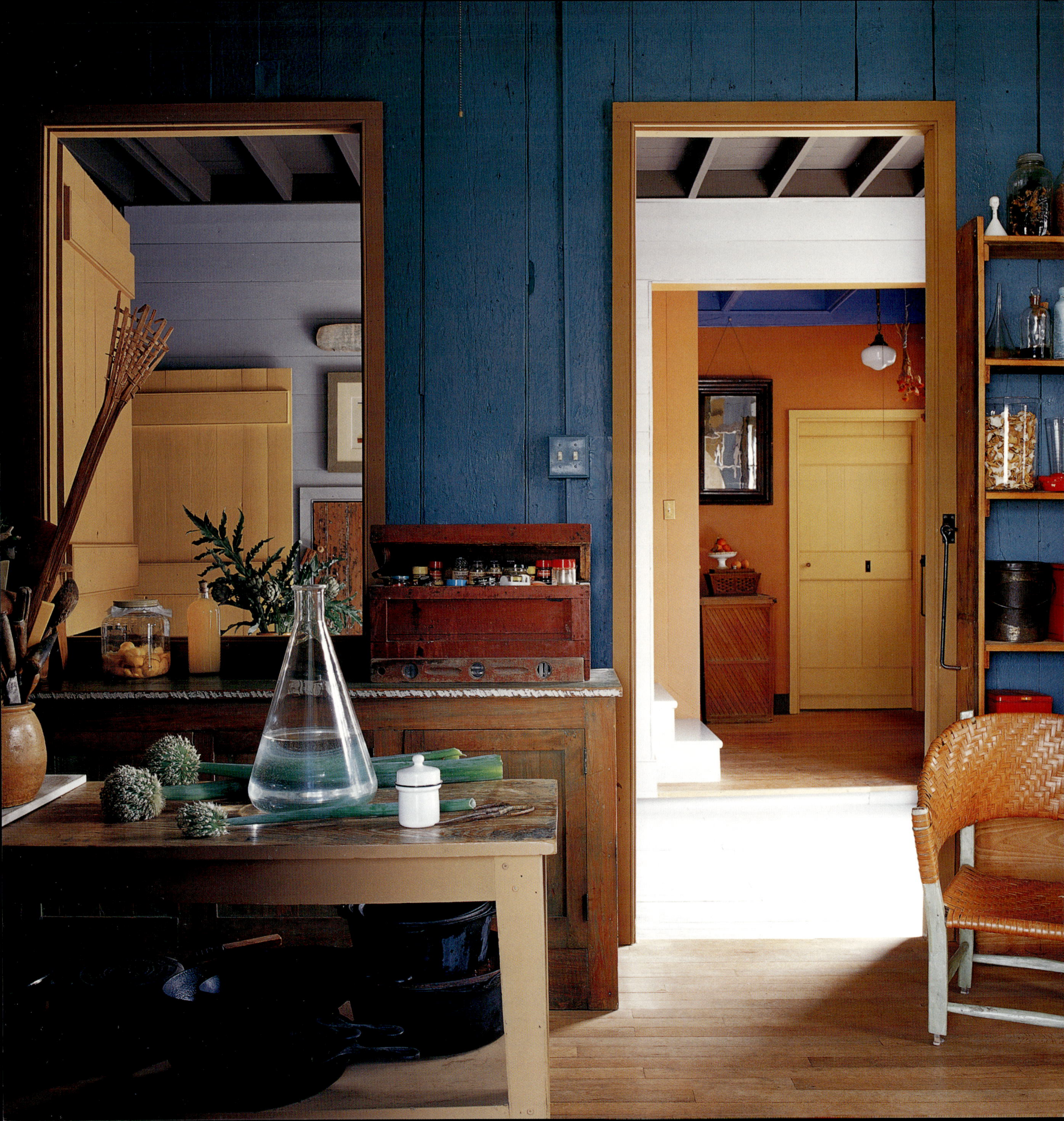

Like the exterior, the interior is chromatically exuberant; the paint colors were discovered as the renovation progressed. A restrained selection of warm ochres and grays counterbalances intense shades of indigo, chartreuse, and turquoise. The eight rooms are filled with architectural elements—millwork, mantels, hardware—that were either unearthed during the renovation or salvaged from other buildings of the same era. Nineteenth-century Louisiana-made furnishings coexist with carefully chosen items from other periods and cultures.

The backyard combines elements of a potager, or kitchen garden, with a host of decorative plants that are either native or naturalized varieties introduced to the area centuries ago. Rosemary, sugarcane, satsuma trees, and artichokes share space with old roses and angel trumpet in a parterre plot created with irregularly shaped flagstone paving. Both the house and garden bear the current owners' personal stamp while remaining true to the property's history, resulting in an urban space that is eminently functional, beautiful, and livable.

OPPOSITE
The vertical planks or bargeboards that make up the kitchen's vividly painted walls were recycled from unpowered flatboats that carried cargo from the upper Mississippi Valley downriver to New Orleans in the early 1800s; unable to make the return trip upstream, the barges would be disassembled and used for building materials. Most Bywater houses of the period were made of bargeboard.

ABOVE
The porch adjoining the kitchen is painted Spanish brown, one of the building's original colors, and is decked with teak. A cypress worktable displays some of the garden's bounty: nasturtiums, cherry tomatoes, and Japanese sweet potatoes. Tomio Thomann fashioned the benches from reclaimed lumber.

LEFT
An upstairs bath was created in an addition made in the 1960s. In one corner is a cypress storage cabinet. The upper part of the door is glazed, with divided lights, and a simple linen towel provides privacy.

OPPOSITE
The dining room occupies what had been a breezeway connecting the living areas and the kitchen, formerly an outbuilding. Surrounding the massive cypress table is a collection of Southern chairs; Mary Cooper herself caned or rushed all the seats. As elsewhere in the house, the walls here are wooden; these are the weatherboards that once clad the exterior. The low wooden door to the left gives access to a storage closet, or *cave*, under the staircase.

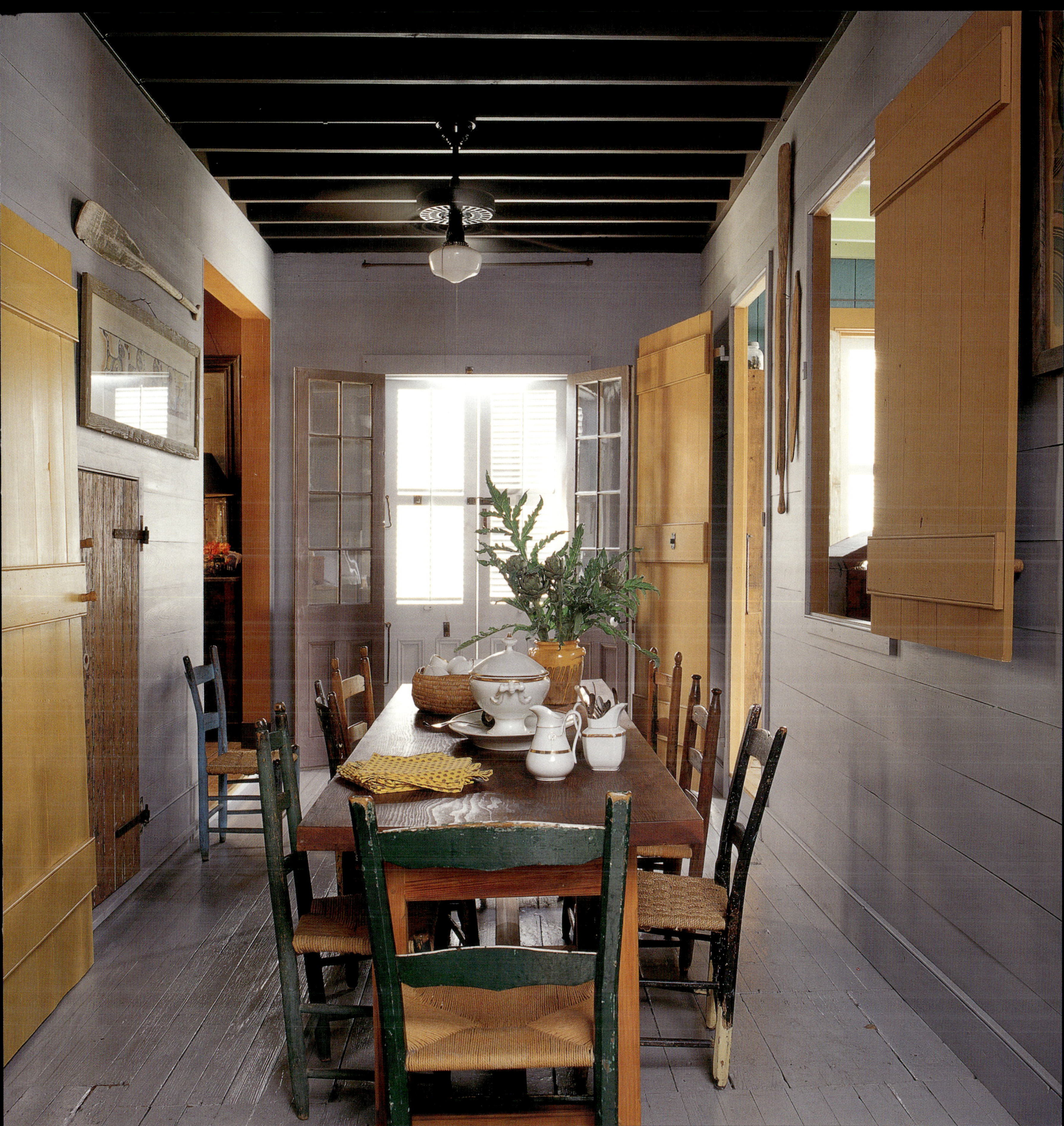

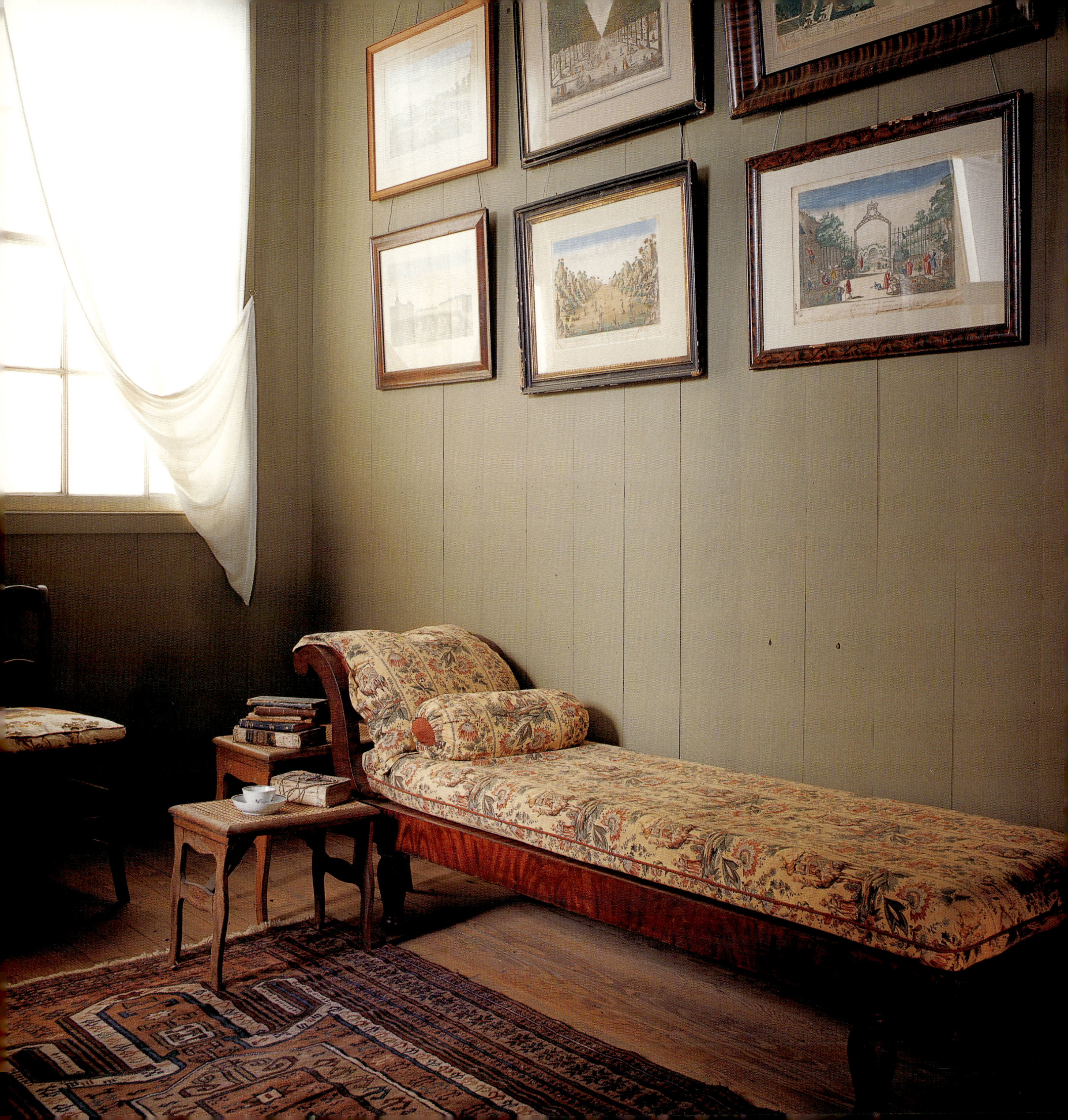

OPPOSITE
Folding stools made in France for picnics or fishing trips are used here as tables. A collection of nineteenth-century *vues d'optique* (perspective views) of France hangs above a daybed painted to resemble rosewood and covered in an Indian-inspired toile.

TOP RIGHT
The small parlor looks into the dining room through door and window openings, giving a glimpse of a monumental woodcut by Mississippi artist Walter Anderson (1903–1965). The mahogany table in the parlor holds a mirrored armoire used for doll clothes and a portable writing desk that belonged to Mary Cooper's grandfather.

BOTTOM RIGHT
The upstairs bedroom's Acadian cypress bed dates from the mid-nineteenth century; a ring of mosquito netting hangs above. A toile curtain on a blacksmith-made iron rod covers the doorway. The French-inspired box mantel (wherein the mantelpiece extends around the chimney) is original to the house and a typical Creole design feature. Its black paint is also typically Creole—a traditional way to hide soot. The floors throughout the house, with rare exception, are unfinished pine patinated by a century-and-a-half of mopping, scrubbing, and sweeping.

Patout Cottage

Traversing the 120 feet from the Bourbon Street sidewalk to the far end of the Patout property takes less than thirty seconds but transports you back in time more than a hundred years. The sounds of the street quickly disappear behind the garden enclosure, where fragrance and lushness command the senses. The interior of the house, filled with eighteenth- and nineteenth-century furnishings, reinforces the impression of time travel.

Buildings in the Vieux Carré, or French Quarter, the original city of New Orleans, date from the eighteenth through the twentieth century. Like many of its neighbors, the double shotgun cottage on Bourbon Street currently owned by Peter Patout has evolved since its 1887 construction to embody elements of different periods, styles, and tastes.

The shotgun is a classic New Orleans architectural type: typically one story high, narrow, and deep, with several rooms connected in a direct line. They come in single and double (or two-family) configurations, some with side halls or side galleries. The camelback variation has a second story rising over the rear rooms, so it appears at street level to be a one-story dwelling.

Shotguns began appearing in the mid-1800s, and many are adorned with gingerbread trimmings and the other embellishments that proliferated with the mass production of architectural ornamentation. What distinguishes Patout's house from innumerable shotguns is its simplicity. If the jigsawed brackets were removed from the facade and the ornate detailing on the fireplaces disregarded, it would resemble a house built much earlier in the century. Inside and out, the Patout cottage conjures the spirit and style of days gone by.

ABOVE
The sitting room, set toward the rear of the house, has views of the kitchen and the courtyard. Between the doorways to them is a marble-topped French desk, which holds a large eighteenth-century French faience tureen that is perfect for serving gumbo. Above hang framed equestrian prints based on portraits of Southern horses by Edward Troy. Candlesticks of Old Paris porcelain (on the table in the foreground) are family heirlooms from Fuselier de la Claire Plantation on Bayou Teche, near Franklin.

OPPOSITE
The cottage's blue and yellow scheme was inspired by a trip Peter Patout made to Cuba—like New Orleans, a former Spanish colony with many brightly painted residences. Like all exterior colors in the Vieux Carré, these were selected from a list of historically appropriate choices and approved by the Vieux Carré Commission. The box steps of stuccoed brick, probably dating from the mid-1900s, are durable, low-maintenance replacements for wooden originals. Neighbors traditionally gathered at these stoops.

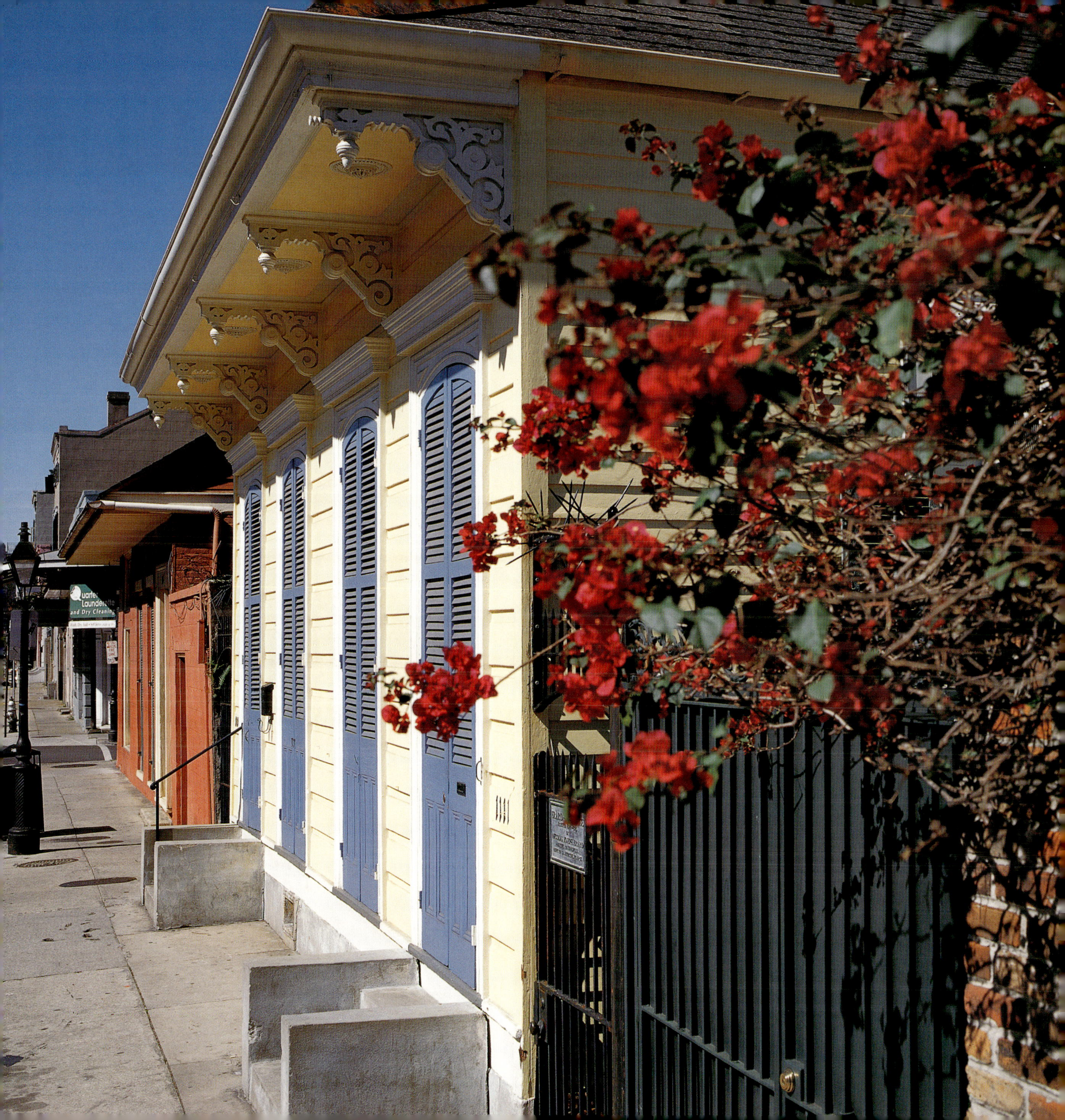
Quarter
Launderette
and Dry Cleaning
1111

LEFT
In the patio courtyard, on a marble-topped garden table from France, a small curio cabinet is filled with religious images, artifacts, and votive candles. The marble plaques (ex-votos) from the Ursuline Convent on Dauphine Street (the third of the nuns' four convents, used from 1824 to 1912) are typical of those that supplicants placed in chapels as thanks to saints for answered prayers.

OPPOSITE
A brick-paved court with cast-iron furniture separates the main house from a two-story masonry building that had been built more than sixty years earlier, in 1824. Just one room deep, it is set nearly against the rear property line. The solid wood shutters, emphasizing security rather than ventilation, reflect a much earlier style than the louvered ones on Patout's cottage at the front of the lot.

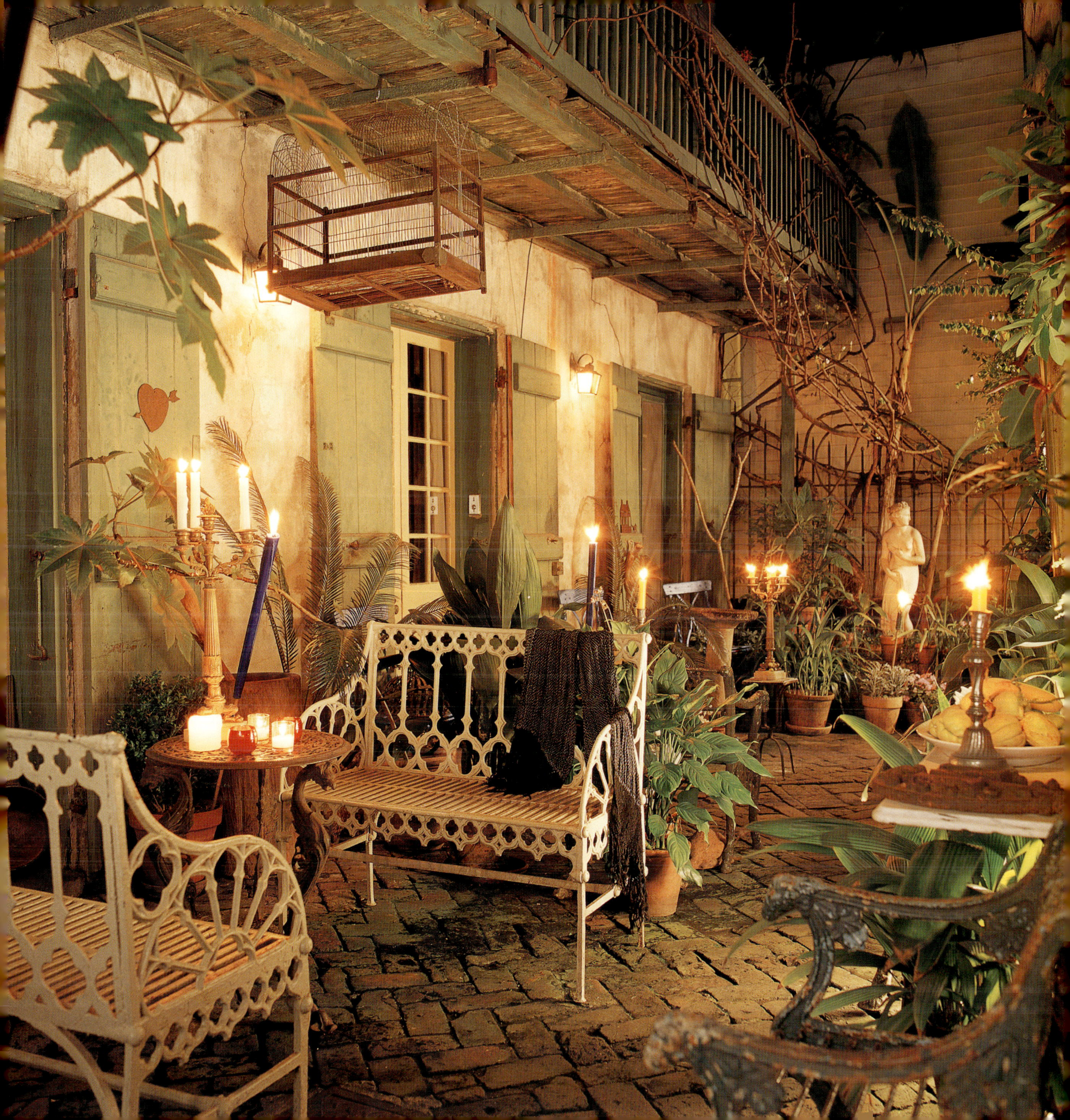

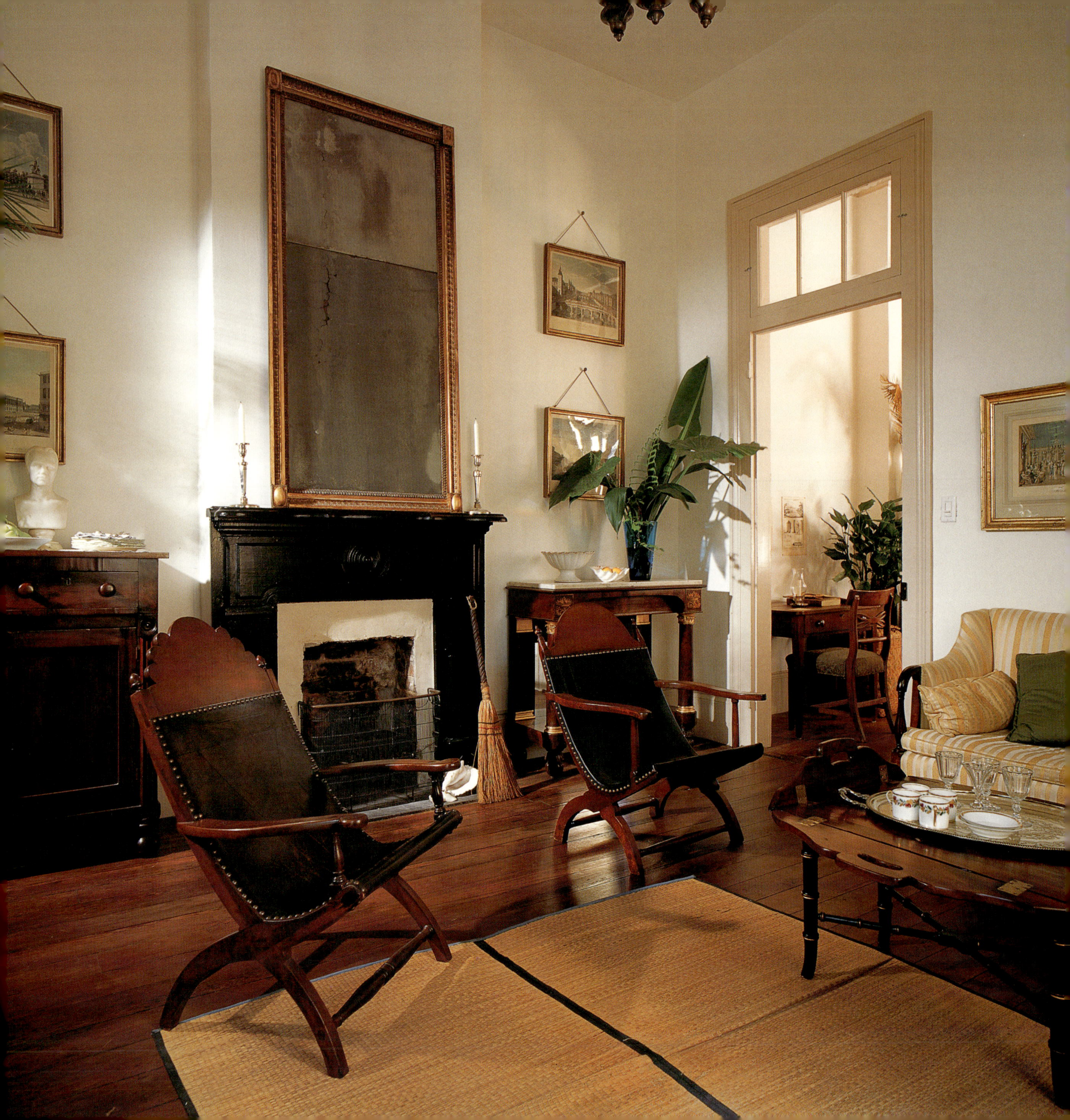

OPPOSITE

The *butaca*, a lolling chair with a wood frame and leather sling seat, was popular in Spain's New World colonies. (Many were manufactured in Mexico's Campeche district, hence the alternate name: campeche or campeachy chair.) The two here are cherrywood and of Louisiana origin. Hanging on the walls are *vues de Paris* prints and a classical mirror, which dates from the early 1800s and belonged to New Orleans descendants of Confederate president Jefferson Davis. The Canton matting is a traditional nineteenth-century floor covering used especially in the summer months, when the straw provided a cool, crisp alternative to woolen rugs.

TOP RIGHT

Dominating the sitting room is a monumental sacristy cabinet from the Ursuline Convent. Made of cypress, it dates from about 1915. The window covering is a reproduction of an 1820s English fabric purchased for five dollars at a local recycling center. The drop-leaf table dates from about 1820 and is made of Cuban mahogany with turnings in the French taste. The Federal-period lyre-back armchairs were made about 1825 by one of New Orleans's most accomplished cabinetmakers, François Seignouret, for Saint Louis Cathedral.

BOTTOM RIGHT

A mantelpiece with a bull's-eye motif holds an antique French tole wineglass rinser filled with mirlitons, a winter squash. It is flanked by a turtle skull and a flower-filled Old Paris cup. These French porcelains were much in vogue with Louisiana Creoles. French goods had great cachet, whether imported to New Orleans or acquired through travel, business, and family ties.

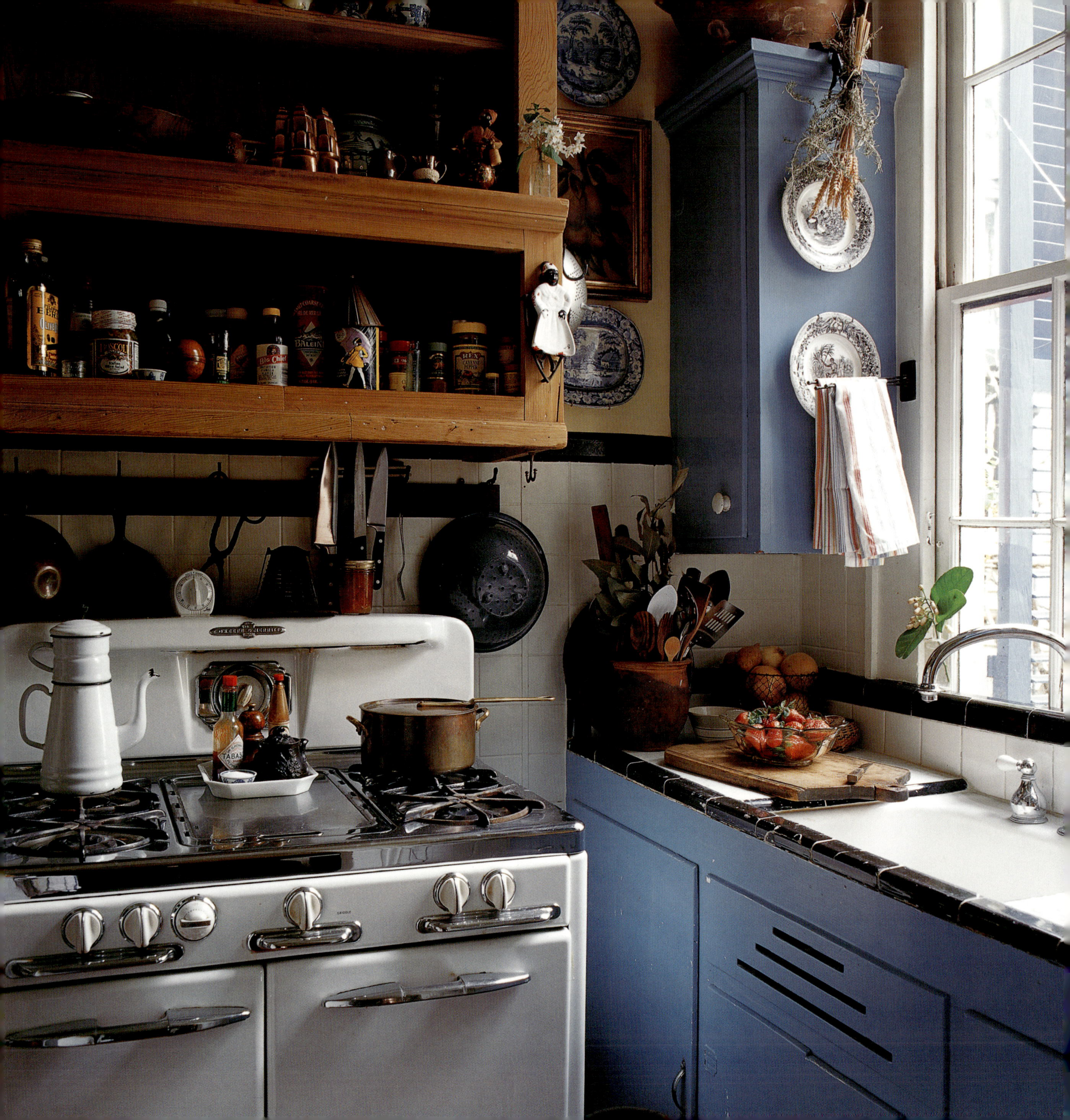

OPPOSITE

The diminutive kitchen boasts a 1950s-era O'Keefe & Meritt range, on which Peter Patout prepares such Creole specialties as gumbo, chicken stew, crawfish étouffé, and red beans and rice. Sitting on the stove top are a traditional enameled-steel drip coffeepot and a selection of local pepper sauces. Seasonings like filé (powdered sassafras leaves used to thicken gumbo), bay leaves from a local garden, and raw sugar from the Patout family's 1832 plantation fill the cypress shelves above the range.

TOP RIGHT

Azure shades, including the rich Provencal blue of this bedroom, pervade Peter Patout's home. The sharp tracery of the brass bed (c. 1880) contrasts with the diaphanous mosquito netting suspended above it. The 1878 Currier & Ives print of an African-American woman references the significance to Louisiana's culture of its eighteenth- and nineteenth-century community of *gens de couleur libres*, or free people of color.

BOTTOM RIGHT

This bed, found in the Spanish Custom House on Bayou Saint John and locally made of mulberry, exhibits a style—the melon headboard with turned finials—favored by Creole families throughout southern Louisiana. The mix of toile and checked fabrics also reflects Creole tastes. The miniatures grouped to the left are of the family of Valcour Aime, a prominent sugar planter and Peter Patout's ancestor. Grandmère Patout's plantation garden furnished the palm fronds that bracket a nineteenth-century French crucifix crafted of wood and ivory.

The Pontalba Buildings

Cities planned and built by French engineers are scattered throughout North America and the Caribbean basin, from Quebec City and Louisbourg, Nova Scotia, down to Mobile, Alabama, and Haiti's Port-au-Prince. Of the French-built cities on this side of the Atlantic, New Orleans alone retains its original street layout, which was established in 1721, three years after the city's founding, from the plan drawn by Pierre Le Blond de la Tour. Central to a French plan was a principal square, the *place d'armes*, or parade grounds. Jackson Square, an emblem of the city, has ably served as that public gathering place for centuries.

It is anchored on the north side by three significant buildings of eighteenth-century origin: Saint Louis Cathedral; the Cabildo, or town hall; and the Presbytere, used for commerce before becoming a courthouse. The trio of religious and government buildings makes a grand statement, dramatically addressing the Mississippi River at the square's southern, open end.

But it is the magnificent Pontalba row houses that account for the square's rare elegance. They were built on the east and west sides in 1848–50, adding a graceful symmetry. Each building comprises sixteen row houses, with street-level commercial space under a continuous gallery and two and a half stories of residential space above. Their hard red bricks (so unlike New Orleans's soft, crumbly bricks), thin mortar joints, severe granite pilasters and lintels on the ground level, and lacy cast-iron galleries all contribute to the success of the overall design. Though the buildings along the square have been restored periodically, the Pontalba ensemble has not undergone major change for more than 150 years.

The formidable Baroness Micaela Almonester de Pontalba was the visionary responsible for their construction. She was born in 1795, the daughter of

ABOVE
Framed by cast-iron arabesques, the view from the front of the apartment gives onto Jackson Square and its live oaks. The public square, though modified over time by landscaping and the 1856 addition of Clark Mills's equestrian monument of Andrew Jackson, was part of the original 1721 plan for New Orleans.

OPPOSITE
The Lower Pontalba Building ("lower" referring to its downriver location relative to the Mississippi's current) faces Saint Ann Street, now a pedestrian mall, and Jackson Square. The first-floor gallery creates a sheltered walkway in front of the businesses that occupy the street-level spaces.

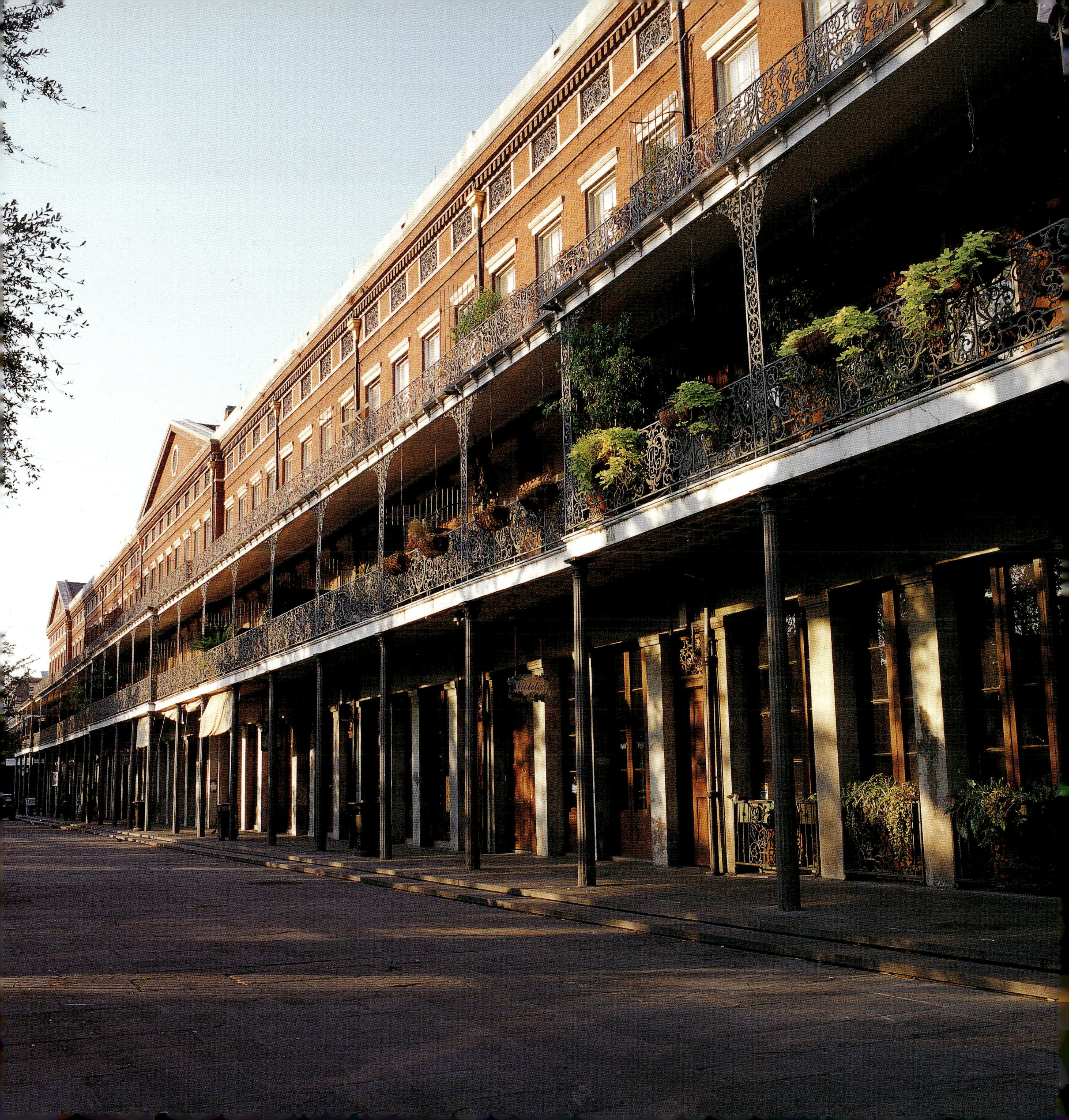

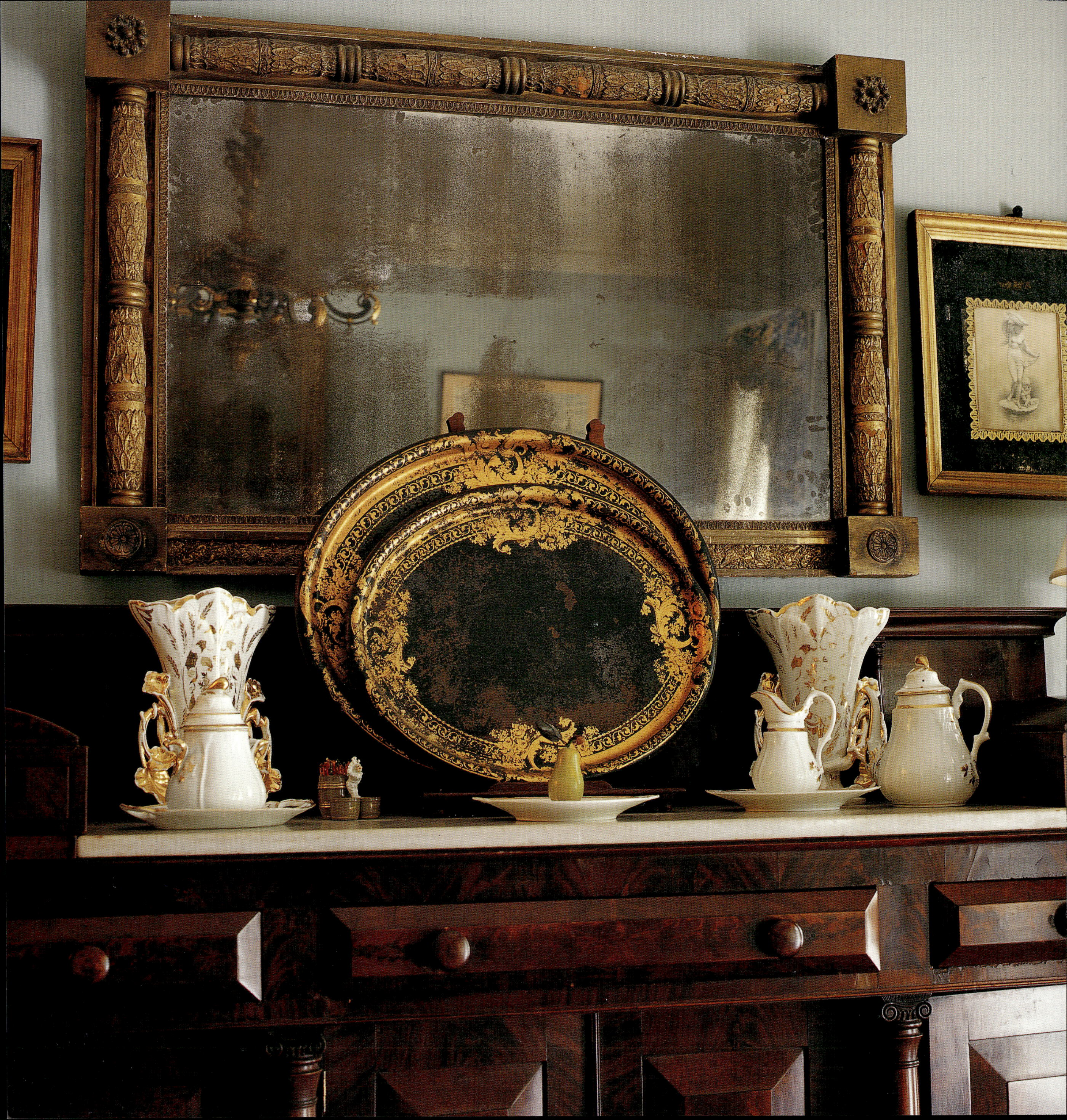

OPPOSITE
The salon's furnishings reflect the building's mid-nineteenth-century construction. A mahogany Empire-style marble-topped sideboard is set with tole serving trays and an assortment of Old Paris vessels. The Federal-style mirror above, its silvering clouded with age, exudes the atmosphere of a distant era. It faintly reflects the room's chandelier.

ABOVE
The apartment's two-room service wing overlooks a small rear courtyard. It is reached by an exterior covered passageway, screened with moveable lattice panels.

a Spanish grandee who had made a fortune in New Orleans real estate. After an arranged marriage at age fifteen to a French cousin, she moved to Paris, whose architecture would inspire her own building projects. Decades later she returned to New Orleans to build on the land she had inherited.

The baroness hired the renowned local architect James Gallier Sr. to design the Pontalba Buildings but personally supervised their construction from scaffolding and ladders. (Her initials, "A" and "P," are woven into the design of the ironwork galleries.) A shrewd businesswoman, and the wealthiest woman in the city, she was also responsible for the renovation of the *place d'armes* that faced her new buildings, landscaping it in the French fashion and installing the statue of Andrew Jackson, for whom the park was named in 1851.

The Vieux Carré's status as a fashionable place to live has waxed and waned through the centuries, but the Pontalba Buildings have always attracted artists of various disciplines, some of them great celebrities. An early, brief visitor was Swedish singer Jenny Lind. In the twentieth century, the writers Katherine Anne Porter, William Faulkner, and Sherwood Anderson all lived here, as did the photographer and author Clarence John Laughlin. It remains a most desirable address today.

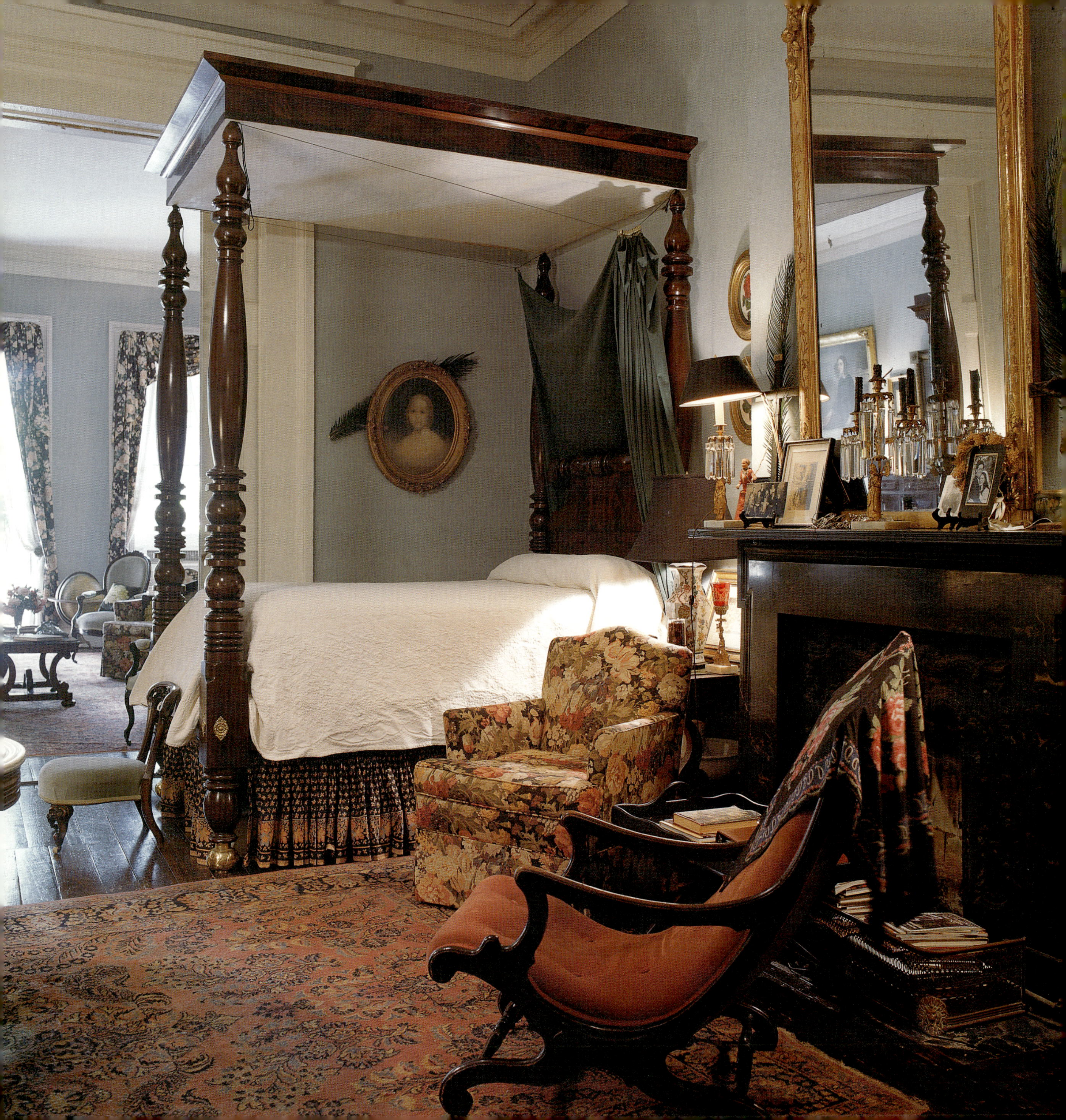

OPPOSITE

The second-floor Pontalba apartment shown in these photographs is currently home to Dr. and Mrs. Jack Holden. It has two large front rooms that, before the row houses were divided into apartments, were used as the salon and dining room. Today, a high-post full-tester Louisiana bed of cherry occupies one of the rooms, but bedrooms originally were on the third floor. The attic was used for storage and servants' rooms.

RIGHT

Arrayed upon the secretary and in the bookcase are books and photographs by some of the apartment's previous residents. Among them were archaeologist Frans Blom, celebrated for his discoveries in the 1920s and 1930s pertaining to Mexico's Maya culture, and photographer/filmmaker Carolyn Ramsey, whose darkroom was located in the apartment's service wing.

O'Brien Cottage

"I fell in love with the setting," says Pat O'Brien, "before I fell in love with the house." That was in 1969, when she bought the property, which lies on a large urban tract formed of several lots on a square just north of the Vieux Carré, in the Faubourg Tremé. The generously sized grounds, deep front gallery, and dormered front give O'Brien's cottage the feel of a country home. A traditional board fence enhances the sense of seclusion. Inside the gate, brick pathways and brick-bordered planting beds lead from the street to the house, past camphor and cedar trees and camellias. The garden continues in the back, all the way to the next street.

The house itself, an 1842 structure, was likely the first one built on the square, but in time the neighborhood grew up around it, with the construction of other Creole cottages, Victorian shotguns, and early-twentieth-century bungalows. The house was built for Charles Martinez, a free man of color, and his wife, Adélaïde Olivier, a free woman of color. Its builders, also free men of color, were Pierre Théodal Olivier and François Muro.

It is a relatively rare form of urban Creole house, the galleried Creole cottage. Like other Creole cottages, it is of brick-between-posts construction and, local brick being soft and fragile, is plastered on the front and sheathed with thick clapboards on the sides and rear. Its steeply pitched gabled roof and shuttered, symmetrically spaced doors and windows are also attributes of one Creole cottage style. Beyond the front gallery are two rooms, with two cabinets connected by an enclosed gallery at the rear; two more rooms are upstairs. The original kitchen, a separate three-room structure, is no longer extant. The current, miniature kitchen was created from one of the cabinets, which is a few steps above the main level to accommodate the *cave*, or storage room, below; a rare feature to survive, it makes the house even more

ABOVE
Next to the front French doors, whose louvered shutters are original to the house, stands a rustic olive jar. Partially glazed vessels like this were used to transport and store foodstuffs from Europe; by the late 1800s they had become decorative staples in New Orleans courtyards and gardens.

OPPOSITE
The O'Brien property suggests an urban oasis. A front garden with brick paths buffers the house from the street and is original to the date of construction. The shade provided by the deep gallery and lush plantings are key to combating New Orleans's intense summer heat. This is a house of tasteful simplicity, appealing proportions, and restrained architectural ornamentation: Box columns support a simple entablature with a dentil course, and wide, flat moldings surround the four full-length openings across the facade.

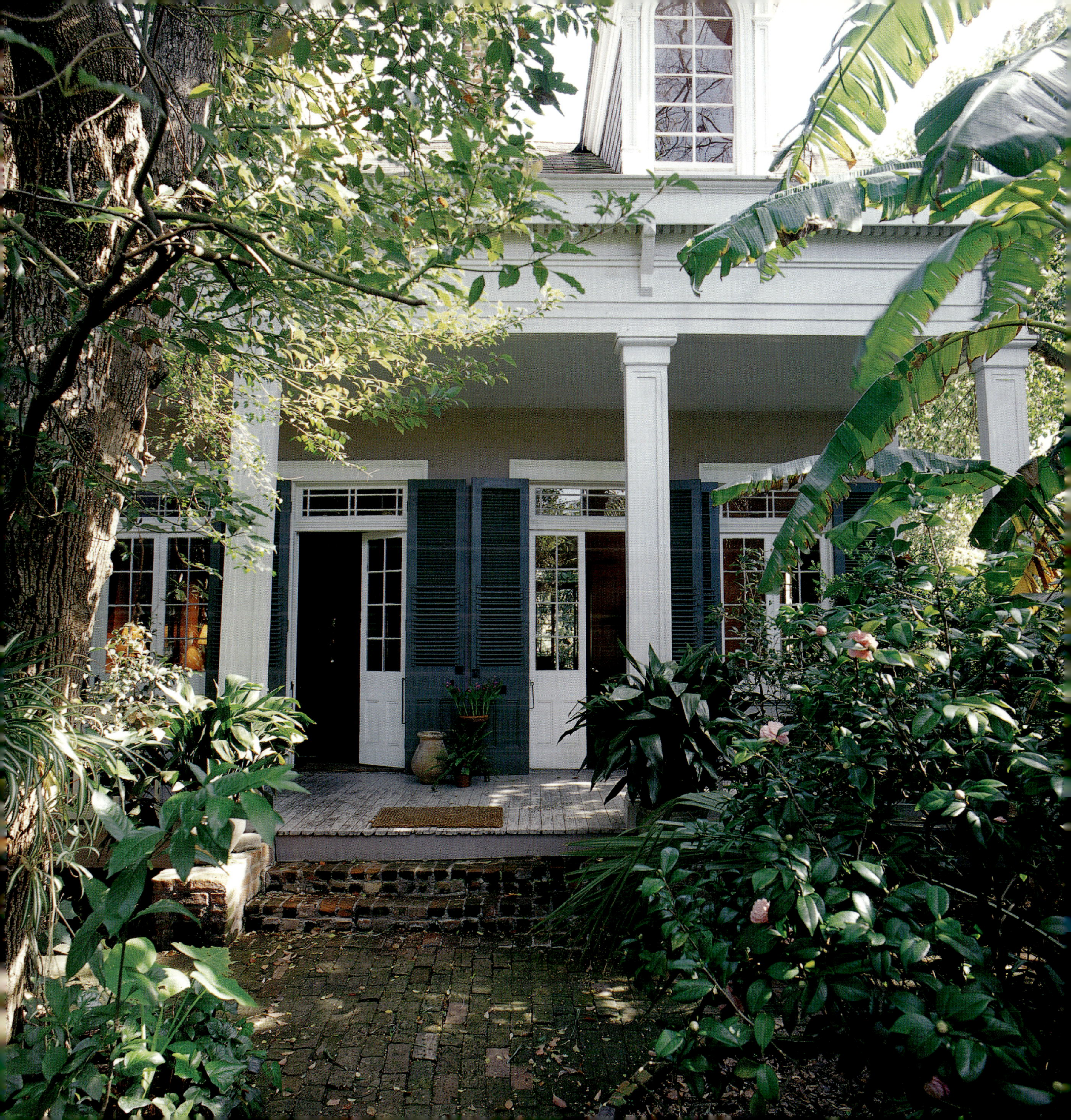

special. The other cabinet now houses a winding stairway to the second floor.

The cottage was home to one family for many, many years. Philomene "Mémé" Abadie, her sister, Pauline (Miss Popo to the locals), and her brother, Louis (Looloo), grew up there after the Civil War. The garden was the centerpiece of the Abadies' social life. Neighborhood children were given plots to call their own, and each May a statue of the Virgin Mary was crowned in the garden, a tradition celebrated by Catholic Creole families. Miss Mémé long outlived her siblings, but remained in the house—without electricity, gas, telephone, or other modern amenities—until 1954, when she moved to a nursing home. At the time, New Orleans resident Sylvia Saunders Davis wrote in an unpublished manuscript that the house appeared to have a broken heart.

Under Pat O'Brien's loving care, the garden and the house it surrounds are thriving, just as they did during the previous residencies of generations of Creoles. The house's broken heart has mended.

ABOVE
A portrait of O'Brien's great-grandmother hangs in the parlor; where New Orleans–made armchairs flank a gaming table in the Directoire style. The side windows are double-hung sashes rather than casements or French doors, a signal of tastes and building practices that were changing by the mid-1800s. Paints were matched to colors uncovered during renovation and believed to date from the 1842 construction.

OPPOSITE
Hurricane shades around the Wedgwood candlesticks ensure that breezes wafting through the open French doors do not extinguish the flames. A pair of ceramic Queen Anne–style potpourri baskets completes the garniture of the marbleized mantel. The portrait above is of O'Brien's grandfather. Below, the fireplace is dressed for summer with palmetto fronds.

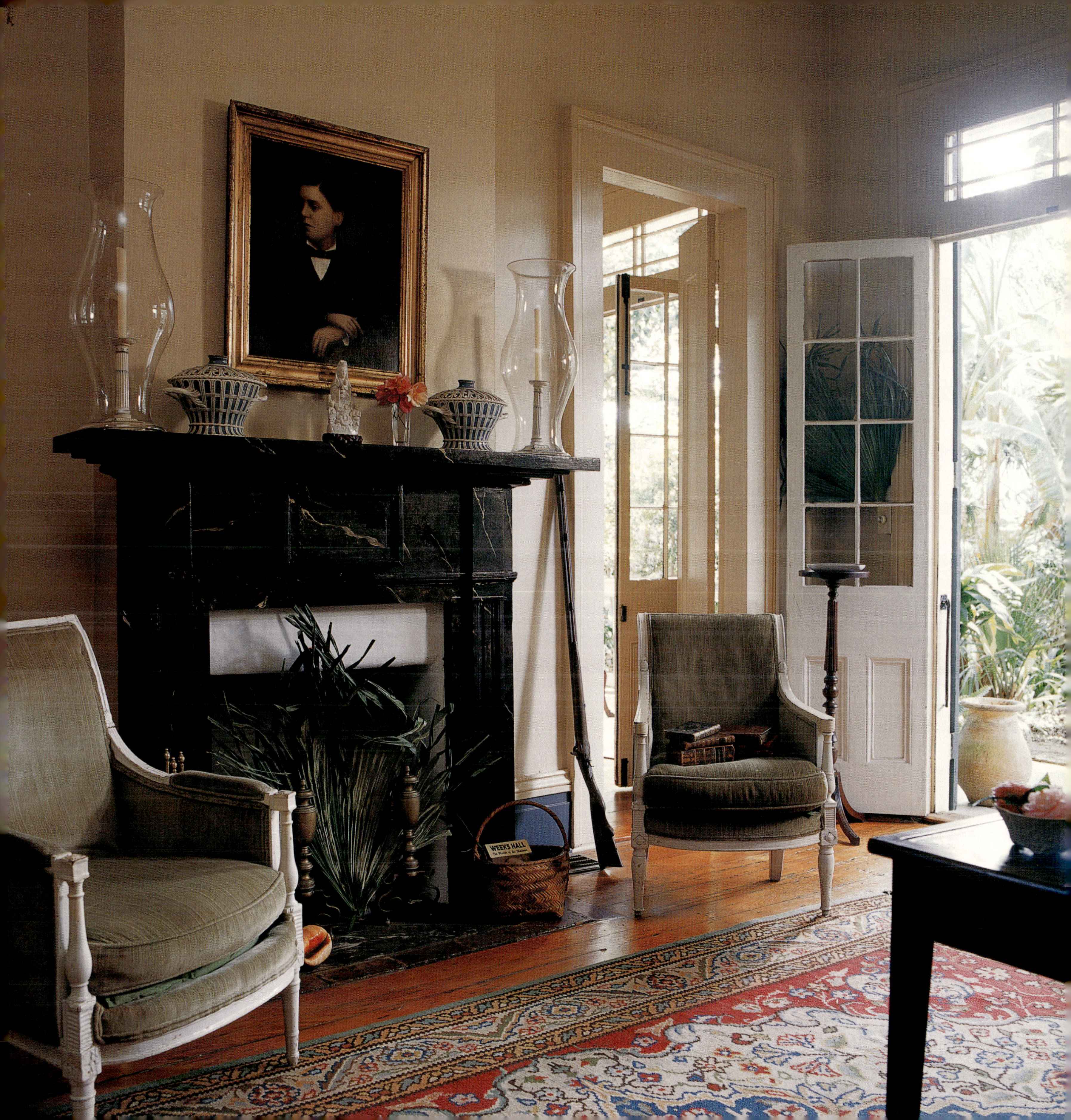
WEEKS HALL

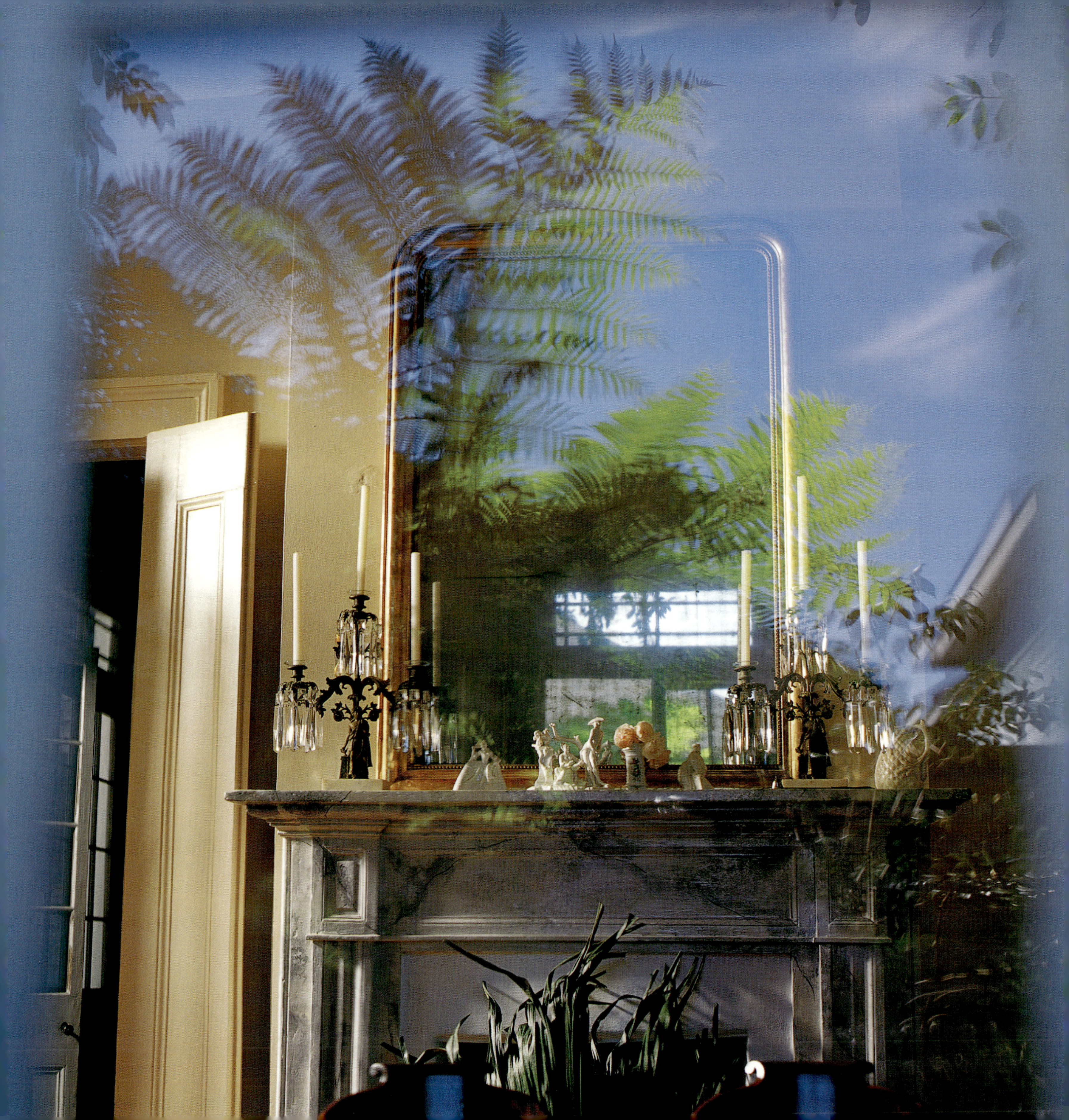

OPPOSITE

Photographing through a windowpane provides a glimpse of the house interior, with reflections of the garden superimposed. Design that allowed for easy transitions between indoors and outdoors was an important Creole architectural development. The nineteenth-century Louis-Philippe mirror over the mantel is from a friend's home on Bayou Teche. A pair of American mid-nineteenth-century girandoles flanks some samples from Pat O'Brien's porcelain collection.

TOP RIGHT

The pigeonholes and work surface of an Empire-style desk are filled with family photographs and objets trouvés. The inkwell, adorned with two pheasant feathers, was found in the backyard. The basket, probably of Choctaw origin, is from the O'Brien family home in southwest Louisiana.

BOTTOM RIGHT

A casement window in the tiny kitchen, where a comfortable chair is positioned, provides a view of the back garden, lush with its loquat tree, elephant ears, ginger, and crepe myrtle tree. Hanging from the ceiling are some of Pat O'Brien's collection of baskets, which she uses to gather herbs and flowers.

River Road

Louisiana's fabled River Road runs along both sides of the Mississippi River for about eighty miles, from New Orleans north and slightly west to Baton Rouge. It is part of the Great River Road developed in the 1930s along the Mississippi, which courses through ten states. But before there was a River Road, the river itself served as roadway. Notwithstanding the twists and turns, bars and logjams, cutoffs and chutes that sometimes made for a treacherous route, the Mississippi was the continent's primary watercourse, and into it flowed dozens of other rivers. It was a principal conduit of exploration, colonization, and commerce, and the rich land bordering it was ripe for development.

During the eighteenth-century colonial period and in the early nineteenth century, planters of French, Spanish, German, and English extraction established hundreds of lucrative indigo, sugar, and cotton enterprises along the river, where they built grand plantation houses that are considered the apotheosis of rural Creole style.

As periodic flooding was inevitable, the principal buildings were often raised above the earth by as much as a full story, creating a ground-level space that was most often used for storage. The elevation preserved the main living area from the risk of high water and allowed its large and numerous windows to capture the meager breezes off the river. Wide galleries, shaded by overhanging roofs, protected the house from the sun's blaze and had the additional benefit of adding outdoor living space that could be used much of the year.

Many of the Creole plantations that lined the river have vanished over time. When sugar fortunes swelled during the antebellum period, some houses were replaced by sumptuous Greek Revival or Italianate mansions (a number of which themselves eventually succumbed to a changing economy). Others fell to flooding, the shifting course of the Mississippi, or industrial development. Indeed, the River Road corridor today is largely industrial, not agricultural. But a few of the plantation houses of the eighteenth and early nineteenth centuries yet remain, having been saved from demolition and meticulously restored. Within their walls, River Road's Creole past lives on.

The *pigeonnier*—for raising squab—was a signature feature of wealthier Creole plantations. This one is from Magnolia Mound.

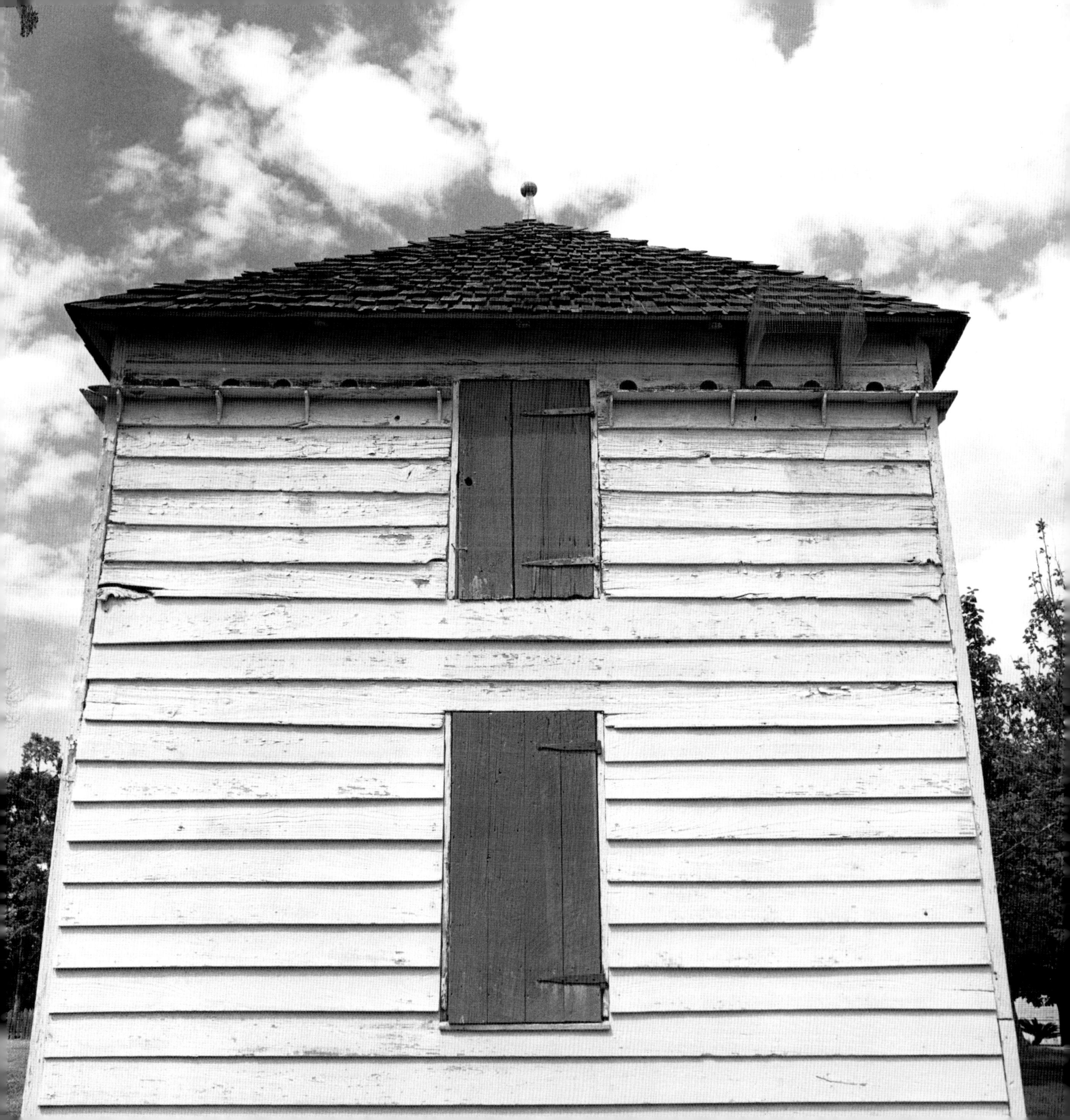

Laura Plantation

Norman's Chart of the Lower Mississippi River, brilliantly drafted by Marie Adrien Persac, is a cartographic landmark published by Benjamin Norman in 1858. It depicts the hundreds of plantation properties lining the river's banks, including Laura Plantation—known by another name at the time—near Vacherie.

Laura stands among enormous live oaks, and some of the surrounding locale still is planted in sugarcane, the crop that once drove its fortunes. The original core of the house, ten rooms (five across and two deep), dates from 1805. Although it is large, it is not among the grandest plantation houses along the river, a number of which are guised in the chaste white of classical antiquity. Laura—garbed in yellow, green, red, and white—fairly shouts that it is a Creole building, native to the subtropical climate.

Its building techniques are synonymous with early Creole architecture: The house is of *brique-entre-poteaux* (brick-between-posts) construction, a traditional French colonial method wherein the timber frame is filled in with masonry; raised on brick piers; and covered by an enormous umbrella roof, a variant of the single-pitch hipped roof, supported by a Norman truss. The construction type may seem heavy in contrast to that seen in other sultry climates, but the thick walls, shaded by the roof and galleries and raised so that circulating air could cool them, proved to be effective insulation from heat and humidity.

The plantation's history is as colorful as its paint scheme. Guillaume Duparc and his wife, Nanette Prud'Homme, constructed it on a 13,000-acre federal land grant, and Nanette managed it after Guillaume's death—the first of four generations of women to oversee the place. Her daughter Elisabeth and son-in-law Raymond Locoul, a French vineyard owner, made the plantation a distribution center for Bordeaux wine. The house ultimately passed to Elisabeth's

ABOVE
This cast-iron jardinière has a timeworn quality that suggests centuries of use. It stands near the *maison de reprise,* a two-story retirement home built in 1829 for Nanette Prud'Homme Duparc, matriarch of the family that built Laura. In the background are several of the outbuildings that testify to the site's history.

OPPOSITE
Gardening was important to Creole lifestyle for pure visual pleasure as well as for sustenance. Laura's *jardin français,* or French garden, embodies the former principle. Access to it was reserved for the plantation owners. Beneath a canopy of Canary Island date palms, gravel paths and boxwood define flower beds, emulating the formal, geometric designs of French taste. The cast-iron sugar kettle at the center of the bed references what was once Laura's predominant cash crop. An overseer's house stands in the background.

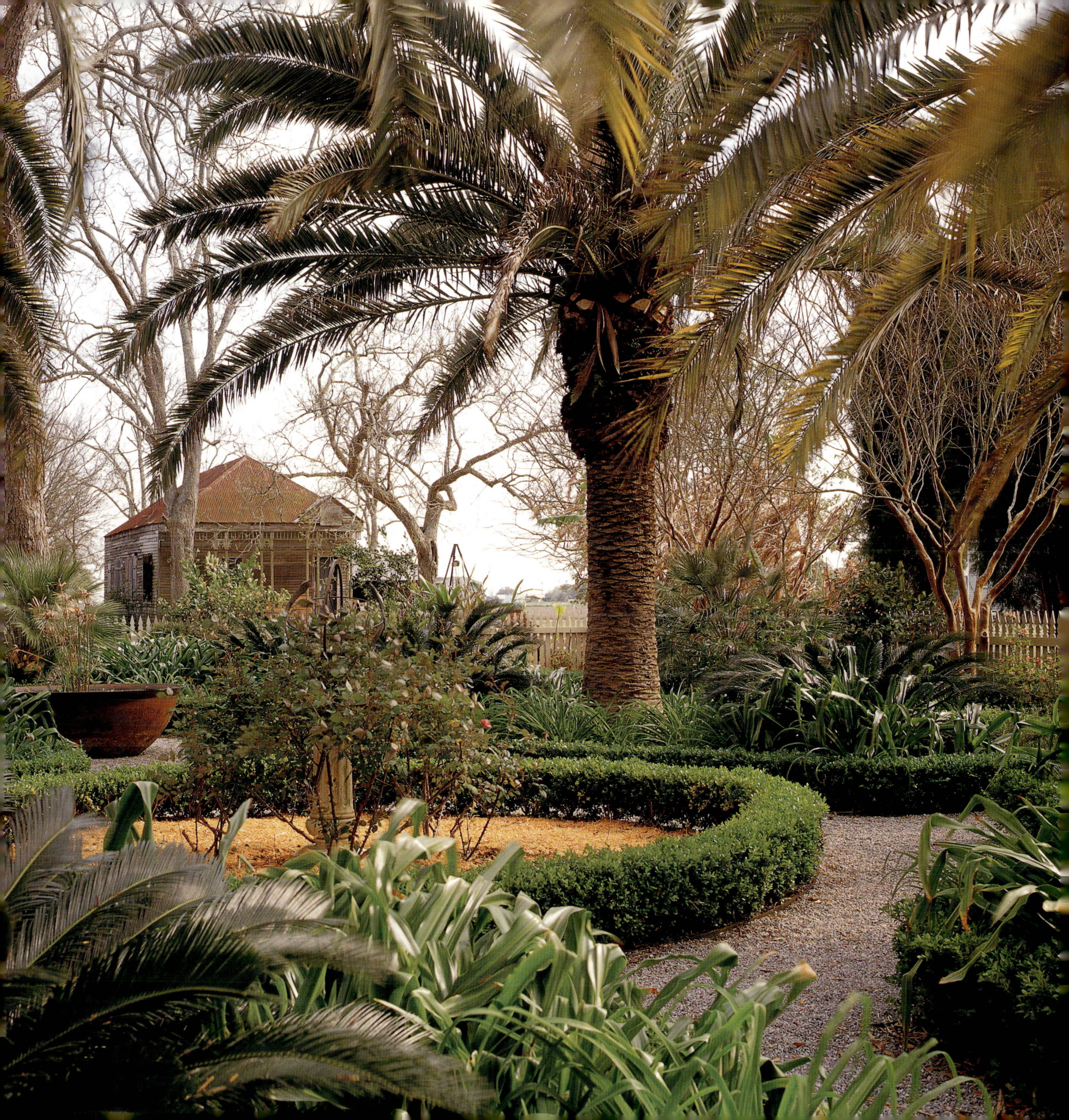

granddaughter, Laura Locoul Gore, who sold it in 1891 to Florian Waguespack with the stipulation that it bear her given name. Laura Gore's 1936 memoir has been an invaluable resource in the property's restoration.

Like any substantial plantation, Laura was surrounded by a coterie of dependencies, buildings that housed people and functions crucial to the business. Most riverside dependencies have succumbed to the elements, fires, or demolition, but still surviving on Laura's grounds are a house built for Widow Duparc, a barn and other farm structures, and six slave cabins. These outbuildings help convey nineteenth-century Creole plantation life to the tens of thousands of visitors who tour the property each year.

Laura's size, relatively early construction, and extant dependencies make it one of Louisiana's most significant Creole structures, but it has suffered the ups and downs attending any long life. When the property went into receivership, in the early 1990s, Sand and Norman Marmillion and a group of stockholders saved the house from the wrecking ball and began its restoration. It opened to the public in 1994. Ten years later, a fire destroyed more than half the main building, and this River Road landmark is once again undergoing a painstaking restoration.

ABOVE
The dining room connects to the front parlor with French doors, which can be opened to create a continuous large space and to provide cross-ventilation from the front of the house to the rear. Beyond the dining room is the pantry, where food prepared in the kitchen (almost always detached from the main house, to avoid heat and risk of fire) was transferred to fine china before being brought to table.

OPPOSITE
Creoles often reserved elaborate furnishings for areas their guests would use. Private rooms were simpler, sometimes bordering on austere, as suggested by the spare furnishings now in the lady's bedroom: a bed, two chairs, a chest, and a framed print. The wooden ceiling of plain boards and exposed beams was a colonial-era technique that remained in style into the early 1800s.

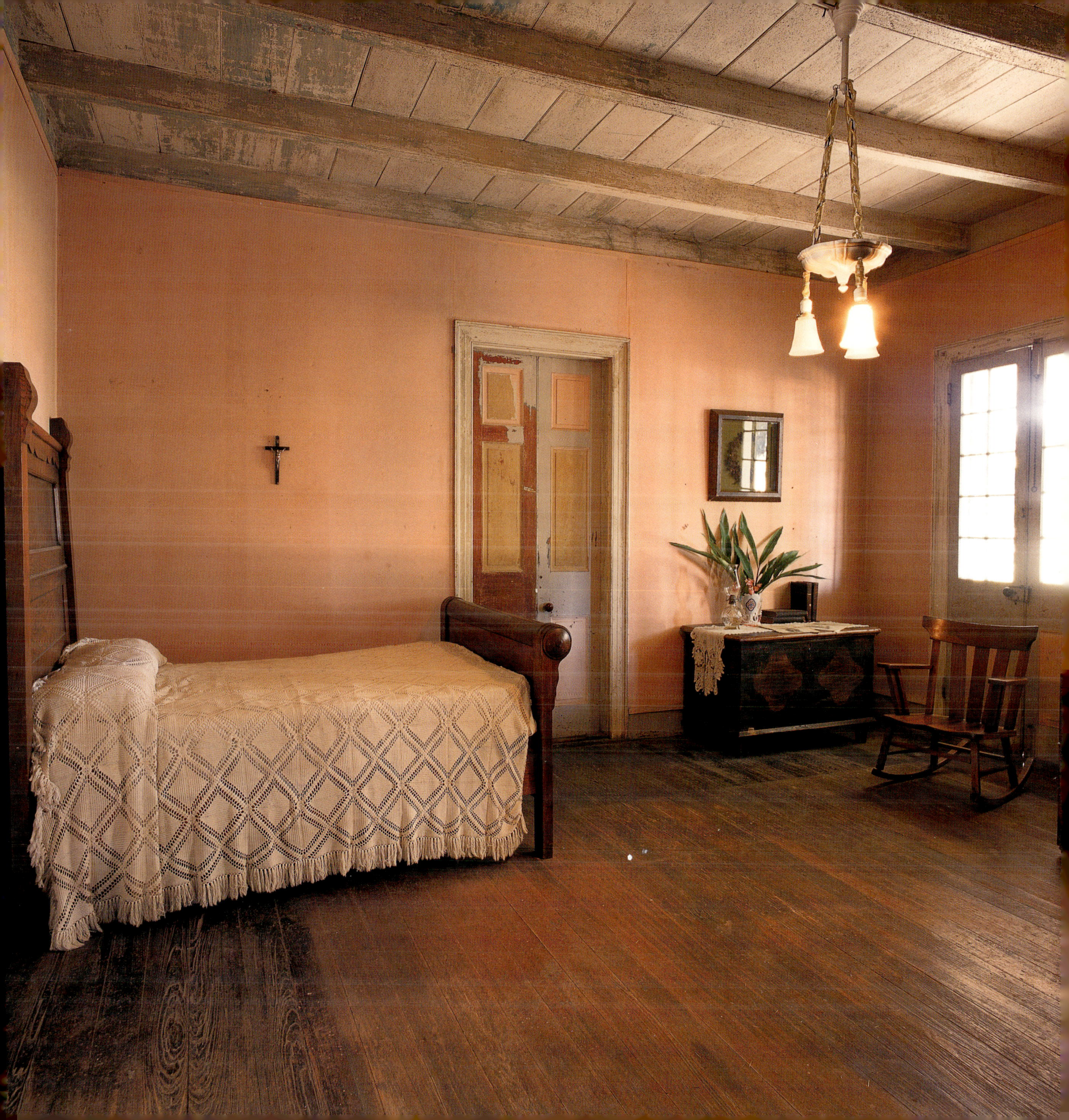

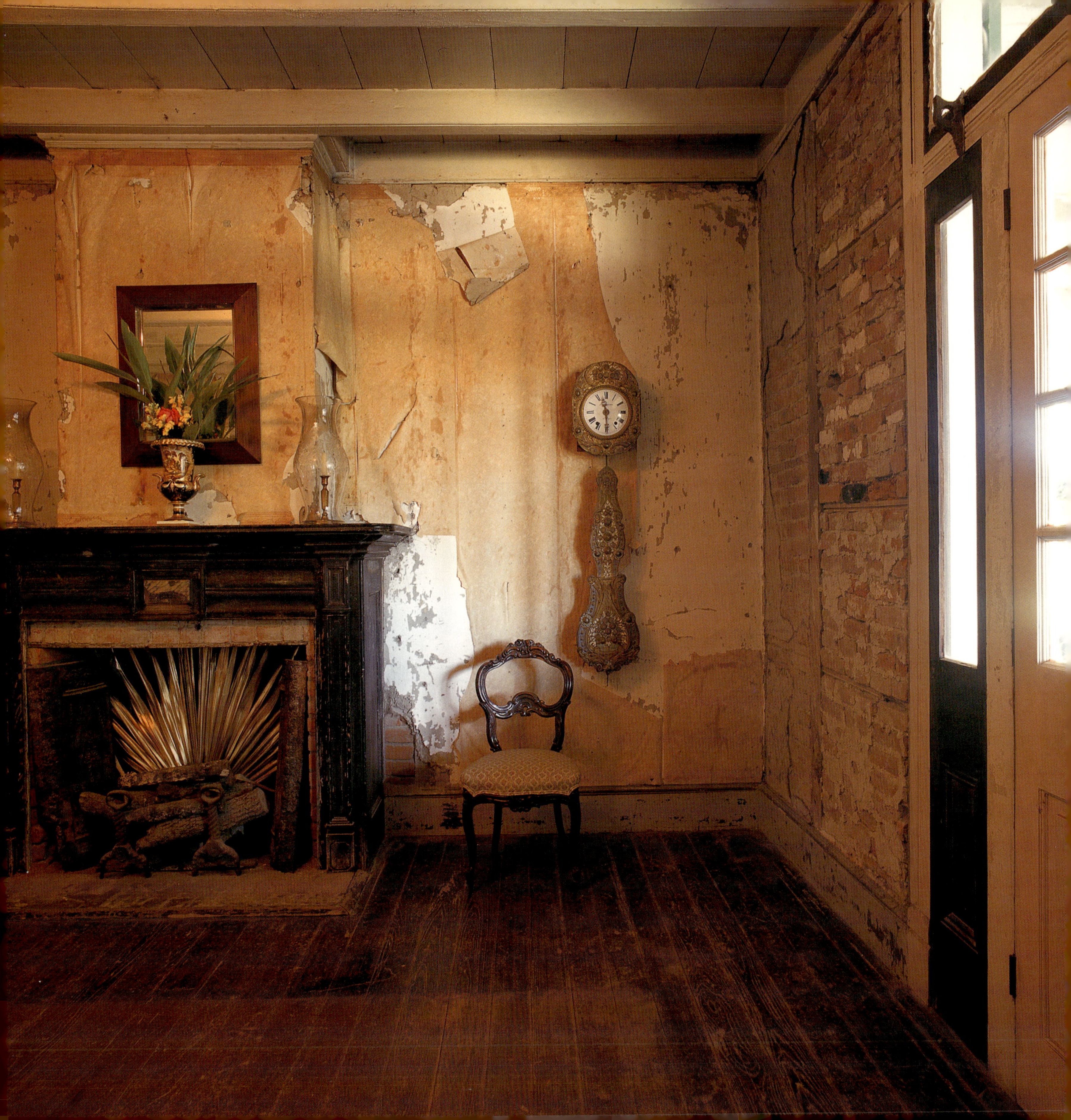

OPPOSITE

In the front parlor, with its peeling wallpaper evoking layers of history, the brick-between-posts construction can be seen to the right; when built, the bricks would have been covered with a layer of smooth plaster or whitewash. The typical Creole box mantel that wraps around the chimney is accessorized simply, with an Old Paris vase, two candles protected by hurricane shades, and a mirror. The rosewood parlor chair with needlepoint seat was acquired from Laura Gore's grandson and returned home.

TOP RIGHT

This locally made cypress table with graceful cabriole legs was charred by the fire that swept Laura in 2004. Now more funereal than functional, it supports a still-life arrangement with an Old Paris vase. "The table was damaged beyond repair," said Sand Marmillion, "but I'm too sentimental to throw it away."

BOTTOM RIGHT

In the ladies' parlor—where women of the household entertained their guests with coffee, tea, and conversation—the box mantel is cypress with a faux marble finish. Although the plantation's owners had the means to install genuine marble, Creole disposition was to save such refinements for the city rather than lavish them on a country home. The hand-painted silk fan above the mantel was an engagement gift to Désirée Archinard, Laura's mother, from her fiancé, Émile Locoul.

TOP LEFT
A wooden cistern set high atop this thick brick foundation collected rainwater, which gravity directed through a pipe into the ground-level kitchen. The opening in the foundation leads to a vegetable storage area, kept cool, dark, and dry by the thick brick walls and the water tank above. In the foreground blooms a type of amaryllis known locally as Saint Joseph's lily.

BOTTOM LEFT
The silvery gray patina of timeworn cypress clapboards and shutters provides a foil for the fruit and foliage of a Japanese plum tree, or loquat. Cypress forests once blanketed southern Louisiana, and the finished wood they yielded was used for everything from framing buildings to making delicate furniture. Called "the wood eternal," cypress was resistant to rot and insects and easily worked with tools.

OPPOSITE
Farming was but one aspect of plantation activity, which typically included processing or manufacturing the cultivated crops into finished products. Large plantations were akin to villages, with various outbuildings dedicated to blacksmithing, stables, sugar refining, and other such needs. Several cypress farm buildings remain scattered throughout Laura's pastures. The ones pictured here once housed chicken, guinea fowl, and rabbits, all raised as food for the residents.

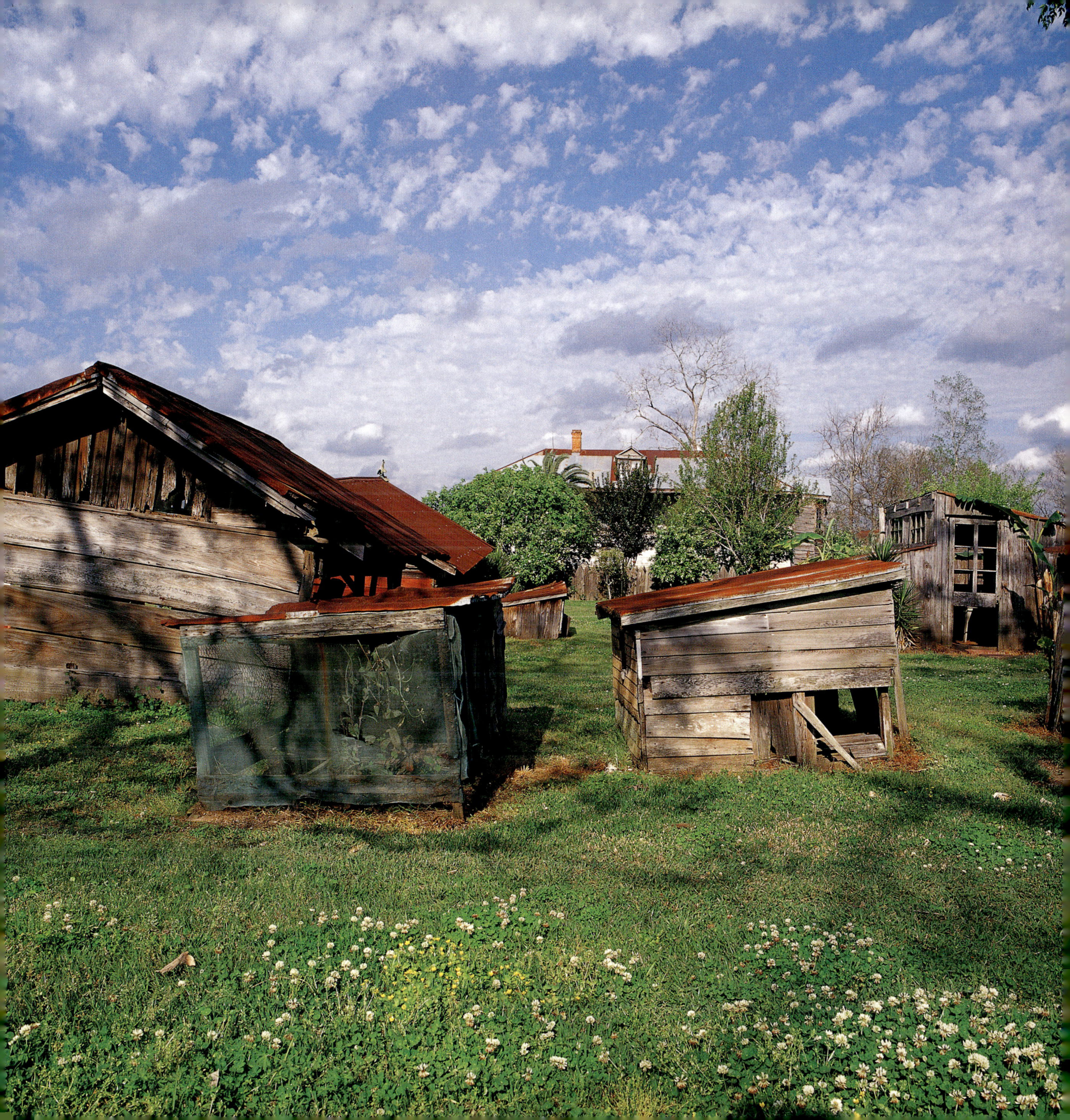

Chêne Vert

The architecture of Chêne Vert (Live Oak) is insistently French Creole, though it was constructed in 1830, almost thirty years into the United States' possession of Louisiana. A classic raised plantation house, with an umbrella roof, exterior stairs, and hall-less floor plan, it is set amid an impeccable formal garden.

Chêne Vert was built by Benôit Vanhille and Caroline Fontenot. Benôit was a French soldier who served in France's Saint Domingue campaign at the beginning of the nineteenth century. (A number of decorative items at Chêne Vert today relate to Benoit's former commander in chief, Napoléon Bonaparte.) Benoit arrived in Louisiana unexpectedly—via shipwreck—but there he met and married Caroline, the daughter of a prosperous cotton and sugar planter.

Their house, unoccupied for many years, was on the verge of ruination when it was acquired by Wayne and Cheryl Stromeyer, who moved it from its original location near Washington, Louisiana, to Baton Rouge—a four-day, eighty-mile trip over highways by truck and across the Mississippi River by barge. They have worked diligently to restore Chêne Vert's original character, viewing their efforts not as a restoration but as a resynthesis of a historic structure, its interior decor, and its grounds.

Guided by a mid-nineteenth-century inventory of Chêne Vert's contents, the Stromeyers acquired and installed furnishings of similar type and quality. An analysis of early layers of paint directed the choice of colors: The blue gray of the first-floor ceilings, the glossy black of the mantels, and the subtle peach and yellow tones washed onto the plaster walls upstairs are as historically accurate as they are lovely.

The Stromeyers also are replicating a Creole plantation setting on the eleven acres the house now occupies. They reoriented a number of vintage outbuildings that were on the site in relation to

ABOVE
Chêne Vert provides a stately backdrop for the parterre. Walkways of pea gravel and rows of dwarf yaupon hollies define the garden beds.

OPPOSITE
The Stromeyers have spent countless hours designing, planting, and maintaining the parterre at Chêne Vert. The original garden had been neglected too long to provide much guidance, so the garden at the new site was based on a plan found in an 1847 drawing in the New Orleans Notarial Archives. Cedars, hollies, crepe myrtles, yaupon, and sasanqua camellias are the principal trees and shrubs. Old roses and annuals add vibrant color.

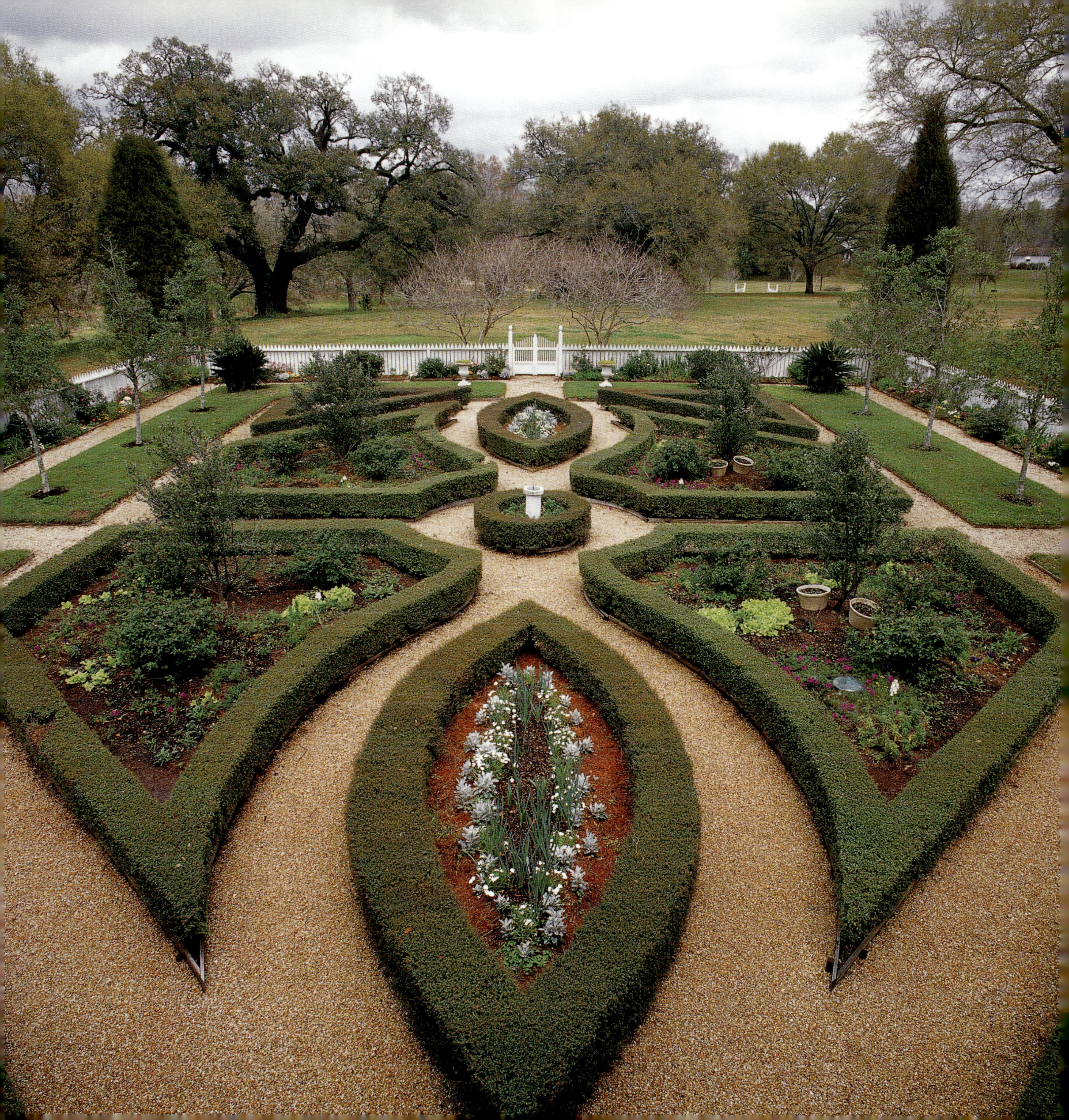

LEFT
Wallpaper borders at chair-rail height and the top of the salon's wall depict Greek motifs, a reflection of the Neoclassical movement that developed after mid-eighteenth-century archaeological discoveries in Italy. Federal and Empire styles, which incorporated many neoclassical motifs, were prevalent in Louisiana from the early nineteenth century into the 1840s. The large mahogany armoire came from Bon Pacquet Plantation in Saint Tammany Parish. All the doorways have curtains as well as doors; in hot weather, the curtains provided privacy without sacrificing the breeze.

OPPOSITE
The salon is furnished with several pieces of Louisiana origin, including a rare wing-back armchair and a small Louis XV–style table with delicate cabriole legs. The campeche or *butaca* chairs, one of which features a rare inlay, are probably Louisiana-made also. To the left of the mantel is a low armoire of mahogany and Spanish cedar, woods that suggest a Caribbean origin and attest to the ongoing exchange between Louisiana and the French and Spanish colonial Antilles. The soft peach paint reproduces the original color.

the plantation house and established an elongated, formal parterre, based on historic garden plans, that incorporates plants from the original grounds. The surrounding landscape is itself an echo of the original, with a low-lying area that has been maintained as a swamp, complete with two hundred newly planted cypress trees, appropriate hardwoods, and many irises. An allée of live oaks, the plantation's namesake and an emblematic feature of the rural Creole landscape, defines one of the approaches to the house. Though displaced geographically, Chêne Vert remains true to its origins.

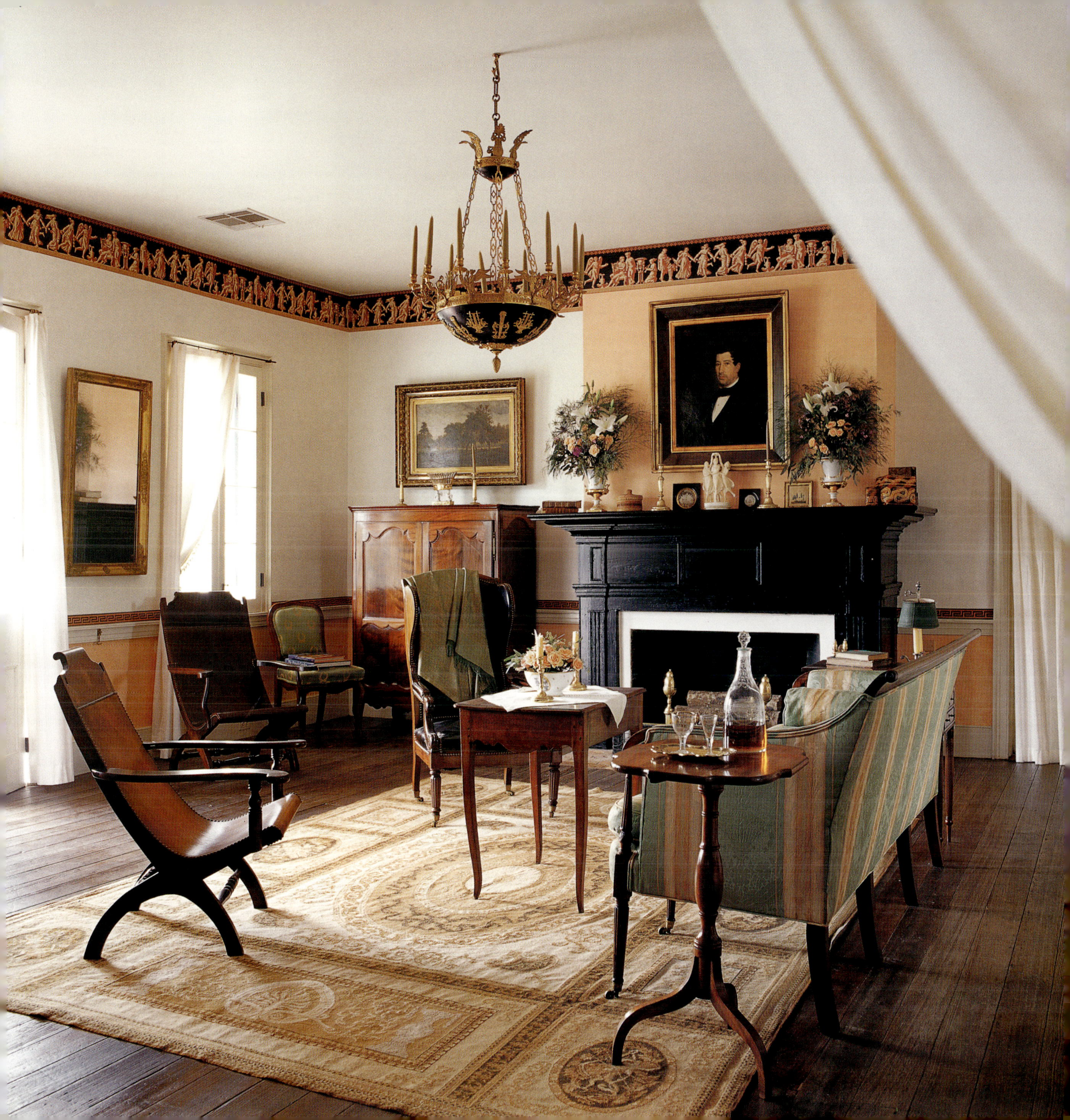

LEFT
A cornhusk-seat ladder-back Creole armchair and a Creole washstand help furnish an upstairs bedroom. The casement windows admit an abundance of light and air. Although sash windows were introduced to the area about 1800, casement windows persisted long after, reflecting both traditional Creole building styles and the greater ventilation a casement window provided over the double-hung sash.

OPPOSITE
An Acadian homespun coverlet from the early twentieth century is folded at the foot of a high-post Louisiana-made bed. Louisiana's Acadians have an expert tradition of spinning and weaving local cotton (their Nova Scotia forebears, who raised sheep, worked in wool). Their plainwoven fabrics, usually in natural white and brown or dyed with indigo, were used for clothing, coverlets, and blankets.

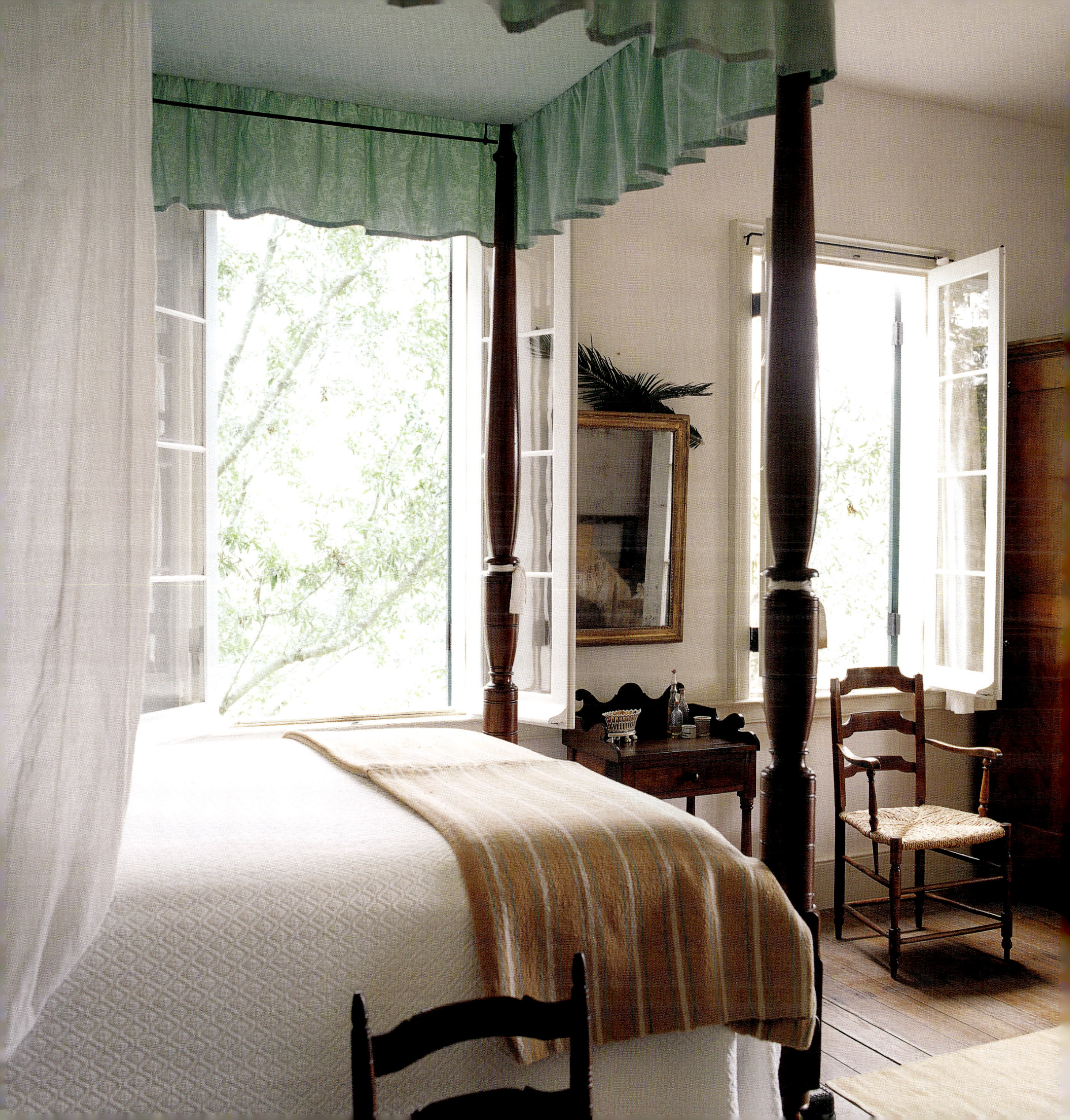

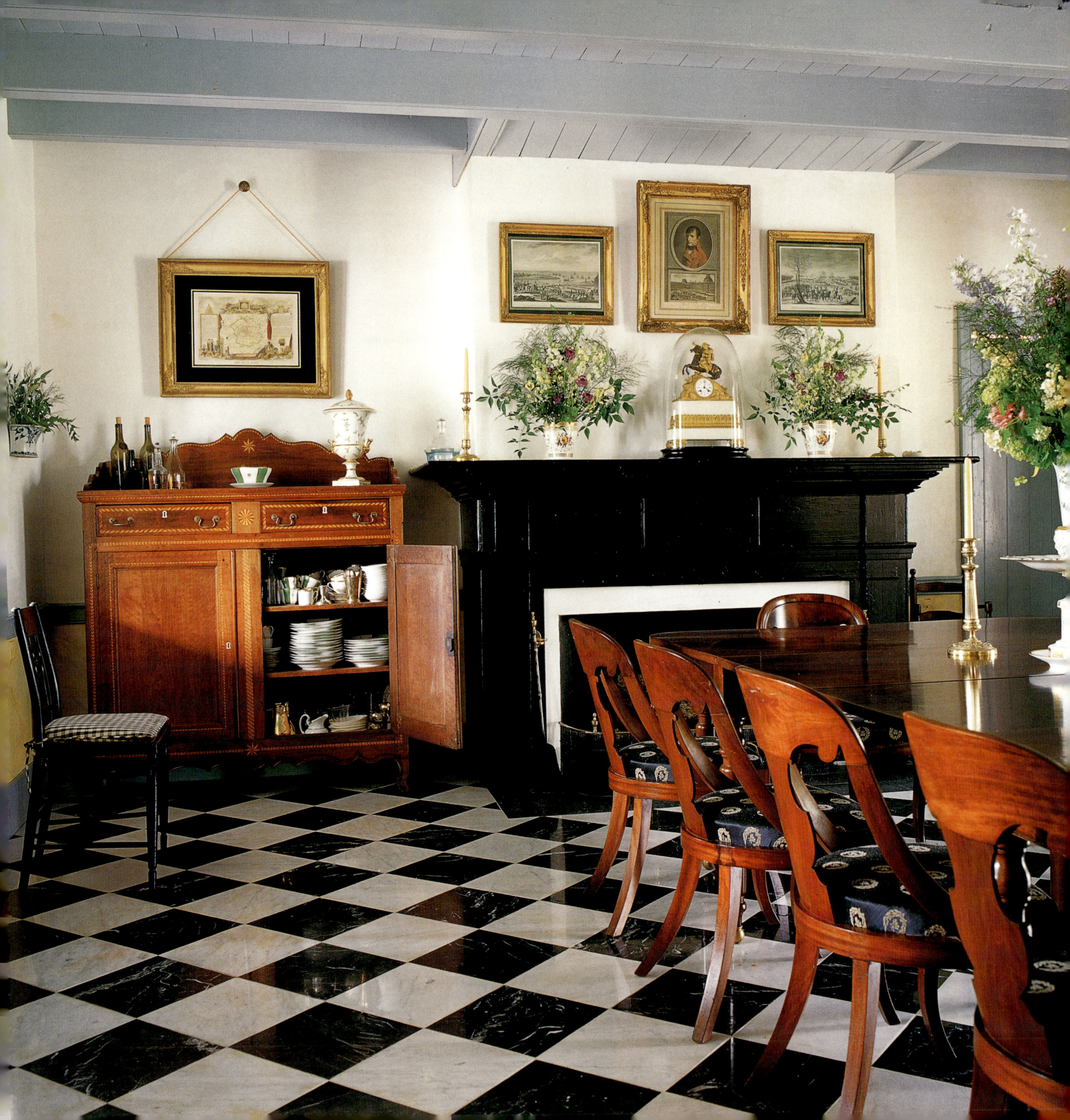

OPPOSITE

The dining room's black-and-white marble flooring has precedent in other southern Louisiana homes of the era and reflects French taste. The massive box mantel is one of six mantels original to the house; it is painted a thick, glossy black, imitative of marble, and bears a figural clock of Napoléon Bonaparte. The prints above the mantel also reference the French emperor. To the left is an unusually tall and narrow sideboard, which is likely from Missouri's upper Mississippi River Valley.

TOP RIGHT

A kitchen building near the main house features an enormous brick fireplace and cooking hearth; five ducks are curing on the rack above. To the right is the iron-doored bread oven; wooden paddles used to remove hot loaves lean against it. The cypress worktable from Houmas House Plantation displays a variety of kitchen utensils and ingredients. The mocha ware ceramics are typical of those original to the house.

BOTTOM RIGHT

Chêne Vert's new Baton Rouge location was already home to other buildings, including this Acadian-style house. Set behind a fence of hand-split cypress pickets, it now serves as a guesthouse. It is built on a foundation of huge cypress logs and constructed in the traditional Creole *bousillage*-between-posts method, which uses a mixture of mud, moss, and animal hair to pack the spaces in the timber frame.

Magnolia Mound

If Creole architecture is a language, then the design, decoration, and influences that shaped Magnolia Mound are components of a seldom-spoken dialect. At an early date the French Creole property acquired an American accent that distinguishes it from its contemporaries.

Built about 1791 on nine hundred acres of farmland, Magnolia Mound and its related structures now occupy but sixteen acres within the urban limits of Baton Rouge. The plantation's chief products have evolved from indigo and cotton to education: It operates today as a house museum. The complex interprets a period spanning some thirty years—from its construction during the late Spanish colonial era through Louisiana's early statehood in the 1820s. The current floor plan generally reflects changes made about 1815.

The building's Creole heritage is seen in its hall-free plan, French doors leading to the covered gallery, and the exposed-beam ceilings in most rooms. Like many rural Creole dwellings, the cottage is raised well above ground level to protect against flooding, capture breezes, and prevent wildlife and livestock from wandering into the house; atypically for a plantation house, the height of the piers does not allow for a full story of ground-level living (or storage) space. Early on, the occupants updated the house to reflect the latest fashions, adding Federal-style architectural details—including reeding, carved mantel motifs, and the parlor's cove ceiling—and enclosing the rear gallery to create a large, formal dining room.

As was the case for many historic structures, Magnolia Mound's charms and importance were long unappreciated, and the property was allowed to decline. It was rescued from demolition in 1967 by a group of concerned citizens. Rehabilitation began in the early 1970s, after careful examination of early-nineteenth-century documents. The plantation

ABOVE
The paneled shutters, which have slots at the top to admit light and air, can be used three ways. When open, as seen here, they allow the glazed upper portions of the French doors to admit the maximum amount of light. Closed against the doors, the shutters form an extra layer of protection against weather and intrusion. With the shutters closed and the interior French doors open, they provide both protection and cross-ventilation.

OPPOSITE
The grounds are planted not only with the namesake magnolia tree but also with live oaks. Eight of the trees on the property were registered and named by the Live Oak Society, which documents specimens that are at least a hundred years old. When built, Magnolia Mound was encircled by its gallery. By the early decades of the nineteenth century, some of the gallery had been enclosed to create additional rooms.

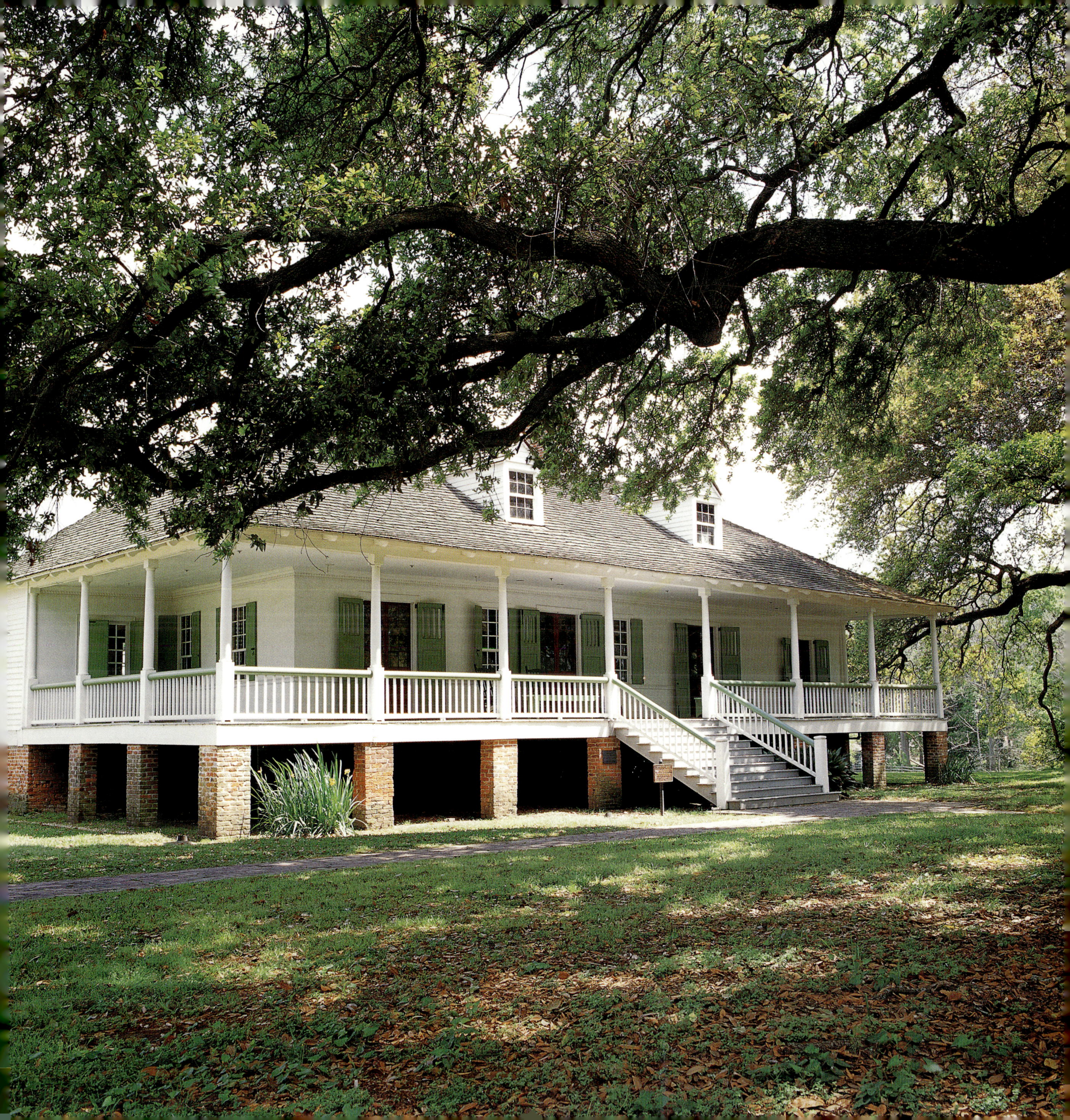

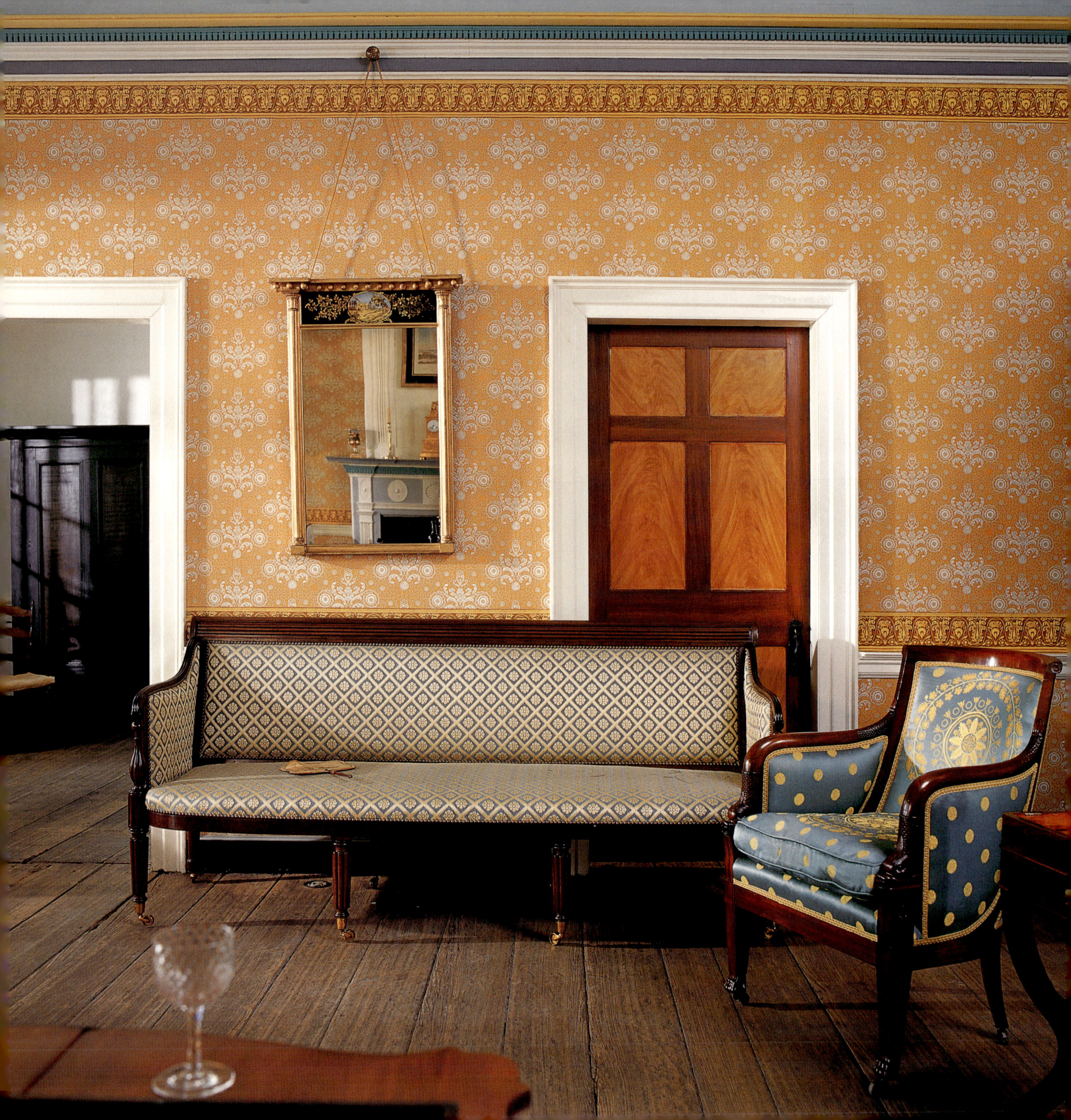

OPPOSITE
Wallpaper generally was used to make a bold, of-the-moment design statement; in the salon it combines with vividly painted millwork to striking effect. The furnishings underscore the house's stylistic mix: The New York–made mahogany bergère exemplifies French Empire design, while the mahogany Sheraton-style sofa, made in Baltimore, is a classic Federal piece.

RIGHT
Mounted by the master bedroom's doorframe is a holy water font, an almost obligatory feature of Catholic Creole bedrooms. Beyond, the door leading from the salon to the gallery displays its faux bois treatment. Cypress was typically used for doors and window sashes, and the exteriors of cypress doors were often grained to simulate a more costly species—in this case, mahogany.

house was furnished according to inventories of contemporaneous estates whose owners' social and economic standing were akin to those of Magnolia Mound's occupants, the widow Constance Rochon Joyce and her second husband, Armand Duplantier, prosperous and prominent planters. Because it is a museum rather than a residence, its furnishings conform to a pedagogic plan to interpret an early-nineteenth-century Creole life-style. However, over the years Magnolia Mound's collections have been scrutinized, updated, and fine-tuned, giving the house a living quality rather than the feel of a stage set frozen in time.

Magnolia Mound retains great architectural and cultural importance, as it bridges not only Louisiana's transition from European colony to American territory and state, but its shift from French and Spanish Creole traditions to tastes shaped by English and continental neoclassicism. It occupies a unique position in the spectrum of Creole style.

TOP LEFT
Creoles valued fine dining and hospitality; they could be lavish entertainers, with meals lasting for hours. Many household inventories list multiple sets of china, silverware, and linens. Magnolia Mound's table is laid with French and American silver in the fiddle pattern Creoles favored and glassware in a quilted diamond pattern. Past the grained paneled doors is a glimpse of the salon and its unusual cove ceiling (the walls curving in near the ceiling line), possibly the earliest example of such a feature in the lower Mississippi Valley.

BOTTOM LEFT
The mantel facade, from a New Jersey residence, expresses both Federal style in its carved decorative motifs and gougework and a Creole preference for box mantels. The Old Paris vases depict the Marquis de Lafayette, with whom Armand Duplantier, an early-nineteenth-century resident, served during the American Revolution; the opposite sides show Native Americans.

OPPOSITE
The dining room's exuberant wallpaper is a historical pattern known as "Les Sylphides," first produced about 1795 and inspired by the discoveries of Pompeii and Herculaneum. The New Orleans–made mahogany table is set for a family meal. Suspended by iron hardware above it is a cypress punkah (painted Spanish brown), a fan that kept dinner guests cool and discouraged insects from alighting; a child slave would pull a cord to move the paddle back and forth. Beneath the table is a painted canvas floorcloth of modern-day fabrication but nineteenth-century inspiration; its design echoes the upholstery on the seats of the carved mahogany dining chairs, which date from 1815–20.

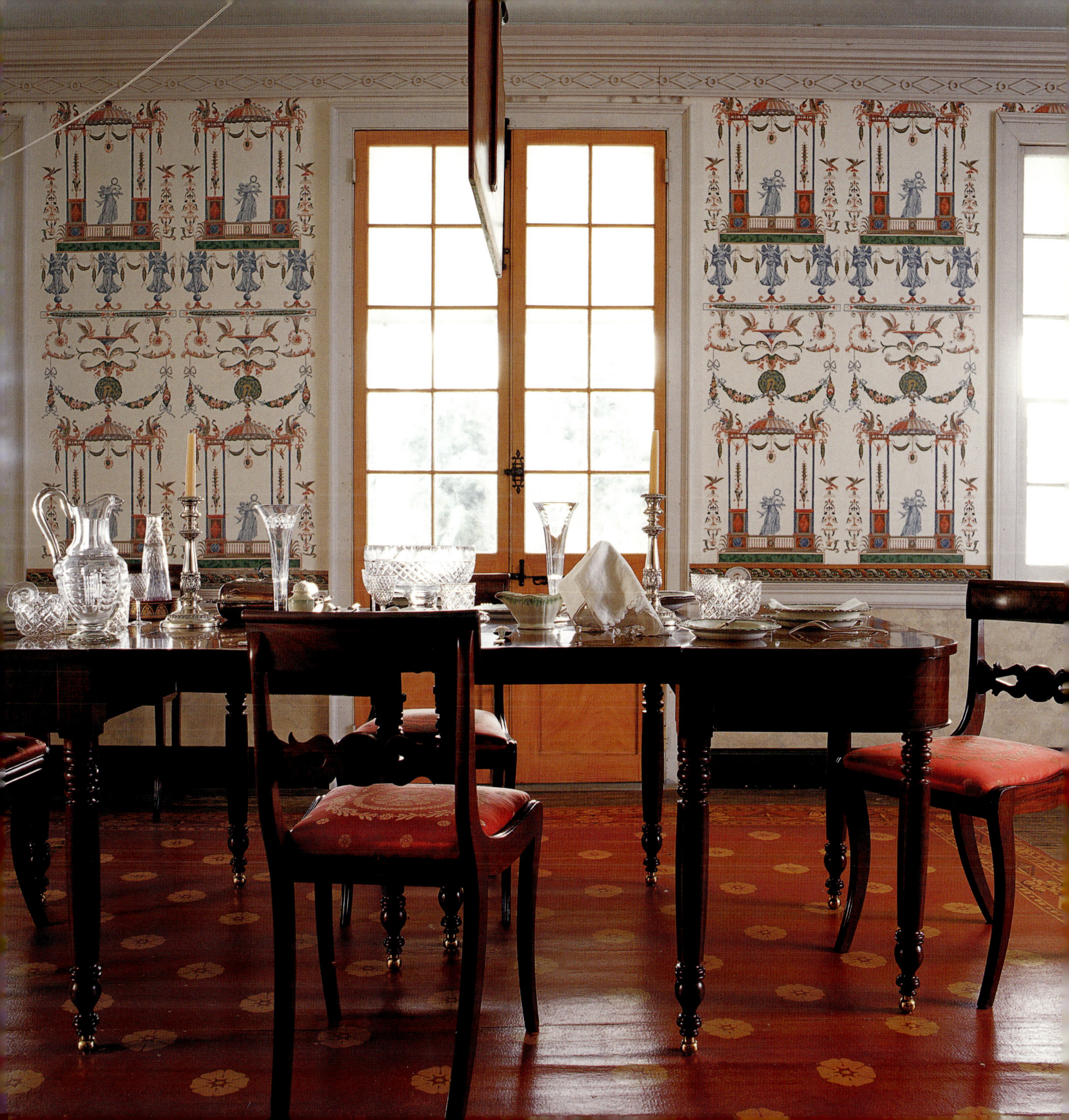

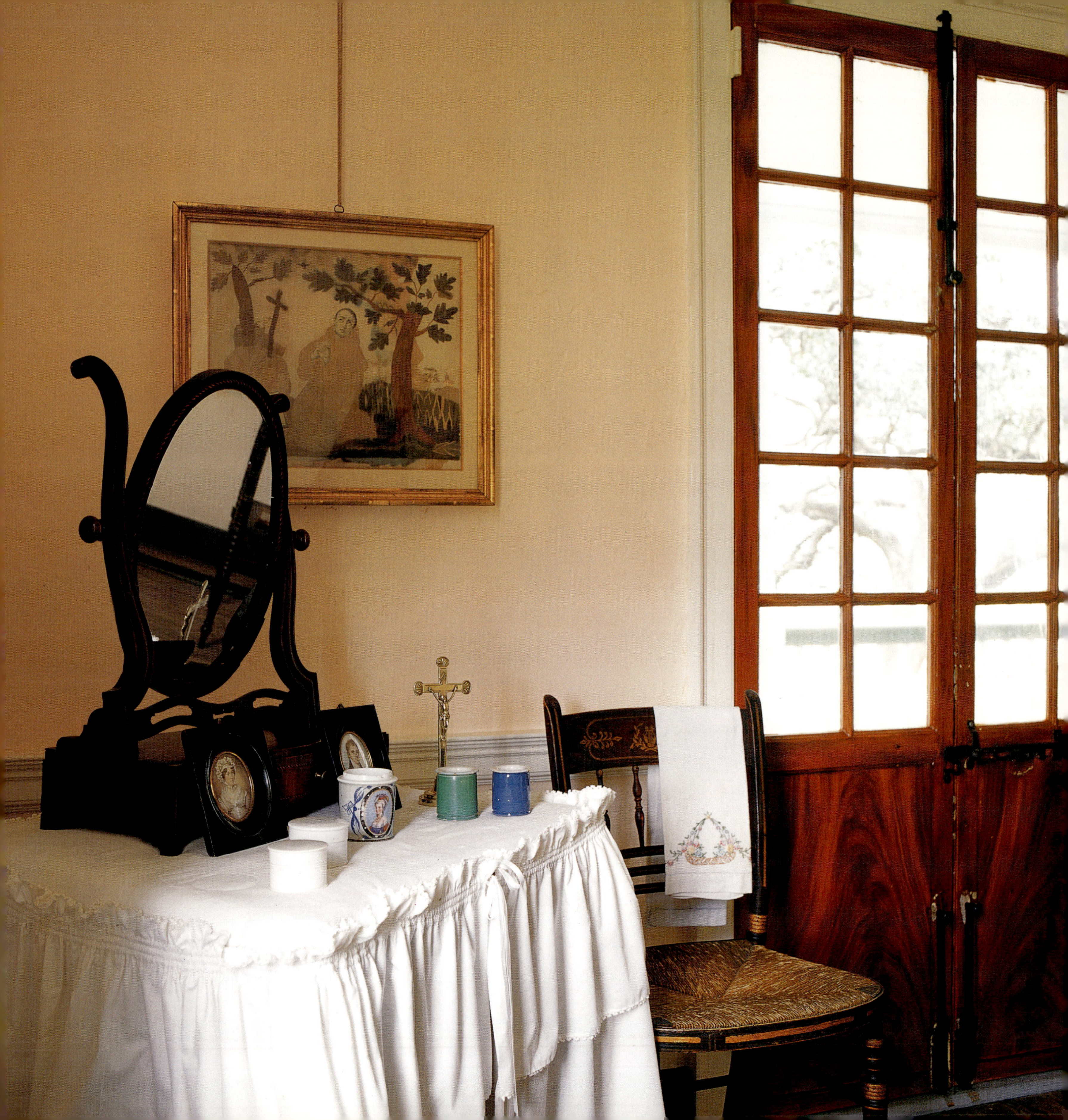

OPPOSITE

In the corner of the girl's bedroom stands a dressing table with a tilting mirror. The blue and green rouge pots were excavated on the property. The embroidered silk picture on the wall depicts a monk bearing the gospels near a tree; along with the crucifix, it attests to Catholicism's permeation of Creole culture.

TOP RIGHT

The girl's bedroom shows off the house's unfinished cypress floorboards. The early-nineteenth-century low-post bed, made of cherry, is topped by a mattress filled with Spanish moss. Moss gathering and ginning was a significant local industry into the early 1900s, when durable synthetics like foam rubber surpassed moss as a stuffing. A voluminous canopy of mosquito netting protects both the post bed and the mid-nineteenth-century pine trundle bed beneath it.

BOTTOM RIGHT

A mulberry and white toile in the "Athena" pattern, designed by J. B. Huet about 1804, dresses the master bedroom. The carved mahogany bed was made in Norfolk, Virginia, before 1800; the cherry prie-dieu (prayer chair) next to it was French-made in the early 1800s.

Pointe Coupée

The Mississippi, like any river, changes course over the years, meandering in search of the shortest, most direct route to the Gulf of Mexico. In 1722 it abandoned a long, deep bend in its main channel, leaving behind an oxbow lake, False River, and rich, alluvial soil in the surrounding area. Shortly thereafter French colonists established a settlement, one of the oldest in the Mississippi Valley, at the river's cut-off point, or *pointe coupée*—which is how the settlement, and later the entire parish, came to be known.

By the mid-eighteenth century Pointe Coupée was a flourishing French colonial community, home to many wealthy farmers. They planted the land—some of the most fertile in the state—first with tobacco and indigo, then with sugarcane. The community prospered and grew, continuing to be French Creole in orientation even as Louisiana's governance shifted from France to Spain to the United States. Unpretentious cottages and impressive plantation houses rose by the score along the river, amid vast cultivated fields, lush pastures, nut-laden orchards, and flowering magnolias.

Many of these eighteenth- and nineteenth-century houses still stand and continue to be used as family homes. In fact, Pointe Coupée Parish is home to one of Louisiana's largest collections of surviving Creole architecture. Most of the buildings remain at their original sites; others, facing destruction elsewhere, were moved here. False River, the sweeping, twenty-two-mile crescent of water that defines Pointe Coupée, lies some hundred miles upriver from New Orleans and thirty miles northwest of Baton Rouge. To this day it supports a number of agricultural communities (including New Roads, Oscar, and Jarreau) where sugarcane, cotton, and pecans still thrive—a fitting setting for these venerable Creole buildings.

Austerlitz Plantation's deep gallery is a tranquil retreat, sheltered from the elements.

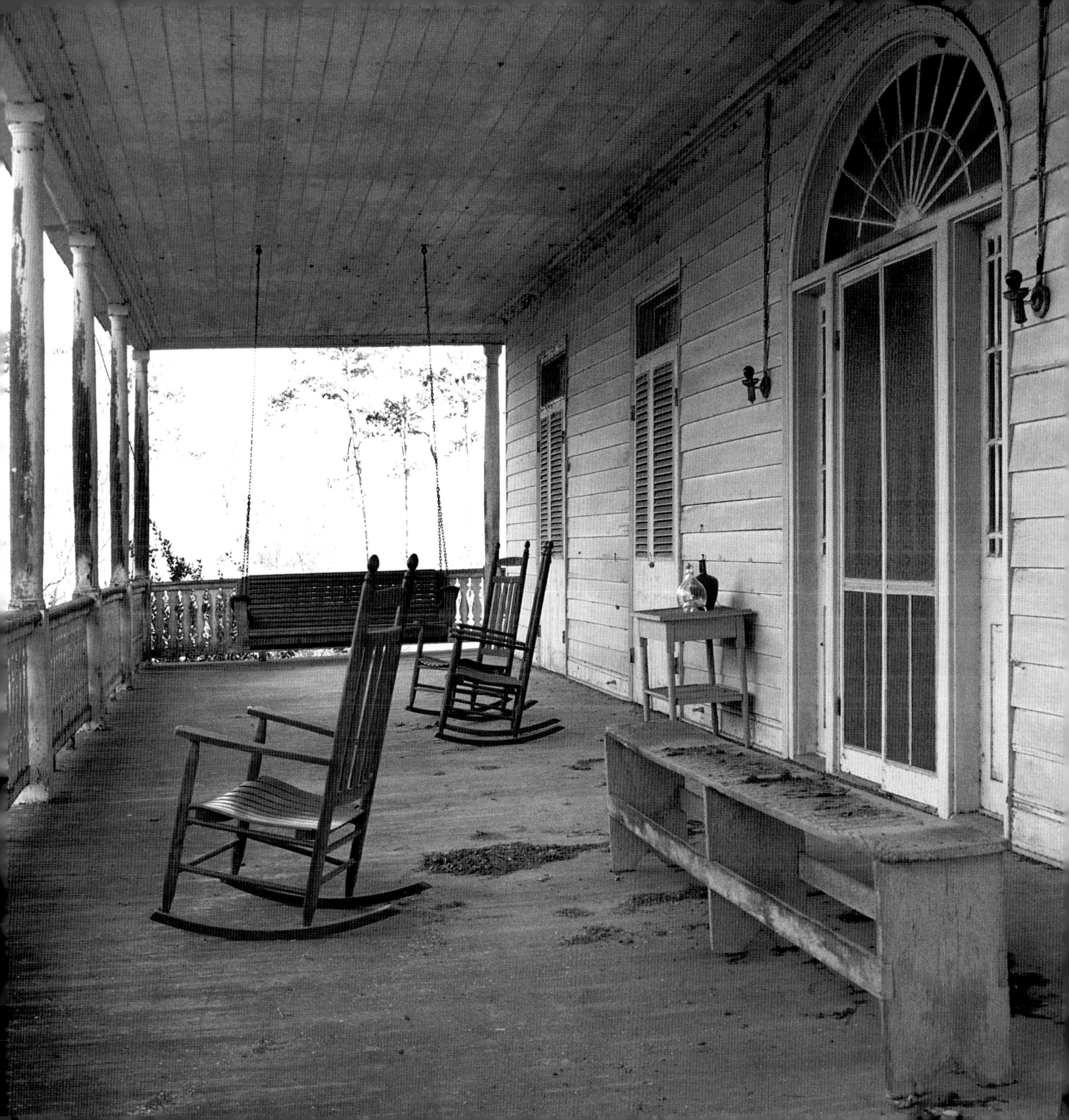

Austerlitz Plantation

Austerlitz Plantation, in Oscar, is like a beautifully patinaed heirloom passed from generation to generation in the finest Creole tradition. The current owners, Joe and Beth Rougon, and their three young children are the fourth and fifth generations of Rougons to live on the property.

The house was built on land purchased from Native Americans in 1783. Construction probably began in 1832 and was completed about four years later for Antoine DeCuir, a wealthy planter and a free man of color. DeCuir was a French-educated admirer of Napoléon, as were many Louisiana French Creoles of that era. The property's name refers to the emperor's 1805 victory at the Battle of Austerlitz.

Austerlitz exhibits many classic elements of the raised Creole plantation house, with a living story above a more utilitarian first floor (originally reserved for storage), deep galleries, and a hipped roof. Also typically, the lower story is sturdily constructed of plaster-covered brick between posts, while the upper story's timber framing is filled with *bousillage*, a mud-based mixture (now covered in weatherboards). A huge roof supported by a Norman truss—another building technique typical of Louisiana Creole houses—surmounts the building. But the wooden columns springing from the ground and supporting the upper gallery are unusual in a raised Creole house; columns of plastered brick were the norm.

The DeCuirs owned the property until about 1855. The next three decades saw a trio of relatively brief ownerships until 1886, when Joseph A. Rougon purchased Austerlitz, thereby initiating the current line of title. In 1899 Rougon added a sizable rear wing; the jigsawed balusters of the upper-level gallery and other ornamental details may also date from this period, or a little later. A subsequent generation of the family, Colonel Henry Rougon and his sisters,

ABOVE
This grafted camellia, one of the 125 Colonel Henry Rougon and his sisters planted in 1939, adds color to the front garden. Their plan included beds of ivy and day lilies, lawns, and roses; an abundance of flowering shrubs, like the camellias and some 250 azaleas; as well as a sundial, birdbaths, and a gazing globe. The current Rougons are renovating the formal gardens, which measure approximately 350 by 250 feet, to include plants from throughout the property's history.

OPPOSITE
Set far from the road, Austerlitz conveys a timeworn dignity and elegance. The placement of the chimney stacks deep within the house, rather than at the ends, is characteristically Creole—and virtually necessitated by use of the hipped roof, which could not support a tall chimney at the outer wall the way a gable-ended house did. Each chimney serves two fireplaces that are placed back to back in adjacent rooms.

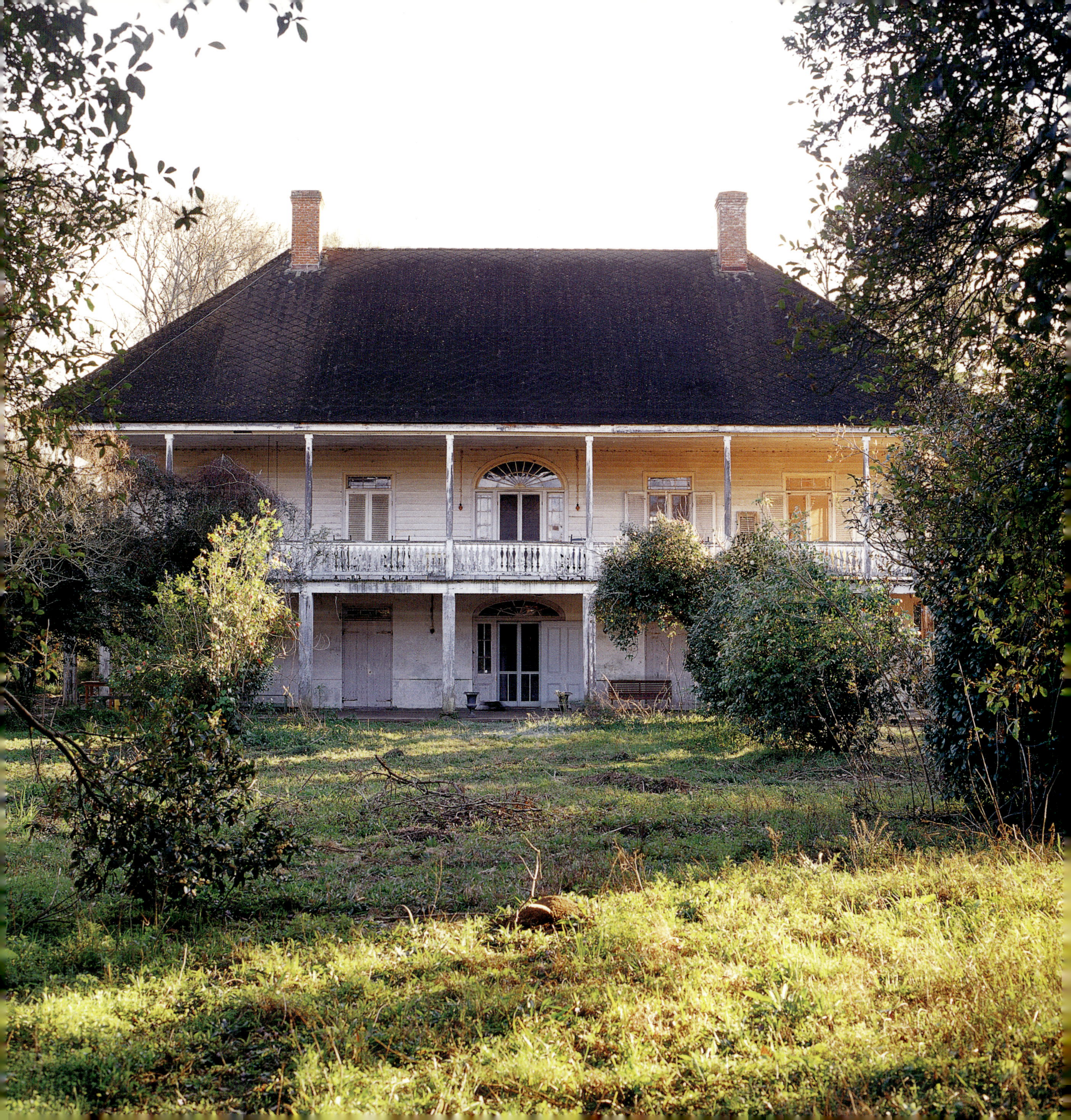

Ida and Itha, extensively landscaped and laid out the formal front garden in 1939.

Consulting with experts and scholars and examining public records and other historical sources, Joe and Beth have judiciously refurbished the twenty-two-room house's architecture and furnishings. In recognition of Austerlitz's historical and architectural significance, it was listed on the National Register of Historic Places in 1991. But Austerlitz is more than a historic restoration project; it is the Rougons' home. Beth describes standing on the deep front gallery and looking toward the sparkling False River as akin to being on a great ship sailing through time.

ABOVE LEFT
A chaise made in Berlin and upholstered in rich blue velvet occupies a corner of Dr. Rougon's bedroom. On the wall is a French clock that Beth and Joe wind daily. The wide flooring planks characteristic of early-nineteenth-century Louisiana Creole houses have been replaced by narrower floor boards, which likely date from the 1899 renovations. An inlaid slant-top secretary holds a pair of cachepots with bouquets of chenille and beads.

ABOVE RIGHT
A gilded wood Venetian side chair, about 1810, is placed to take advantage of the breeze and the view offered by the open French door leading to the front gallery. Family memorabilia covers the table.

OPPOSITE
Like all the original rooms of Austerlitz, Dr. Rougon's bedroom opens onto the deep galleries; set at the front of the house, it has fine views toward False River. The mantel garniture includes a pair of green glass girandoles.

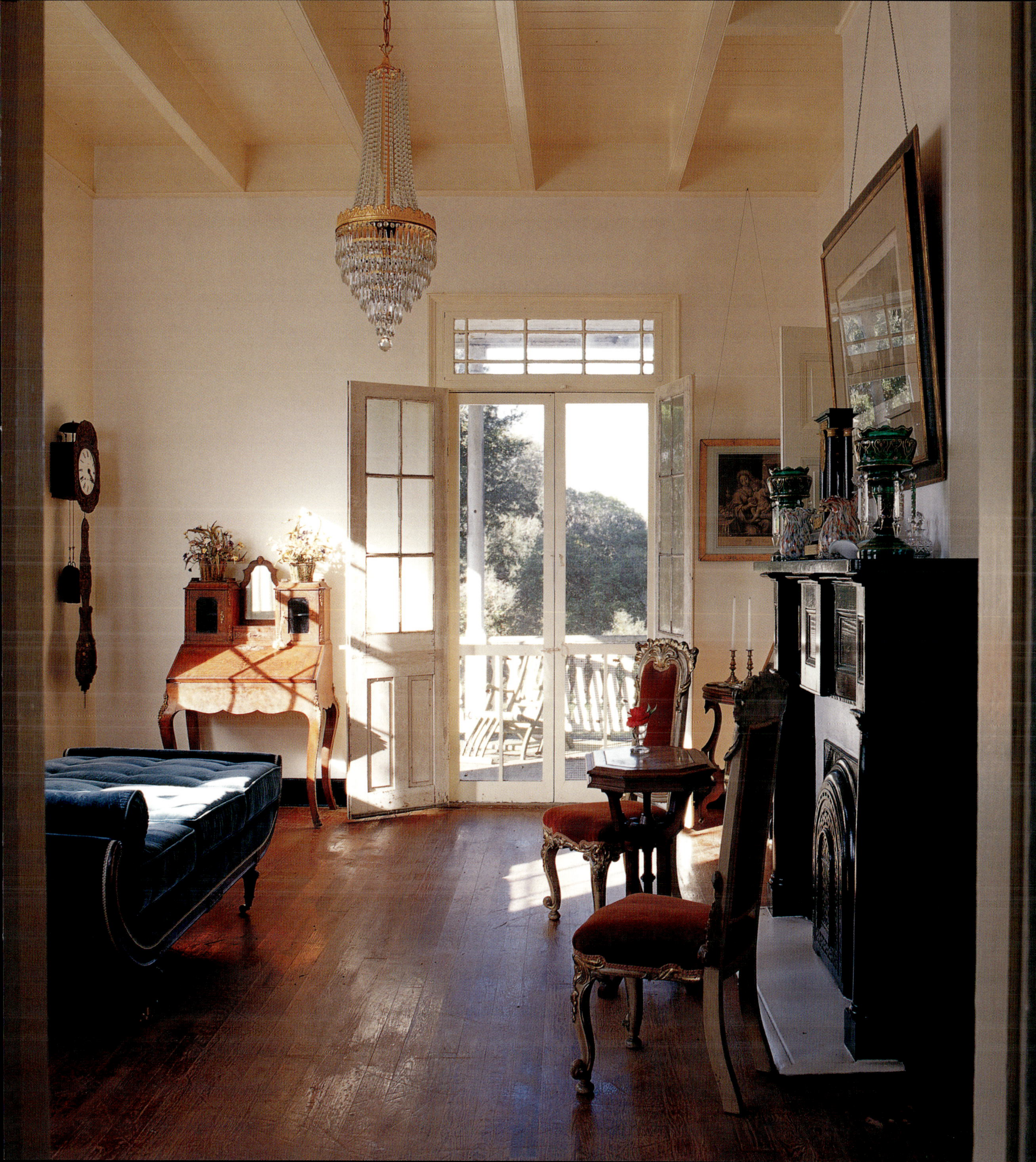

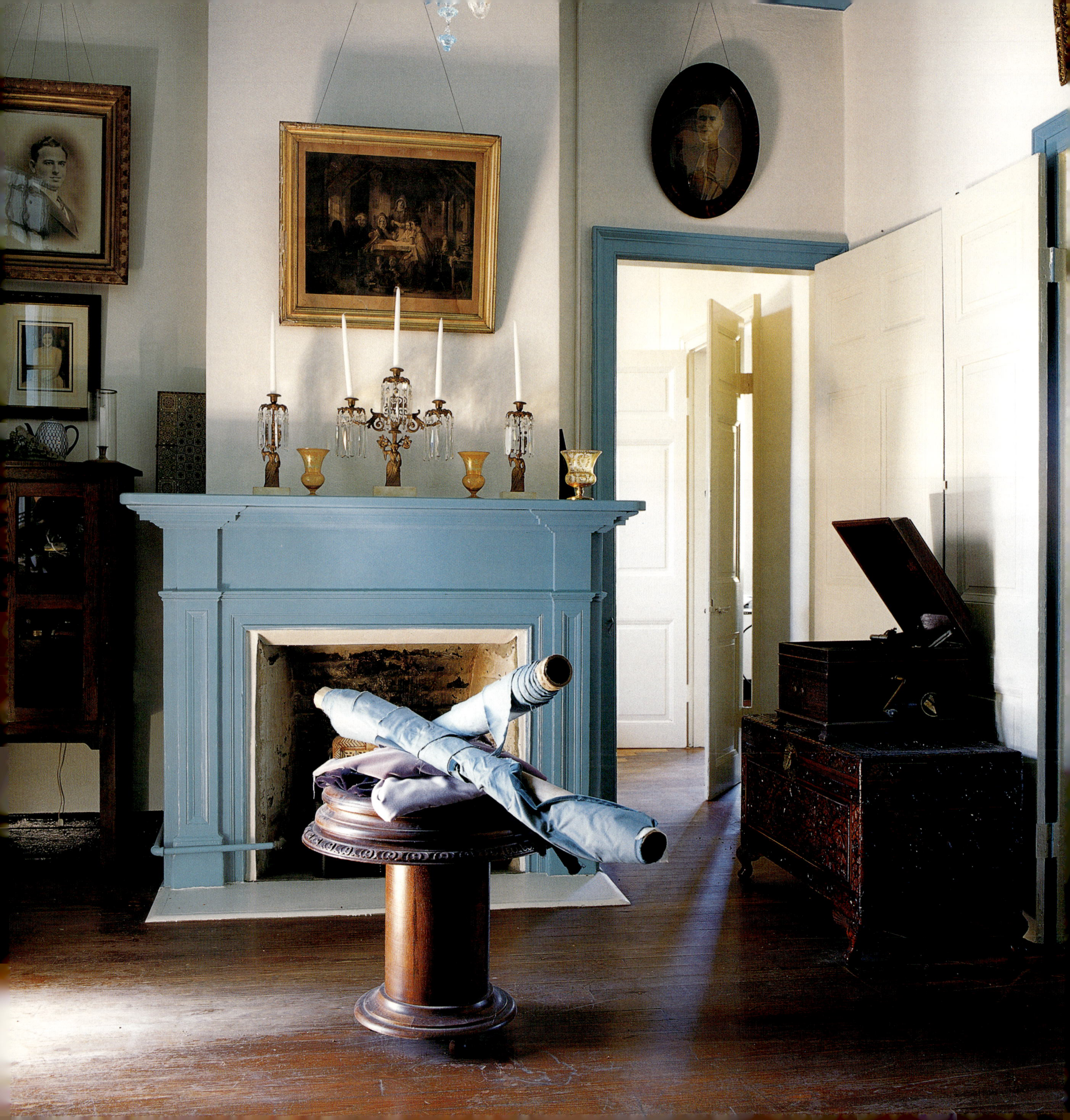

OPPOSITE
An upstairs bedroom is dedicated to Joe Rougon's great-aunt Amelie, an artist active in the early twentieth century, whose paintings and drawings are displayed throughout the house. Portraits of generations of Rougons hang in this room. The mantel is painted in what research indicated was its original shade of blue. This Prussian blue appears on architectural details throughout the house, including ceiling boards and beams, door frames, and other mantels.

TOP RIGHT
Research indicates that Austerlitz once had a room of Napoleonic memorabilia, so Beth and Joe Rougon are collecting objects relating to the French emperor's life and career, including the equestrian portrait hanging above the hall mirror. The interior staircase possibly dates from Austerlitz's 1899 addition. Staircases in raised Creole plantation houses were generally on the exterior, but no evidence has been found of one here.

BOTTOM RIGHT
In the main salon, on the wall to the right, is one of a pair of McKenny & Hall lithographed portraits of Native Americans dating from the early 1840s—an homage to the two chiefs (named Nicolas and Champagne in the act of sale) who in 1783 sold the property on which Austerlitz was later built. Girandoles and an Empire-era clock sit atop the mantel, and a marble-topped center table from the same period occupies the middle of the room.

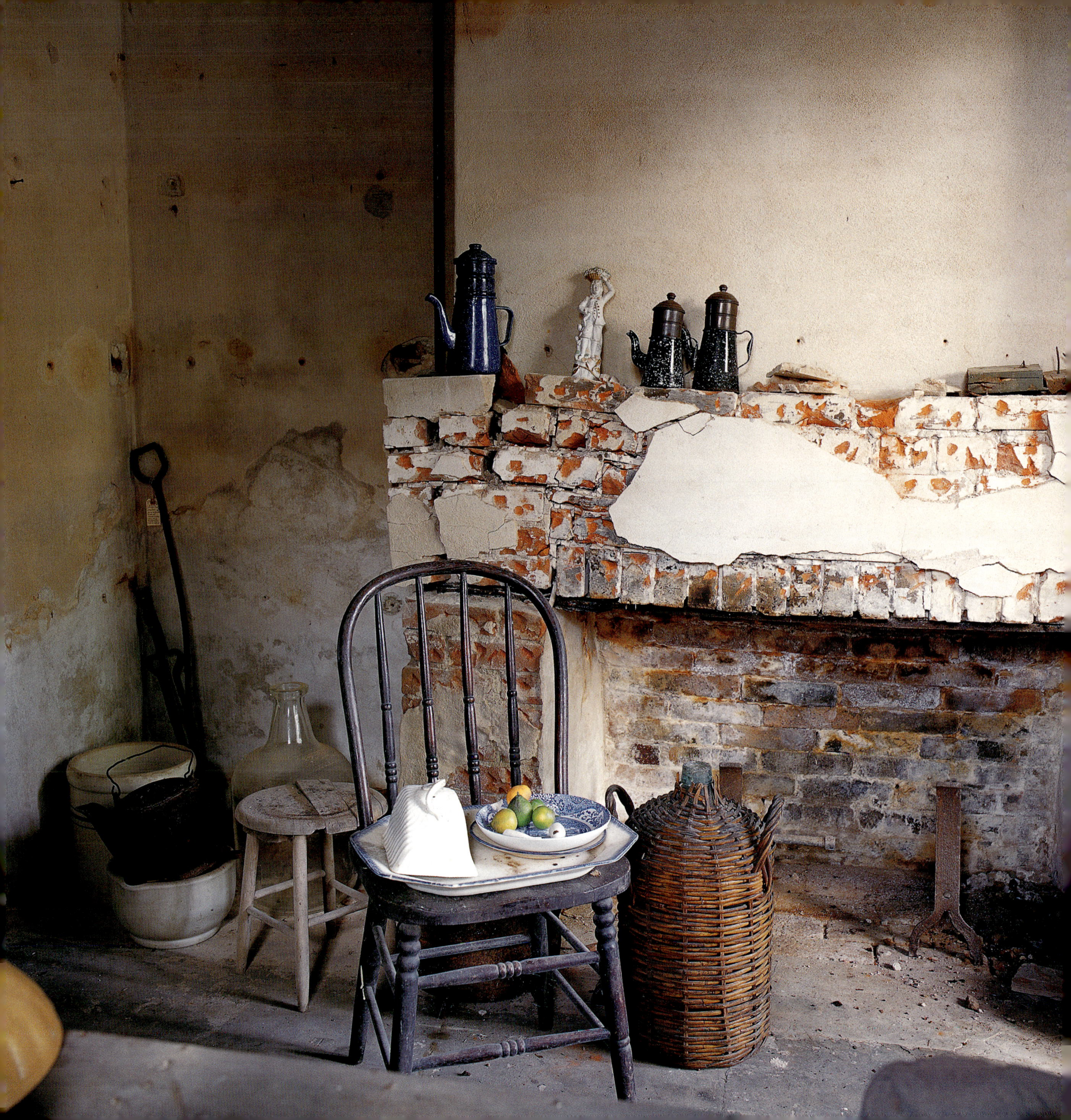

OPPOSITE
Joe and Beth call this ground-level room the "kitchen museum." Its soft, locally made bricks are compromised by the earth's dampness, as happens in southern Louisiana. No Creole kitchen of the nineteenth century would have been complete without an assortment of earthenware crocks like the ones here or the straw-encased glass demijohn, which was used for wine or other liquid cargo. Atop the mantel are three traditional drip coffeepots for preparing the strong chicory-laced coffee beloved by Creoles.

RIGHT
Joe Rougon's aunts, who lived at Austerlitz before him, used this first-floor room as a dining room; today, the Rougons find an upstairs room more comfortable. Now used for storage, it still holds the dining table and chairs from the 1880s, when the first Rougons took possession. Remnants of deep blue paint are visible on the ceiling boards and beams. Supported from an iron hook is a chandelier, its candles the sole means of dispersing the room's darkness after sunset.

Maison Chenal

Maison Chenal and the fine collection of outbuildings that surrounds it found sanctuary in the False River countryside. The buildings originally stood at various sites that were to be cleared for other uses, but Jack and Pat Holden—devotees of architectural and historic research—began rescuing them from demolition in 1975, moving and grouping them here. In addition to the main house, the compound includes a kitchen and laundry building, a barn, a *garçonnière* (young men's quarters), a small overseer's cottage, a *pigeonnier* (dovecote), a privy, chicken coops, a beehive, and animal pens—all the elements of a plantation setting.

The quintessential raised plantation house, Maison Chenal bears physical and technical evidence dating it to the 1790s, but its overall look suggests an update about 1820. It was acquired in 1808 by Julien Poydras, a planter, merchant, jurist, philanthropist, and framer of the state's first constitution. His family held it for almost seventy years, until 1876.

The Holdens focused on the 1820s update when interpreting this, their principal residence. They filled it with Louisiana-made furniture and nineteenth-century paintings and prints by artists who worked in the area. They applied equally careful research to the gardens, delving deeply into memoirs, plans, and manuals of the era. Today the parterres at the front and back of Maison Chenal reflect Louisiana's nineteenth-century gardening practices and serve as a veritable primer on the plant species favored by Creoles.

The Holdens were among the first Louisianans to undertake a private restoration of such depth and quality, and their pioneering example at Maison Chenal inspired other lovers of historic architecture and furnishings to do the same. Painstakingly researched, exquisitely restored and furnished, and in a historically accurate garden setting, Maison Chenal today is a one-of-a-kind treasure that captures the *toute ensemble* of Creole life.

ABOVE
Just behind the main house grow the edible, decorative, and medicinal plants that would have been found in an early-nineteenth-century garden. Beyond the garden is a kitchen and laundry building, which the Holdens moved from Cedar Bend Plantation, near Natchitoches. It is one of several outbuildings they have added to the property to recreate the sense of a working plantation. Its beveled clapboards are fitted together, giving a smooth appearance rather than the shingled look of overlapping weatherboards.

OPPOSITE
Maison Chenal's asymmetry is typically Creole: Doors and windows were placed with little regard for exterior balance until the introduction of the American center-hall plan about 1830. Here, the columns, doors, and windows are irregularly spaced; the staircase and chimney are set off-center. The steep double-pitch hipped roof was a common roofline in southern Louisiana. A traditional picket fence of hand-split cypress guards the parterre.

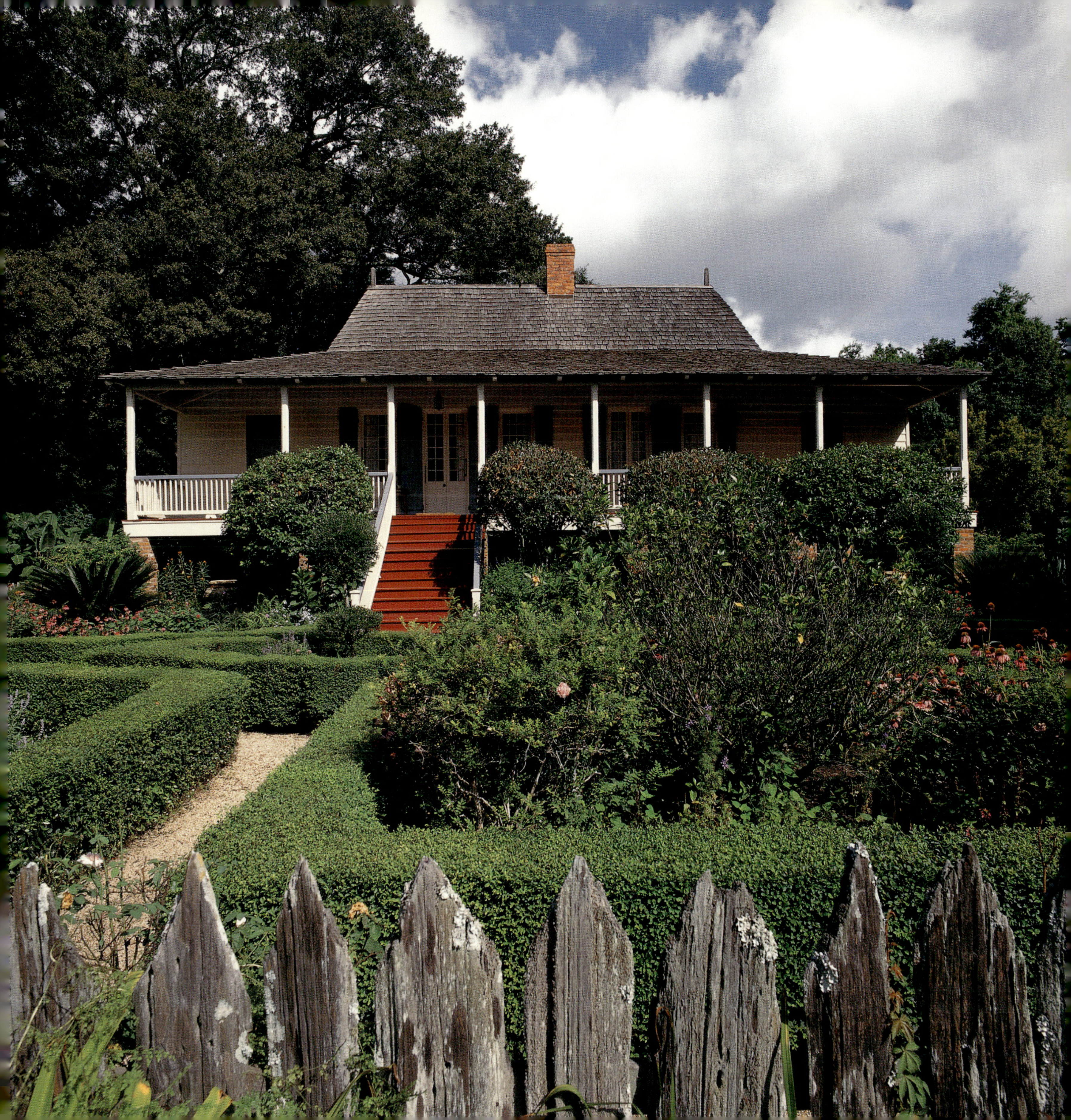

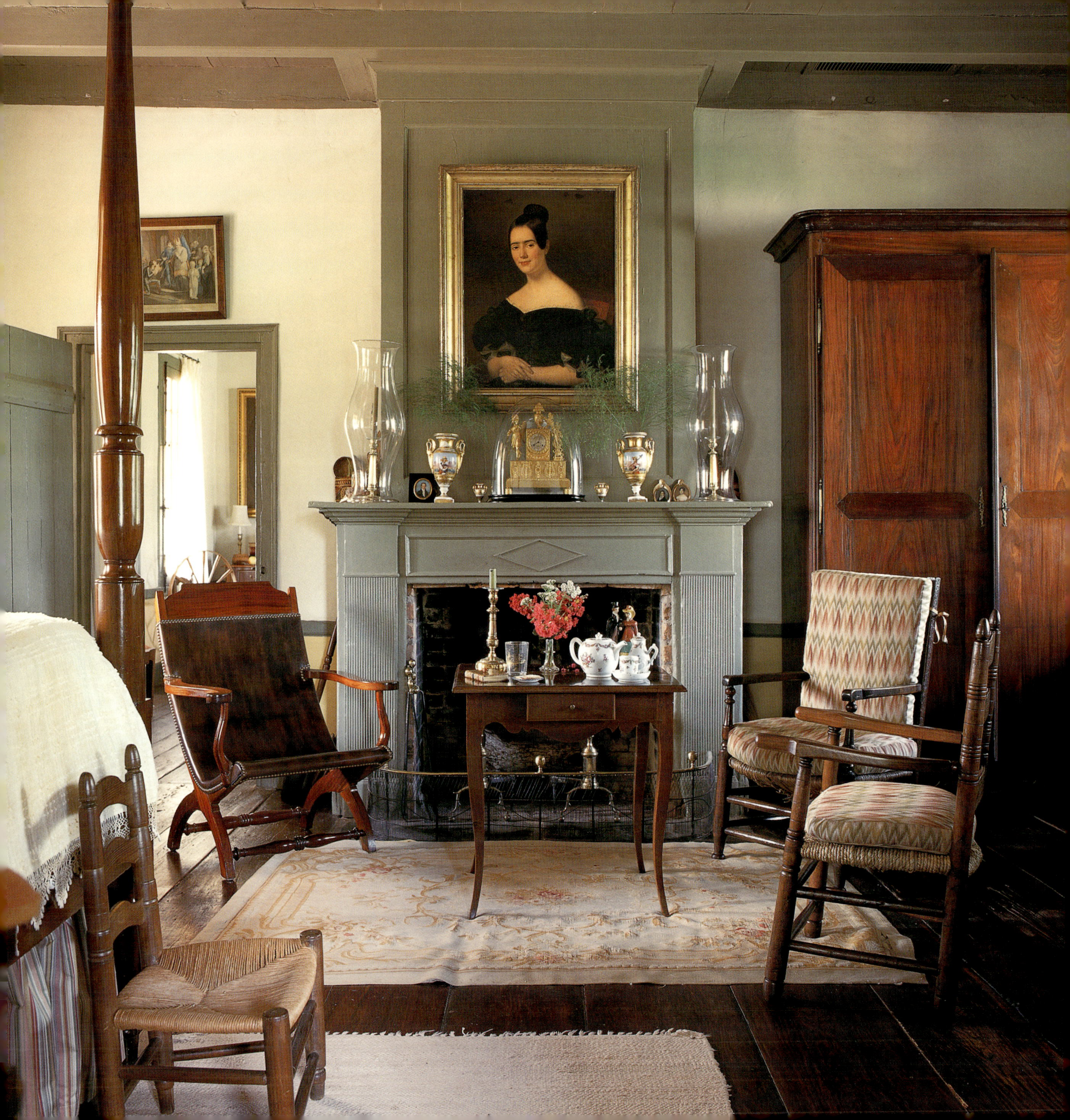

OPPOSITE

The elongated diamond shape on the principal bedroom's box mantel was a recurring Creole ornamental theme, seen in furniture, architectural details, and garden plans. The portrait of a woman above the mantel is by Jean-Joseph Vaudechamp, active in Louisiana in the 1830s. The mahogany armoire's flat-panel door style, emphasizing the wood's grain, superseded an earlier taste for carved, raised-panel doors.

TOP RIGHT

Flanking the salon's doorway are a Louisiana-made ladder-back chair with a rush seat and a tall-case clock, which bears the imprint of S. Fournier, a New Orleans clockmaker. The aquatint engraving above the doorway celebrates the transfer of Louisiana to the United States. Made by J. L. Boqueta de Woiseri in 1803, it shows an eagle flying over New Orleans bearing a banner: "Under my wings, everything prospers." Piled on the edge of the mantel are baskets woven of local cane by the Chitimacha, perhaps the original inhabitants of the southern Louisiana coast.

BOTTOM RIGHT

A full-tester high-post Louisiana mahogany bed with a melon-shaped headboard is dressed with a coverlet from the Holdens' collection of vintage Louisiana Acadian weavings. Other Louisiana-made pieces include the breakfast table with cabriole legs, the ladder-back chairs, and a cherry washstand from the Sacred Heart Convent in Grand Coteau. Many Creole bedrooms also served as a place for prayerful reflection, as evidenced here by the crucifix, prie-dieu, blessed palm frond, and religious prints.

LEFT

The dining table, made in Louisiana of cherry, is laid with a gumbo serving set and early Louisiana silver pieces, including a tumbler and a serving ladle. The hidden lily adorning the table was taken from the gardens. Over the table is a cloth and wood punkah, a hand-powered paddle fan; this one came from Voisin Plantation, on the River Road.

OPPOSITE

A cherry and cypress chest from the upper Mississippi Valley displays an Empire clock and a glass filled with antique pipes. Presiding over the room is a portrait of William Gordon Forman, a principal landowner in Pointe Coupée during the early decades of American Louisiana, painted by José Sálazar. The Holdens' collection includes four works by the Spanish artist, who was active in Louisiana in 1793–1802, during the Spanish colonial era.

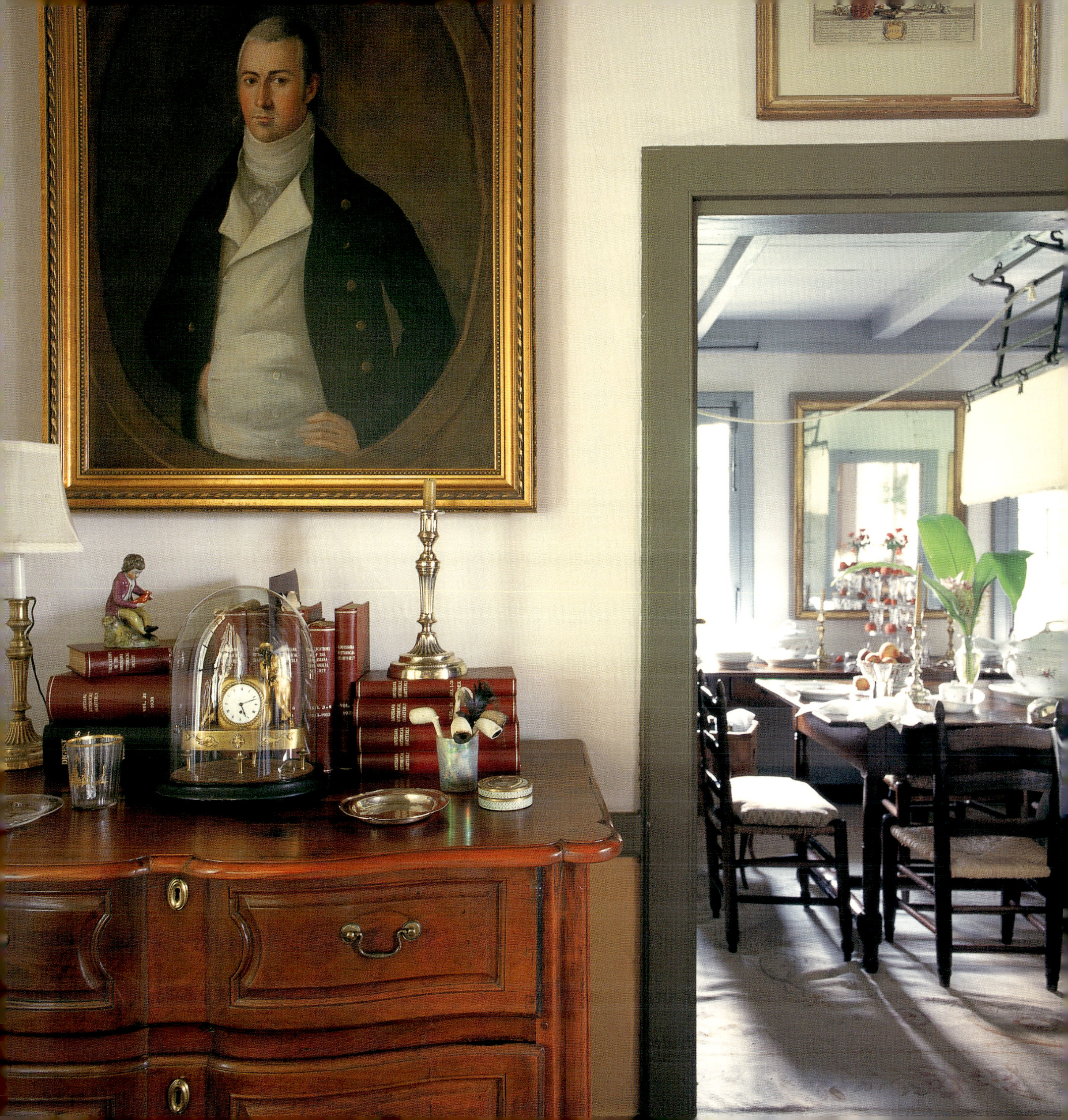

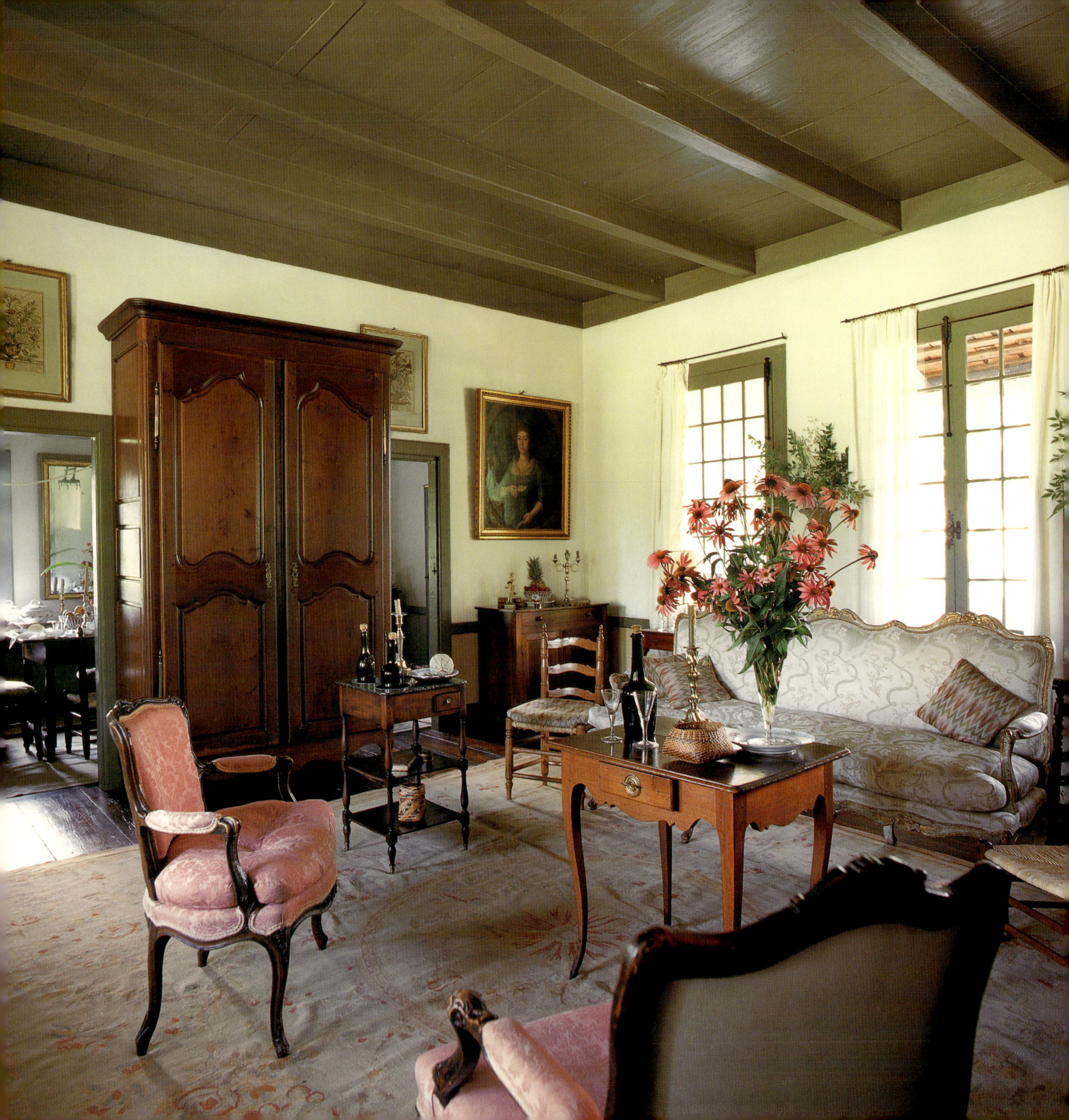

OPPOSITE
The *salle principale* measures twenty feet square. Louisiana-made pieces predominate at Maison Chenal, but the sofa and armchairs are French, as is the wine cooler with two bottles fitted into recesses on top. The armoire and the small table with delicate cabriole legs were made in Louisiana of American walnut. A 1791–92 Sálazar portrait of Comtesse Loubies hangs in the corner. The simple white curtains of muslin or chintz, hung on plain iron rods, are typical Creole window coverings.

TOP RIGHT
The kitchen and laundry building has a brick floor, massive cooking hearth, and a painted cypress worktable. A rack for drying laundry stands in the corner. Louisiana-made ladder-back chairs with cowhide seats support the ironing board, a common improvisation, according to oral histories.

BOTTOM RIGHT
When they relocated Maison Chenal, the Holdens raised it higher to expand the ground level into a full floor of living space, including a kitchen (with modern appliances and plumbing), small dining area, and sleeping chamber. Standing on the hexagonal terra-cotta tiles are a Louisiana-made walnut table, garde-manger, and hide-bottom ladder-back chairs. Two split-oak utility baskets flank the doorway.

Parlange Plantation

In 1947 Louisiana photographer Clarence John Laughlin made a photograph inside Parlange that he used in a haunting photomontage, *The Mirror of Long Ago*. Some sixty years later, Parlange still reflects its rich past. It has remained in the same family for hundreds of years, and the interior, especially, exudes the unmistakable perfume of age-old tradition.

The continuous occupancy was set in motion by Marquis Vincent de Ternant, who built a house here about 1750 on land granted by Louis XV of France. The marquis passed the property to his son Claude, who changed the plantation's focus from indigo to sugarcane and cotton. About 1820, after Claude's death, his widow, Virginie, married Charles Parlange. Today their descendants Lucy and Walter Parlange carefully tend the house and its grounds, where they graciously entertain their numerous guests.

The Parlange of today likely owes its appearance and design to the 1830s, though it is possible that remnants of Ternant's earlier structure were incorporated in a remodeling and enlargement. In typical (though not universal) fashion for raised plantation houses, the upper floor's timber framing has *bousillage* infill, while the lower floor is of brick-between-posts construction—masonry being better at bearing weight than the mud-and-moss *bousillage*. Parlange is elegantly proportioned, though slightly asymmetrical. Characteristically, it has no hallways; the seven rooms on each floor flow directly into each other and open onto the sheltered galleries that surround the living area.

Magnificent live oaks, nearly a hundred feet in height and festooned with Spanish moss, lend a sense of tranquility and permanence. Also prominent on the plantation grounds are two nineteenth-century *pigeonniers* (dovecotes). A large plantation like Parlange would have had many other outbuildings; just prior to the Civil War it housed more than one hundred slaves in thirty-five cabins, but none of the cabins remains.

ABOVE
Lawns and gardens provide lovely walks and varied perspectives of Parlange's architecture. This side view, from beneath a canopy of live oak, shows the plastered brick columns of the lower level, which support the gallery above. Statuary commonly accented Creole gardens.

OPPOSITE
Parlange's overall symmetry is subtly interrupted by the irregular spacing on the main floor. Doors and windows in Creole structures were placed according to the needs of the rooms, rather than for external alignment. The mature landscaping adds to the property's timeless atmosphere.

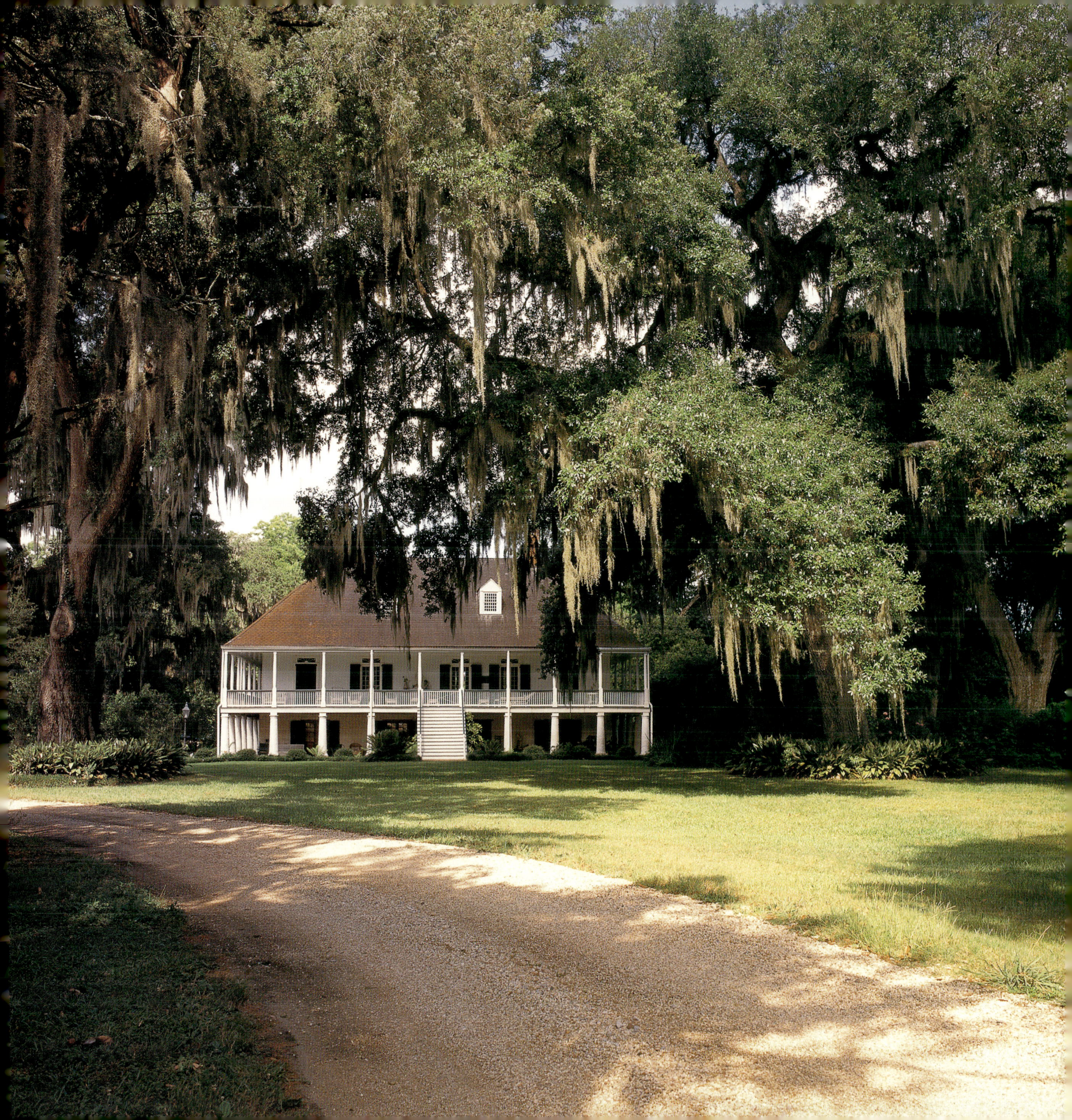

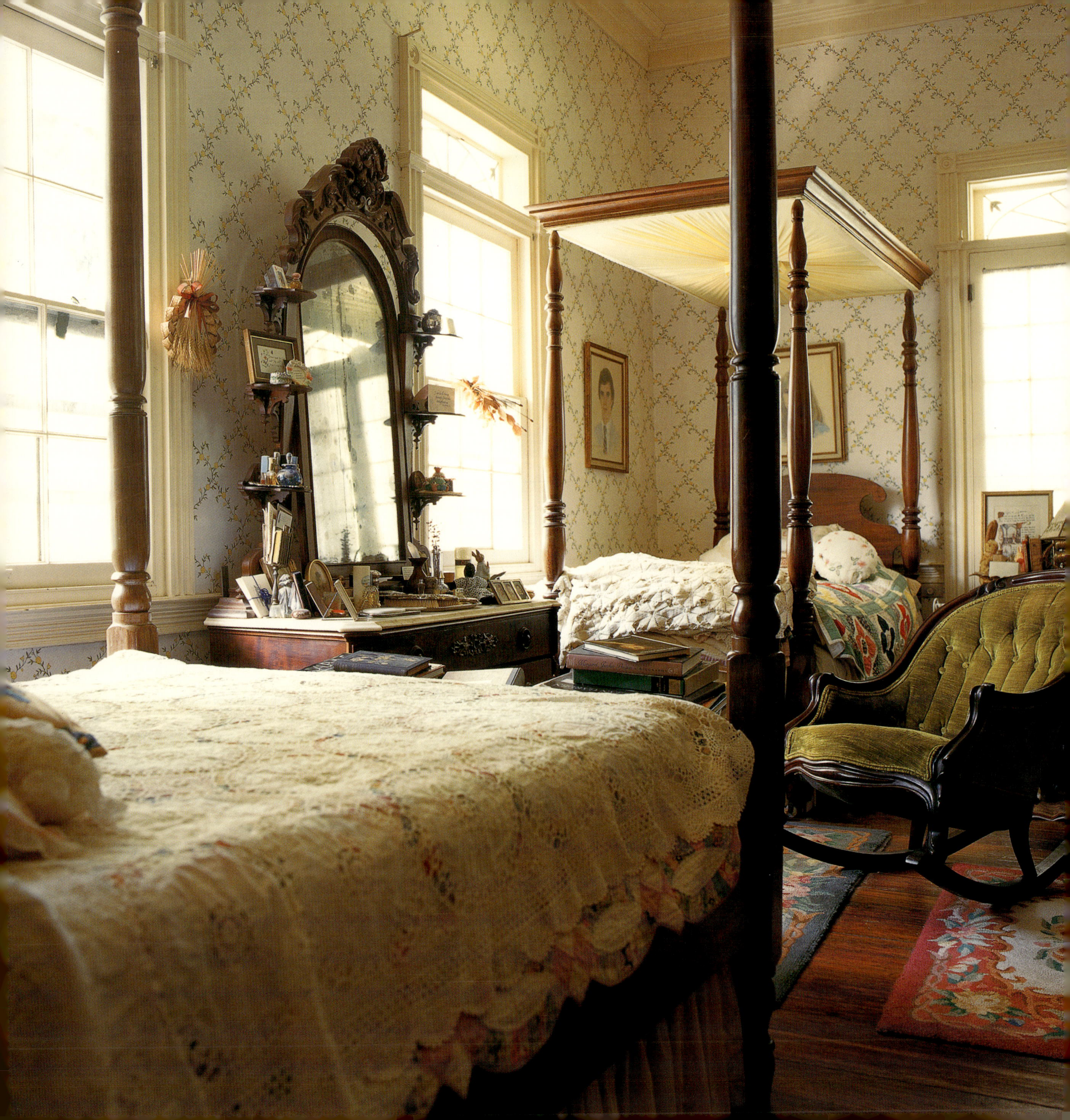

OPPOSITE
The children's tester beds are arranged toe to toe. In warm weather they would have been draped with mosquito netting.

RIGHT
Cushioned wicker chairs and other seating make comfortable perches on the gallery from which to enjoy Parlange's landscape. Slender cypress columns support the hipped roof. The double colonnade is a feature unique to Louisiana's Creole architecture; a single row is the norm.

Parlange's history is populated with colorful characters, but one in particular has drawn attention for more than 125 years: Virginie Amélie Avegno, who spent her early childhood at Parlange, her grandmother's home. After her father died of wounds suffered in the Civil War, the eight-year-old girl moved with her mother and sister to Paris. There she grew to be a celebrated beauty and married Pierre Gautreau, a Parisian banker. She attracted the attention of the American expatriate artist John Singer Sargent, who painted a full-length portrait of her in a bare-shouldered dress with a plunging neckline. He exhibited the work in the 1884 Paris Salon, where *Portrait of Madame X* caused a sensation.

TOP LEFT
A laminated rosewood settee, an ornate type favored by French Creoles in the mid-1800s, sits between doors that open from Parlange's large, central salon onto the deep front gallery. On the opposite wall, other sets of French doors open to the rear gallery.

BOTTOM LEFT
The timeworn keys of the piano and the clutter of family mementos give Parlange a feeling of history as well as of home.

OPPOSITE
In the salon, portraits of Virginie and Charles Parlange's children hang by massive iron hooks in the corners. They are the work of Louis-Édouard Dubufe, a mid-nineteenth-century French painter. The smooth cypress plank ceiling—an exception in the house, most of whose ceilings exhibit their support beams—presents a formal look, with an effect similar to that of a plastered ceiling.

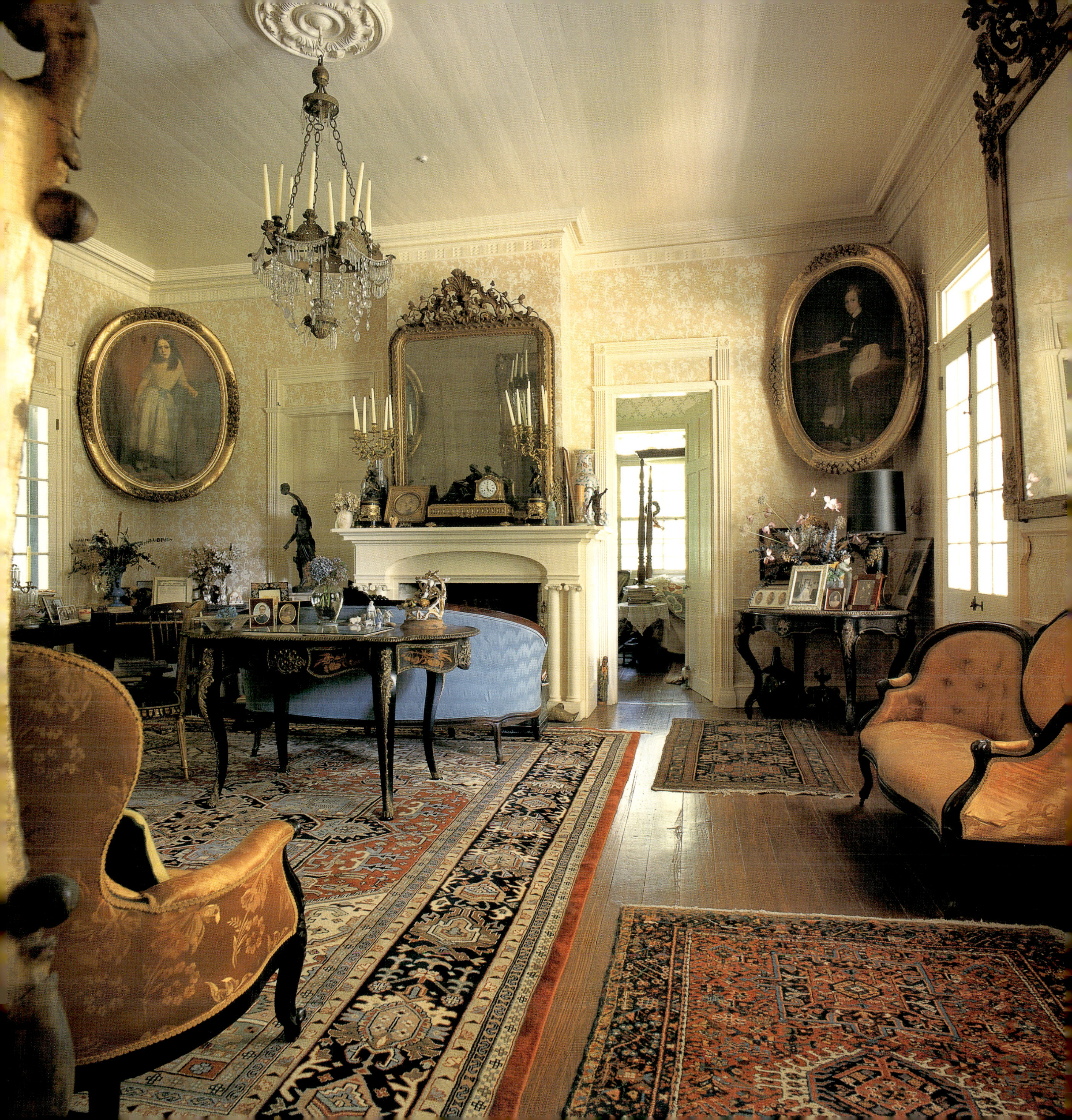

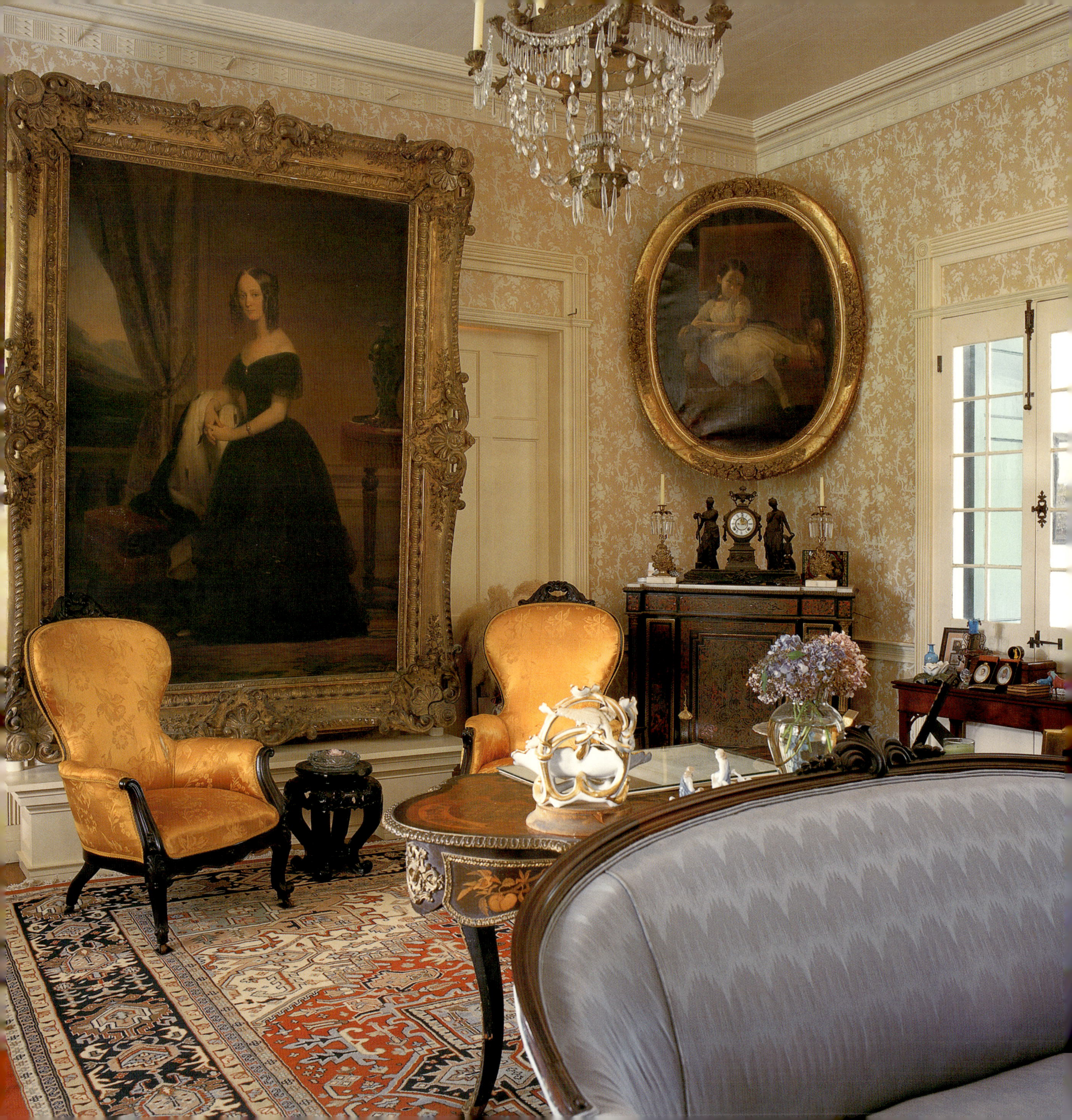

OPPOSITE

The salon is dominated by a monumental portrait of Virginie Parlange by Louis-Édouard Dubufe. In the corner is a portrait of one of her children by the same artist. According to family lore, portraits were placed in the salon's corners to soften the hard angles and to emulate the circular salons fashionable in mid-nineteenth-century France.

TOP RIGHT

French doors lead to the dining room, where a late-nineteenth-century étagère holds an array of serving pieces descended through generations of the Parlange family. One family's long occupancy has given rise to an eclectic array of furnishings, with objects and styles dating from the original construction all the way to the present.

BOTTOM RIGHT

Magnolia boughs and pinecones decorate the dining room's hearth. Above the Federal-style mantel of unpainted cypress hangs a portrait of Mrs. William Lindsay Brandon by Louisiana painter Theodore Sidney Moïse (1808–1885). The sitter is an ancestor of Lucy Parlange, who still owns the necklace in the painting.

LEFT
The two octagonal *pigeonniers* are each two stories tall and made of brick. Such large, elaborate dovecotes were hallmarks of Creole design and something of a status symbol, despite their utilitarian function: to supply squab for the table. The penchant for impressive *pigeonniers* is thought to have roots in France, where only wealthy landowners were permitted to raise pigeons.

OPPOSITE
One of the *pigeonniers* has been converted to a guesthouse. The bedroom is tucked beneath the truss of the roof and the walls are lined with bookshelves. The brick flooring is original; brick was used because it withstood the corrosive effects of the original occupants' guano better than wood. A pecanwood ladder handcrafted by Brandon Parlange, Lucy and Walter's son, provides access from the ground floor to the upper-level sleeping area.

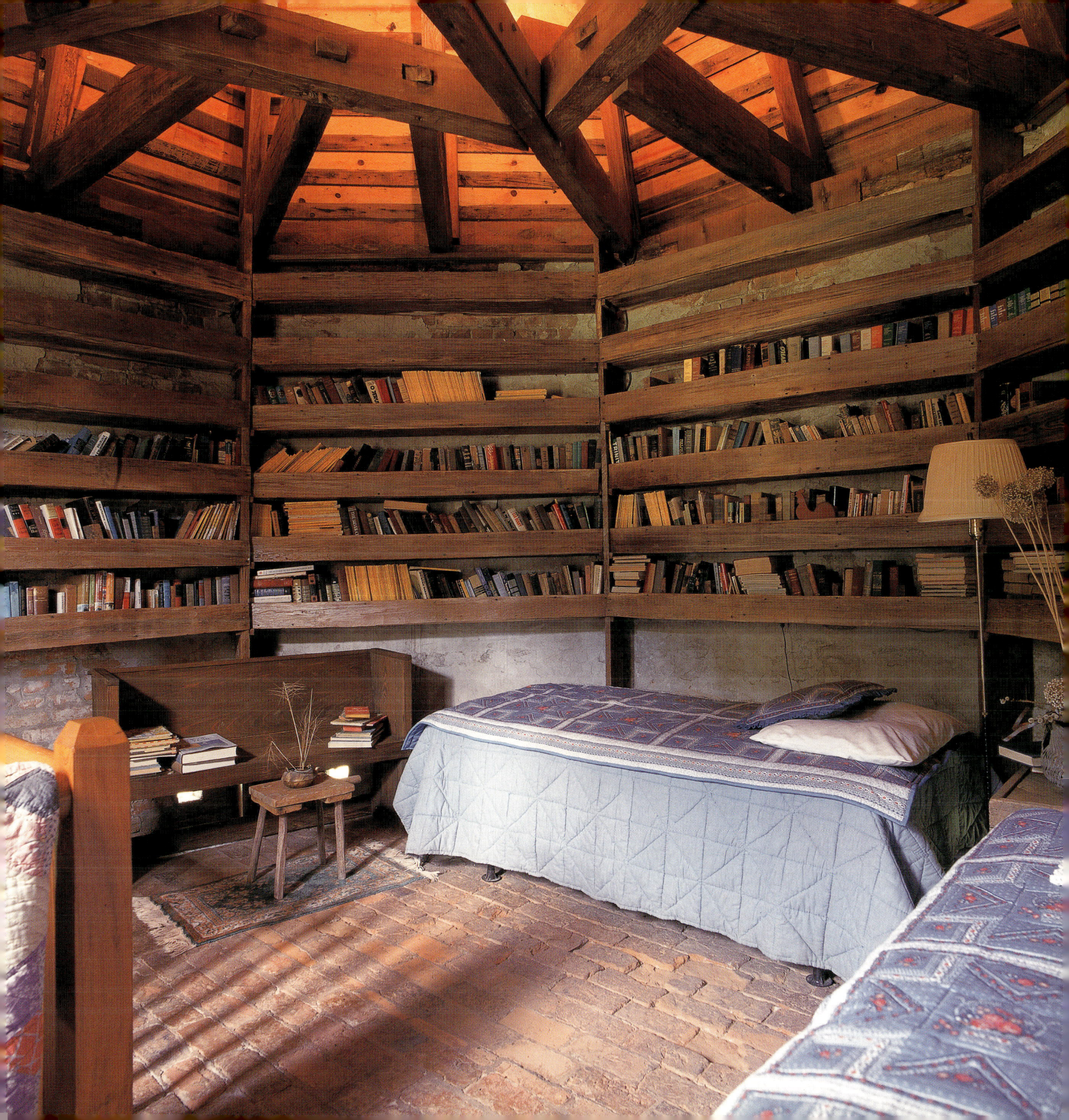

Lacour House

Though Lacour House's original purpose and precise building date have yet to be determined, it certainly ranks among the earliest of Louisiana's permanent French colonial structures. The name springs from Nicholas Lacour, an early French owner of the Pointe Coupée property on which the house was first discovered. He died in 1761.

Today the house stands across the road from Maison Chenal; like its neighbor, it was relocated by Jack and Pat Holden. It had been moved in the 1980s to Jefferson Island, some eighty miles to the south, to be included in a historic re-creation of a sugar plantation. When that project stalled, the Holdens acquired the house and returned it to Pointe Coupée, setting it on the banks of the Chenal, which was once a channel of the Mississippi River.

The house is of *bousillage* construction, and the techniques used suggest a pre-1765 origin, perhaps as early as 1730. Its restoration took cues from the 1745 Ursuline Convent in New Orleans, the oldest documented surviving French structure in the Mississippi Valley. Its uncommonly large rooms suggest that Lacour House may have been associated with one of the French forts built in the area during the early eighteenth century. The rooms' generous proportions accommodate one of Lacour's principal uses today: hosting educational events on Creole architecture, gardening, and culture.

Lacour House's landscaping is the conceptual opposite of Maison Chenal's geometric, symmetrical parterre. Its *jardin anglais,* or English garden, is designed as a more "natural" landscape, filled with unexpected encounters. Paths are winding rather than straight (except in the tidy herb garden); natural and manmade features are carefully framed in distant views. The ancient riverbed provides moderate contours in an otherwise flat terrain, contributing to the bucolic effect.

ABOVE
Lacour House has the double-pitch hipped roof characteristic of many eighteenth-century Louisiana Creole buildings. The roof's principal support is an immense Norman truss, but its overhanging edges are supported by a series of posts secured directly in the earth. That early technique quickly ceded to others that better protected against moisture: first posts on sills, then cypress blocks and brick piers. The gallery's floor is the earth itself, also typical of early houses.

OPPOSITE
Lacour's boathouse stands at the edge of the Chenal, an abandoned channel of the Mississippi River that empties into False River. Bald cypress trees, water oaks, live oaks, and irises create a serene landscape, home to a variety of birds, reptiles, fish, and mammals.

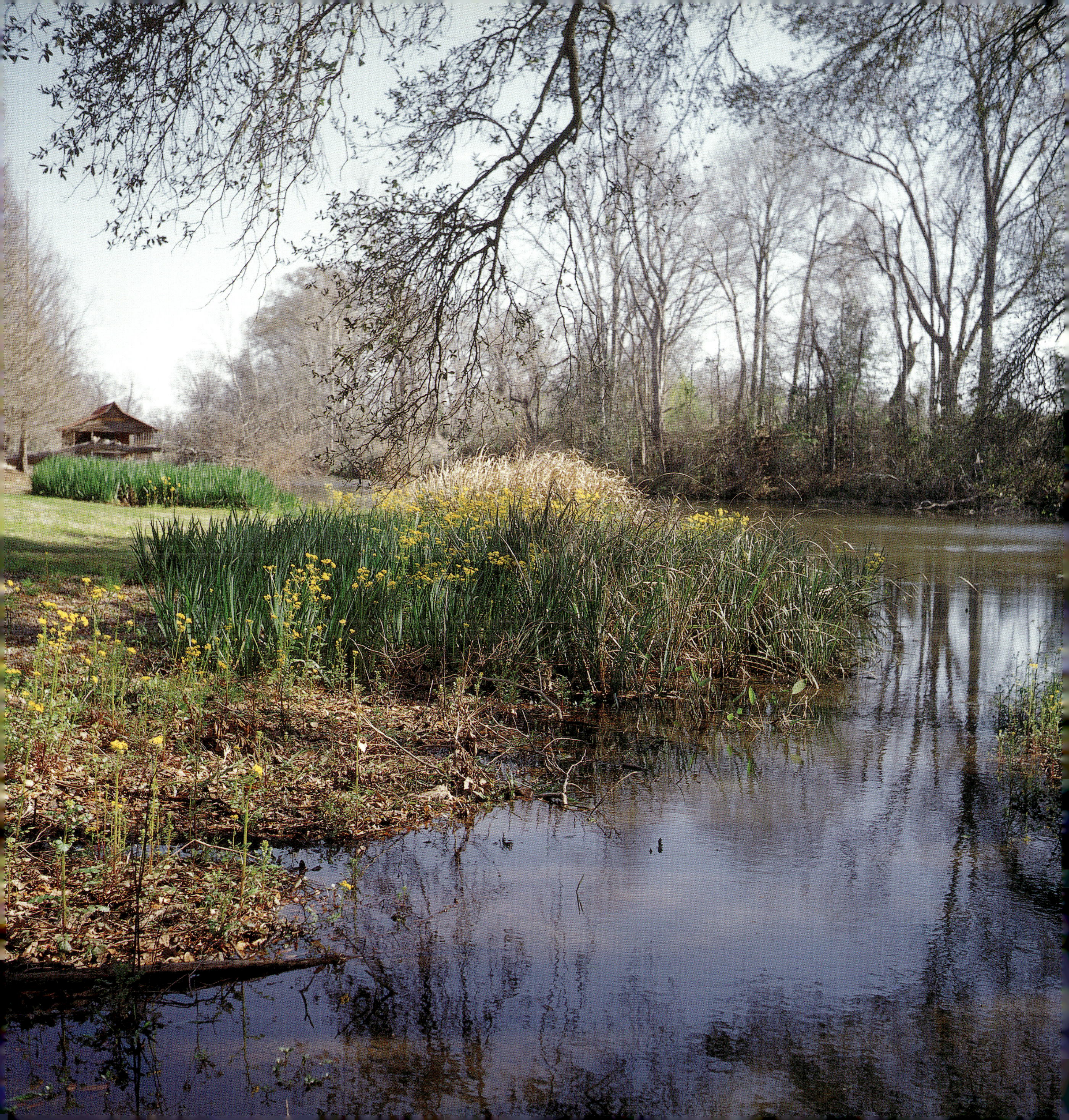

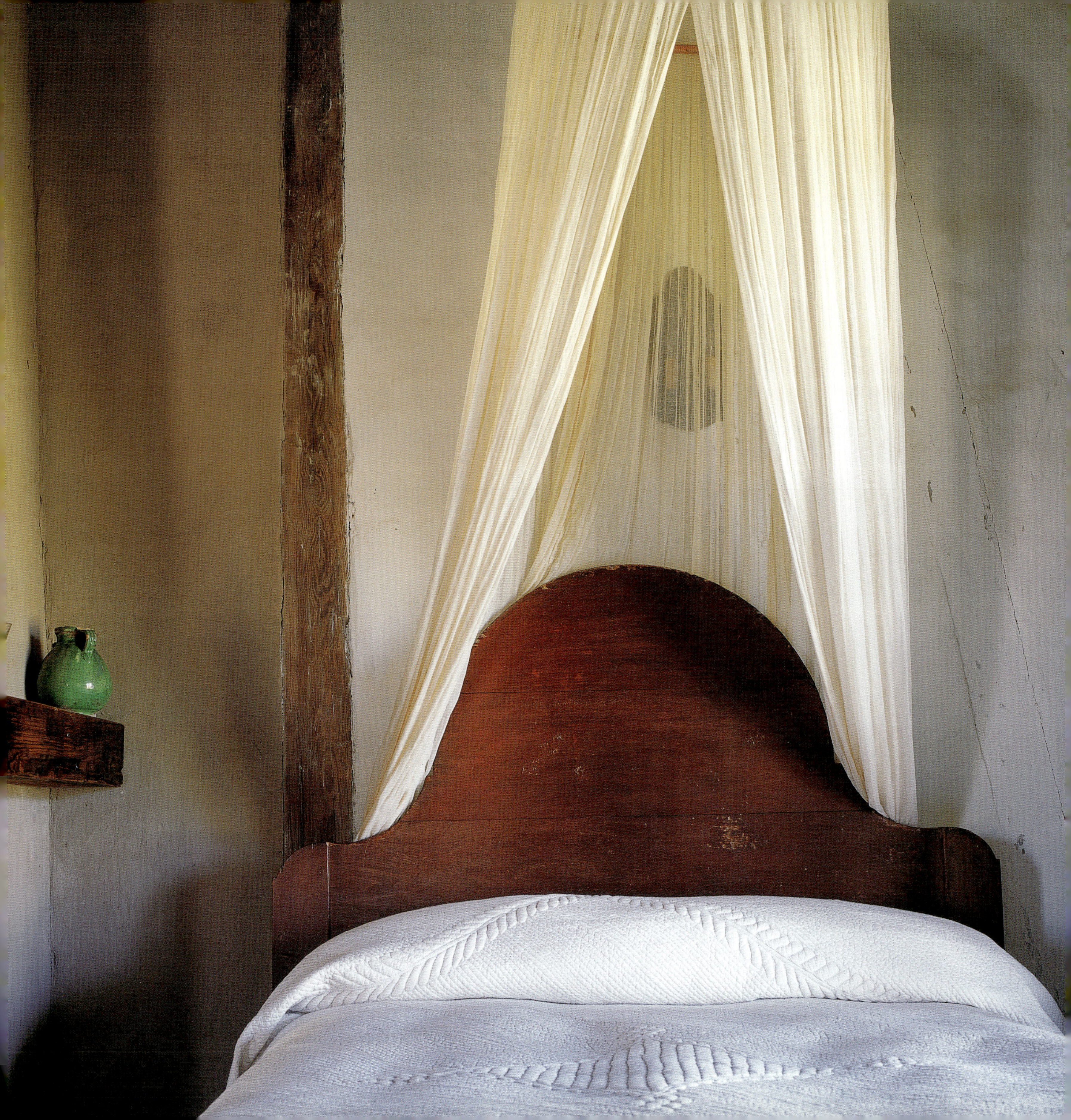

OPPOSITE

Remnants of Spanish brown paint, a color Creoles called *gros rouge*, cling to the melon-shaped headboard of this Louisiana low-post cypress bed. Creoles usually stuffed their mattresses with Spanish moss, which they topped with feathers. During the summer, when the unscreened casement windows would be open, the netting suspended here from an iron ring was an essential defense against vicious mosquitoes, which carried yellow fever as well as a painful bite.

TOP RIGHT

The smaller of Lacour's two rooms measures a generous twenty-two by twenty-five feet. Some of the pots, bowls, jugs, and pitchers on the trestle table were unearthed in Louisiana. In the corner is a Louisiana-made cypress armoire from the eighteenth century, whose proportions and decorative carving suggest a link with Canadian pieces of the time.

BOTTOM RIGHT

Centered on a Louisiana-made table are a green-glazed basin and pitcher—old French types. Behind them, Lacour's timber-and-*bousillage* construction is clearly visible.

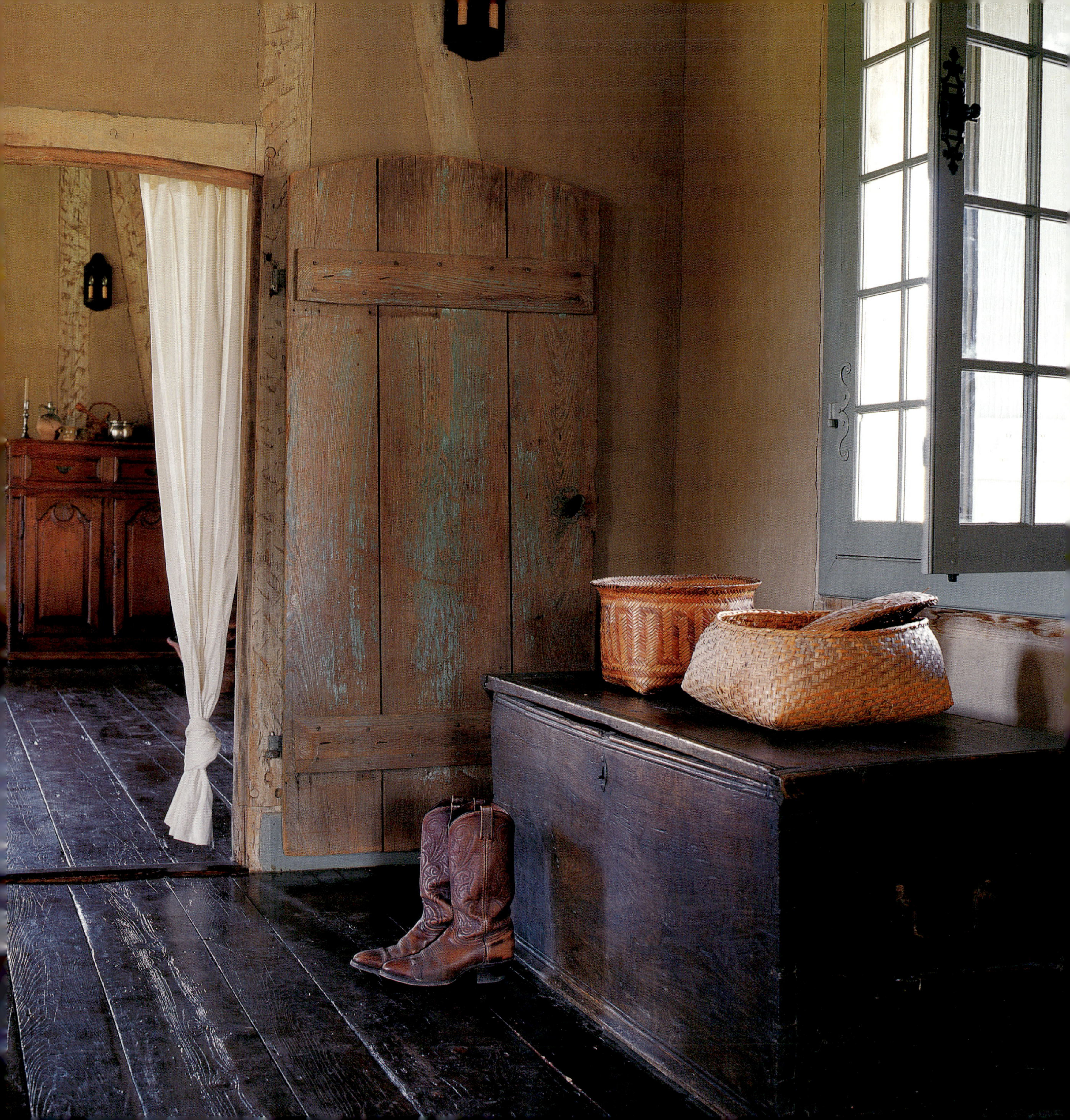

OPPOSITE
Near the doorway between Lacour's two rooms stands a simple French chest displaying Louisiana Indian baskets. A number of local tribes were known for their fine basketry, which they traded and sold in the public markets throughout the eighteenth and nineteenth centuries. The wide-plank floors are cypress.

TOP RIGHT
A roaring fire blazes in Lacour's large room. As is usual in Creole design, the firebox shares its chimney with another firebox directly behind it in the adjacent room. The simple mantel and slope-sided chimney were typical of early colonial buildings. The gentle arch of the firebox and the doorway to its right repeats on the exterior gallery and window openings. The armchairs are reproductions of some used by priests at the nearby Saint Gabriel Church.

BOTTOM RIGHT
Protected by a fence of hand-split cypress pickets, an herb garden flourishes a few steps from the kitchen building. It was inspired by an early-eighteenth-century New Orleans garden plan. Tender early growth is protected beneath glass cloches, which function as miniature greenhouses. At the intersection of the gravel paths stands an indigo kettle. Indigo, which yielded valuable dyes, was the leading plantation crop until the late eighteenth century, when sugar refining was perfected and planters turned to sugarcane.

Jaques Dupre House

The namesake and longtime resident of this 1820s raised cottage, Jaques Dupre, was a major landholder whose property included much of present-day Saint Landry Parish. A cattle rancher, he was active in state politics during the Jacksonian era and served briefly as Louisiana's governor in 1830–31, after the sitting governor died in office.

The house stood for generations near Opelousas, in the heart of Louisiana's cattle-ranching Acadian country, about eighty miles west of Baton Rouge. But it had fallen into disrepair by the mid-1990s, when Sis Hollensworth acquired and relocated it some forty miles east, to a former soybean field near Jarreau, in Pointe Coupée's False River area.

Hollensworth restored and furnished the house with passion and verve, doing much of the work with her own hands. In the late 1990s she planted an allée of live oaks that will in time beautifully frame the entry. That landscaping decision underscores the principle guiding Hollensworth's restoration: It is meant not only for the present, but for the future as well. She also restored some of the furnishings and has undertaken repairs in the upper walls, mixing the mud-based *bousillage* herself.

The ground floor, comprising the dining and sitting room, kitchen, a bedroom, and a bath, was reconstructed with the original bricks and door and window casings, but incorporated electricity and other modern conveniences. The gallery never extended around to the back of the house; there, what may originally have been an open loggia between two cabinets has been enclosed and now contains a staircase.

Hollensworth furnished the house primarily with Louisiana-made pieces. She also incorporated items from her birthplace in Arkansas, carrying on the Creole practice of cherishing family heirlooms by using and enjoying them.

ABOVE
The ground-floor porch beneath the gallery is paved in brick, a traditional treatment found at the original site. The cylindrical columns, composed of courses of bricks shaped like slices of pie, stand upon square brick bases; some of the bricks bear the initials "J.D." (presumably for Jaques Dupre). The wear patterns on the cypress worktable suggest a mid-nineteenth-century origin. Against the wall stand a *pile* (a large mortar made from a tree trunk) and its wooden *pilon* (pestle), used to pulverize corn, make filé of sassafras leaves, and remove the hulls from rice.

OPPOSITE
The massive roof of wooden shingles is supported by a Norman truss. Structural evidence suggests that the house originally had a double-pitch roof instead of this umbrella-style roof. To the right and slightly behind the main house is a cottage that is used as a guesthouse.

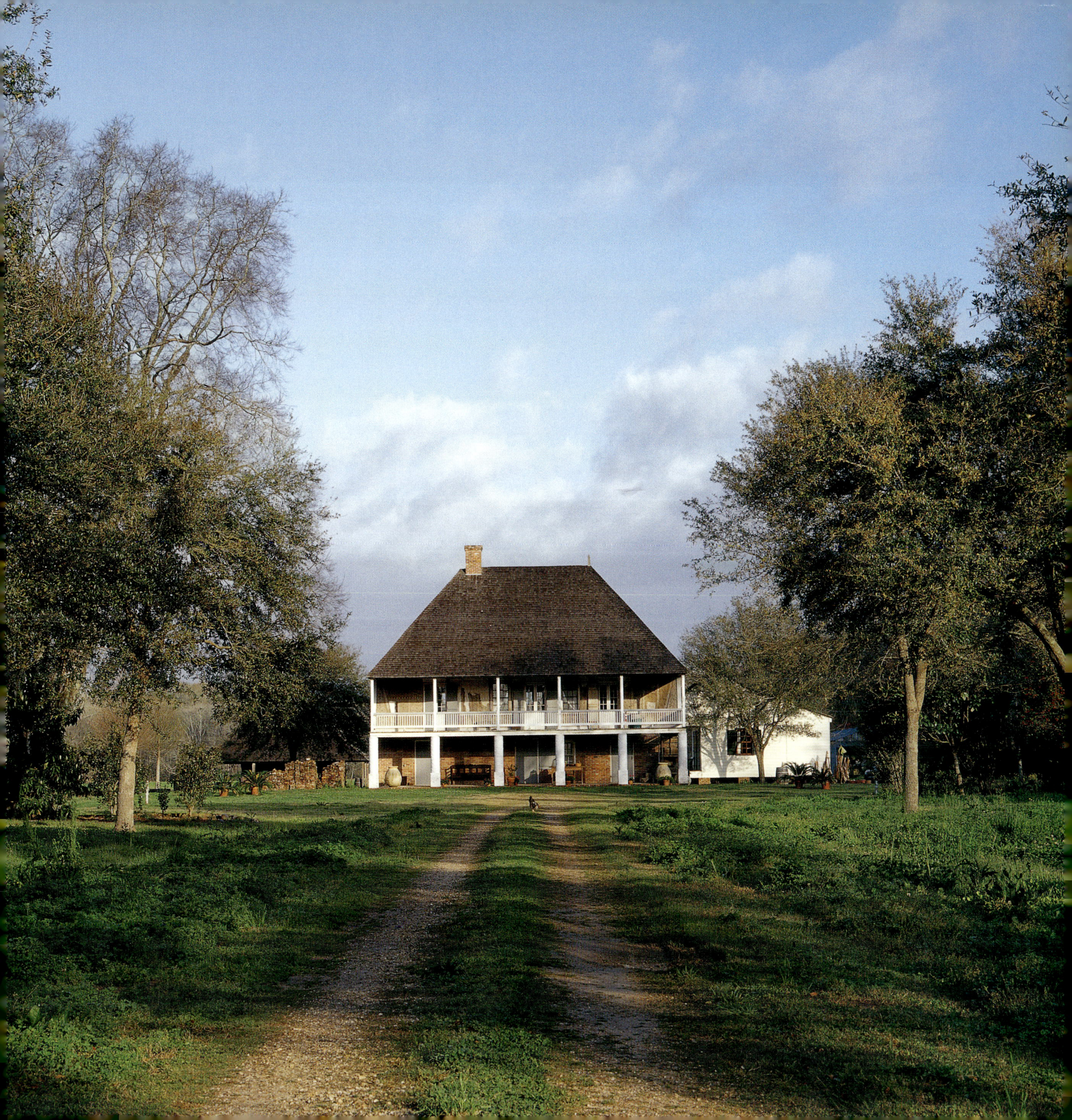

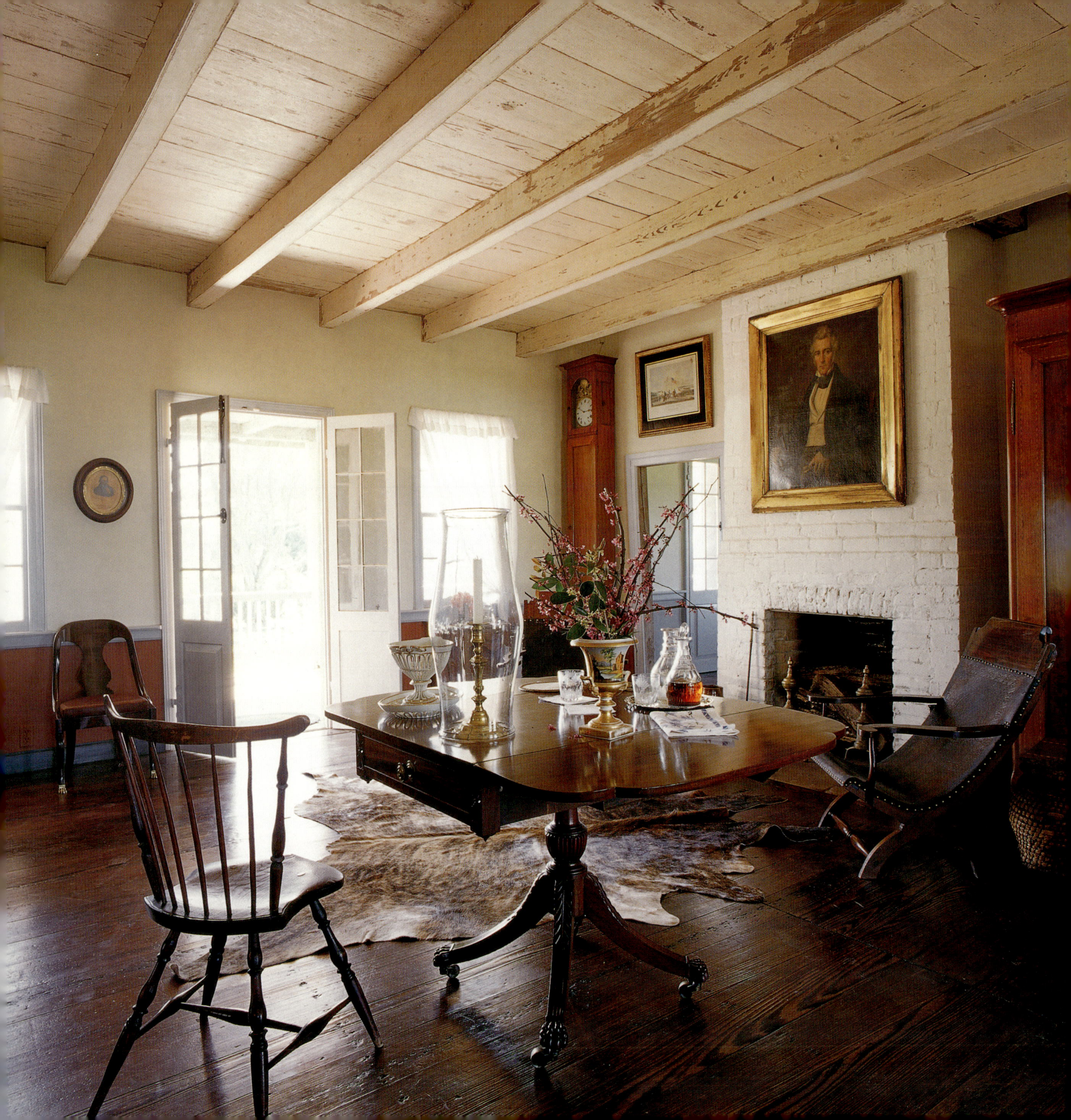

OPPOSITE

Sunlight floods the salon from doors open to the gallery. To the left, above a French side chair with gold-embossed red leather seat, hangs a portrait of Jaques Dupre himself. In the corner stands a rare Louisiana-made tall-case clock with a cabinet of cherry and cypress. The portrait of Daniel Stewart above the fireplace is by Jacques Amans—a favorite painter among Louisiana Creoles in the 1830s and 1840s. The Duncan Phyfe–style mahogany breakfast table is from New York and dates from 1810–20.

RIGHT

The roughhewn beams in the sitting area betray the ground floor's original utilitarian use as a storage space; typically beams used in such houses' living spaces were smoothly dressed. The sandstone flagging is the original flooring. The painted bench with cushions dates from about 1830 and possibly came from Baltimore. The Louisiana walnut table, with turned legs and stretcher, dates from 1820–30. Above the fireplace is a painting from 1884–85 by William Henry Buck, who is associated with Louisiana's "bayou school."

TOP LEFT
The upstairs bath boasts a wood-enclosed, copper-plated tin tub and a hand-colored lithograph of Hayne Hudjihini (also known as Eagle of Delight), whose husband was chief of the Oto tribe. It is one of the rare female portraits from Thomas McKenny and James Hall's American Indian series. To the left is the enclosed loggia, whose lower walls are painted in a terra-cotta matched to a similar paint found in the house. To the right of the bath, past the curtained doorway, is a bedroom with a Louisiana mahogany armoire.

BOTTOM LEFT
A striped Acadian coverlet adorns an upstairs bedroom's high-post Louisiana-made bed of cypress and cherry. A laundry basket of split white oak holds more vintage Acadian bedclothes woven of Louisiana cotton. By the bed, on the cypress floor, is an eighteenth-century Spanish chamber pot. The drop-front desk, made in Louisiana of cypress and cherry, dates from the 1810s.

OPPOSITE
The downstairs bedroom's French-made walnut bed (late eighteenth or early nineteenth century) is dressed with textiles descended through generations of Sis Hollensworth's family in Arkansas, including a quilt and a linsey-woolsey coverlet. The early-nineteenth-century walnut chest at the foot of the bed is also a family piece from Maryland or Georgia. Folded on top is a trio of Acadian woven blankets. Throughout the house, curtains (usually toile) hang from simple forged iron rods and metal rings, a treatment described in early-nineteenth-century accounts.

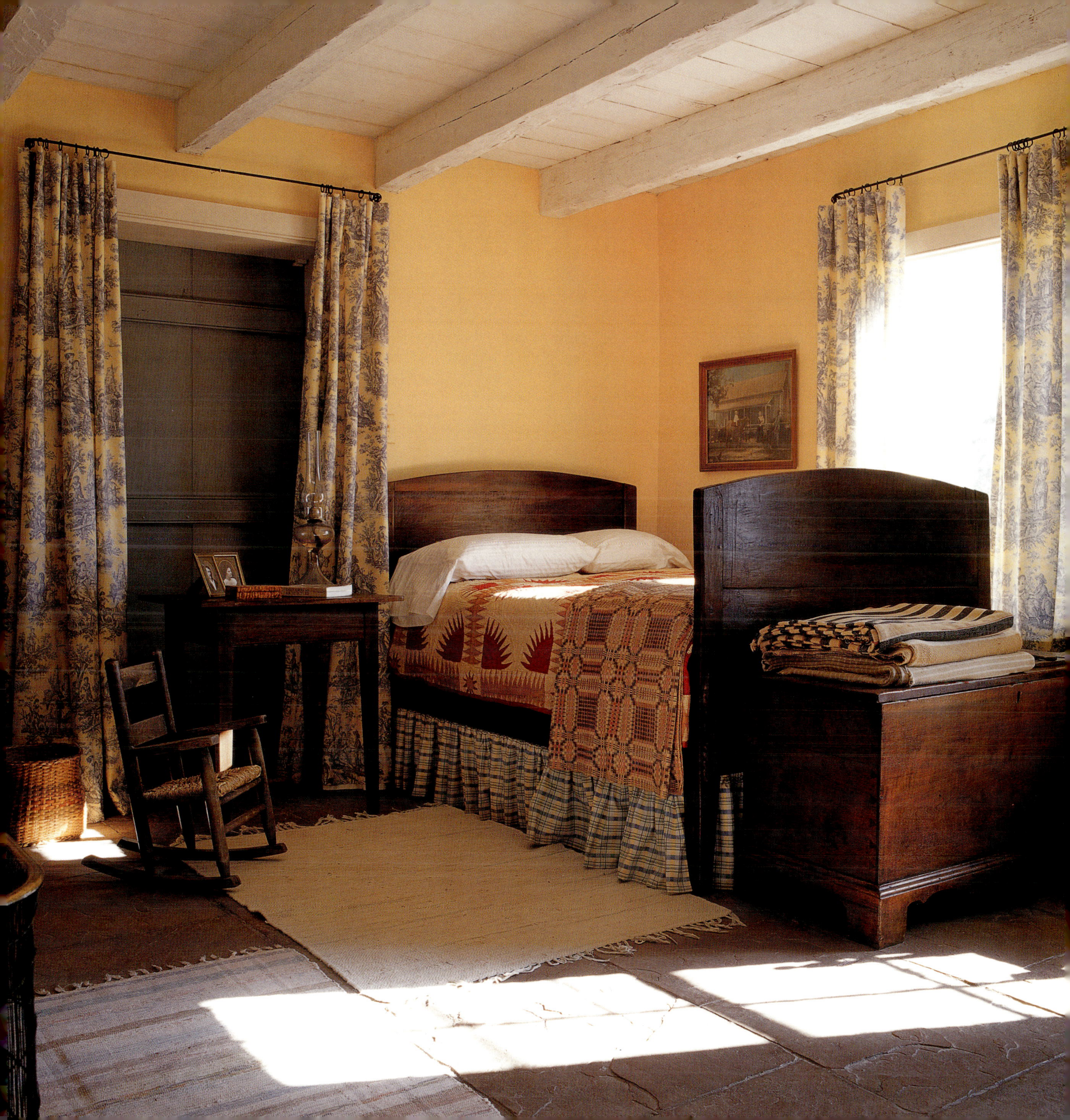

The Bayou Country

Louisiana's early colonists viewed south-central Louisiana—a varied region of dense forests, vast prairies, mysterious swamps, and slow-moving bayous—as a remote and forbidding wilderness. French explorers probed the area in the first half of the eighteenth century but largely left it to the nomadic Atakapas and Opelousas people.

Settlements were not established until the 1760s, when the French-speaking Acadians arrived. In what history calls the *grand dérangement* (great upheaval), they had been expelled from Acadia (today's Nova Scotia) in 1755 for refusing to renounce Catholicism and pledge allegiance to the British crown. Several thousand found their way to Louisiana between 1765 and 1790. Country folk made destitute by deportation, the Acadians did not find a warm welcome from the Creole gentry, despite their shared language, religion, and French heritage. So they pushed into the backcountry west and south of New Orleans, settling along the bayous lacing the region.

They transformed the landscape, raising cattle on the grasslands, fishing the coastal waters, hunting and trapping in the alligator-filled swamps, and cultivating rice and sugarcane on the well-irrigated soil. Today this area is known as the Cajun heartland—"Cajun" being a derivation of "Acadian"—and the core of Francophone Louisiana. Lafayette, the largest city in the eight-parish region, lies at its center, 35 miles north of the Gulf of Mexico.

The Acadians were the first but not the only French speakers to put down roots here: so did Creole planters, French West Indians, patrician refugees of the French Revolution, and Napoléon's loyalists and former soldiers. But while the Acadians built simple dwellings, the subsequent settlers exhibited urbane French tastes. Their homes, generally raised plantation houses, were often decorated in the styles of the ancien régime or the empire.

Although the local economy is now driven by oil and natural gas, old traditions still hold sway: Farmers grow cotton, rice, and sugarcane; cowboys herd cattle and ride rodeos; fishermen harvest seafood; and French is spoken. And a rich mix of architecture—modest Acadian cottages, simple Creole farmsteads, and splendid plantation houses—survives amid a hauntingly beautiful countryside of moss-draped cypress and lazily flowing bayous.

Rienzi Plantation House, in Thibodaux, was built in 1800–10, but mid-1800s updates in the Greek Revival style and the 1930s double staircase mask its early appearance.

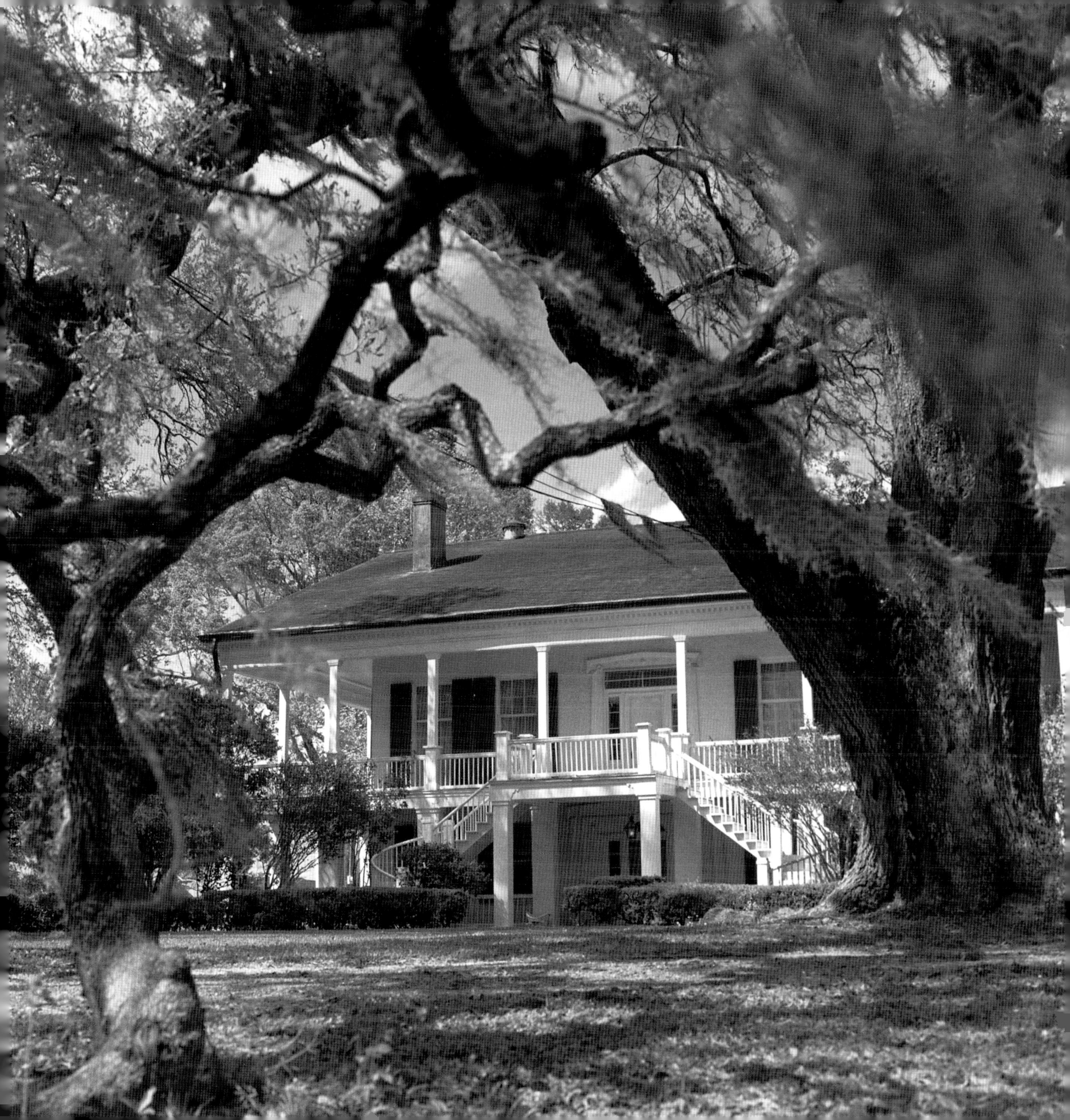

Couret Plantation

The 177 acres Couret Plantation occupies were recently annexed to the city of Lafayette, but not long ago it was a working farm, with cattle, sheep, chickens, and a cash crop of soybeans its most recent enterprises. The plantation once encompassed more than 1,500 acres, and the house's simple lines, millwork, and furnishings reflect its use as a farmstead. The nearby Mermentau River (a source of fine crawfish) yielded the cypress timbers and lumber used in its construction.

Sources generally date the house to 1829–36, which explains its combination of influences: Although it takes the Creole form of a two-story residence without interior halls, it has exterior chimneys at the gabled ends of the house, in the style that had begun penetrating by that time. Adding to its Creole flavor are the covered galleries, eleven feet deep, on the front. There is no evidence that galleries ever were present at the rear. The columns are squared, rather than round. Those on the ground floor rest atop elongated bases, perhaps presaging the classical styles that would prevail in coming decades.

The upper floor is of typical *bousillage* construction, and the lower story is of plastered brick. Research suggests that the lower floor was built on this site, and the upper floor, a structure dating from the late 1700s, was moved from Bayou Vermilion, a short distance away.

Nearly a dozen outbuildings, some thought to be approaching two centuries in age, surround Couret. Its barns, root cellar, storage sheds, chicken coops, hutches, and cistern contribute to its rustic feel.

Couret was held by a single extended family through most of its history, up until 2003. It was built for Gerasin Bernard, whose daughter Clemance married Louis Couret. Their son William passed the house to his two daughters, Agnes and Lucille. Miss Lucille was a beloved local schoolteacher who lived at Couret into her nineties. Those who knew her say it is her gentility and quiet grace that gave the home its special character.

ABOVE
On a cypress-topped worktable near the kitchen, bowls, plates, and pitchers hold fresh ingredients, including a clutch of eggs courtesy of the property's resident fowl. The earthenware storage jars below hold additional foodstuffs. To the left are the traditional mortar and pestle (*pile* and *pilon*) fashioned from a section of cypress log. They were used to make coarse cornmeal or remove hulls from rice, probably a frequent task, as Couret lies close to Louisiana's rice-farming region.

OPPOSITE
Clean lines and an uncomplicated white palette, accented only by green shutters, contribute to Couret's bucolic tranquility. Widely spaced live oak, cypress, catalpa, and other trees and shrubs soften the landscape. By local accounts the Courets were unostentatious people, aptly reflected by their unprepossessing home, but its construction and contents suggest an appreciation of well-crafted things.

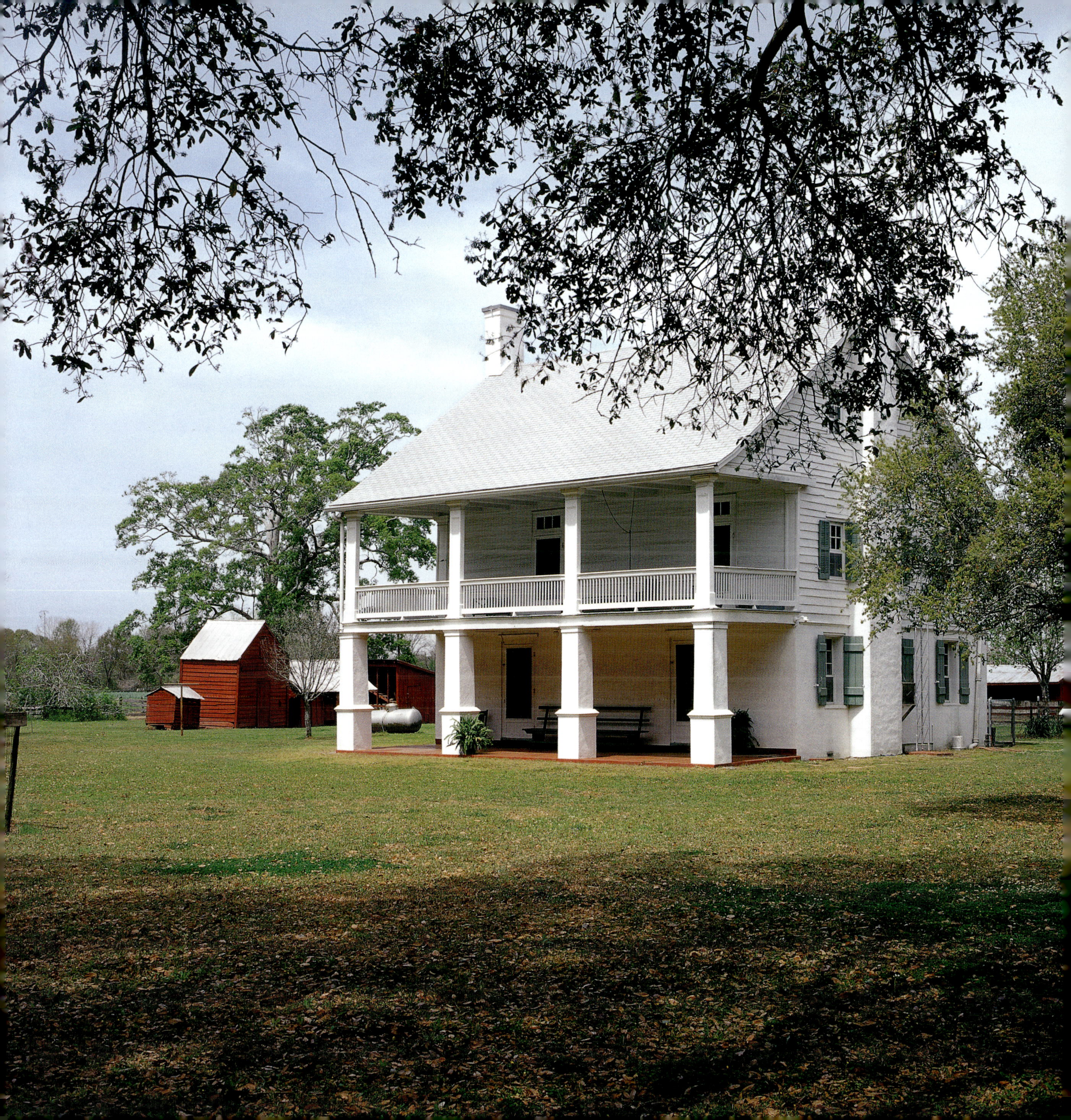

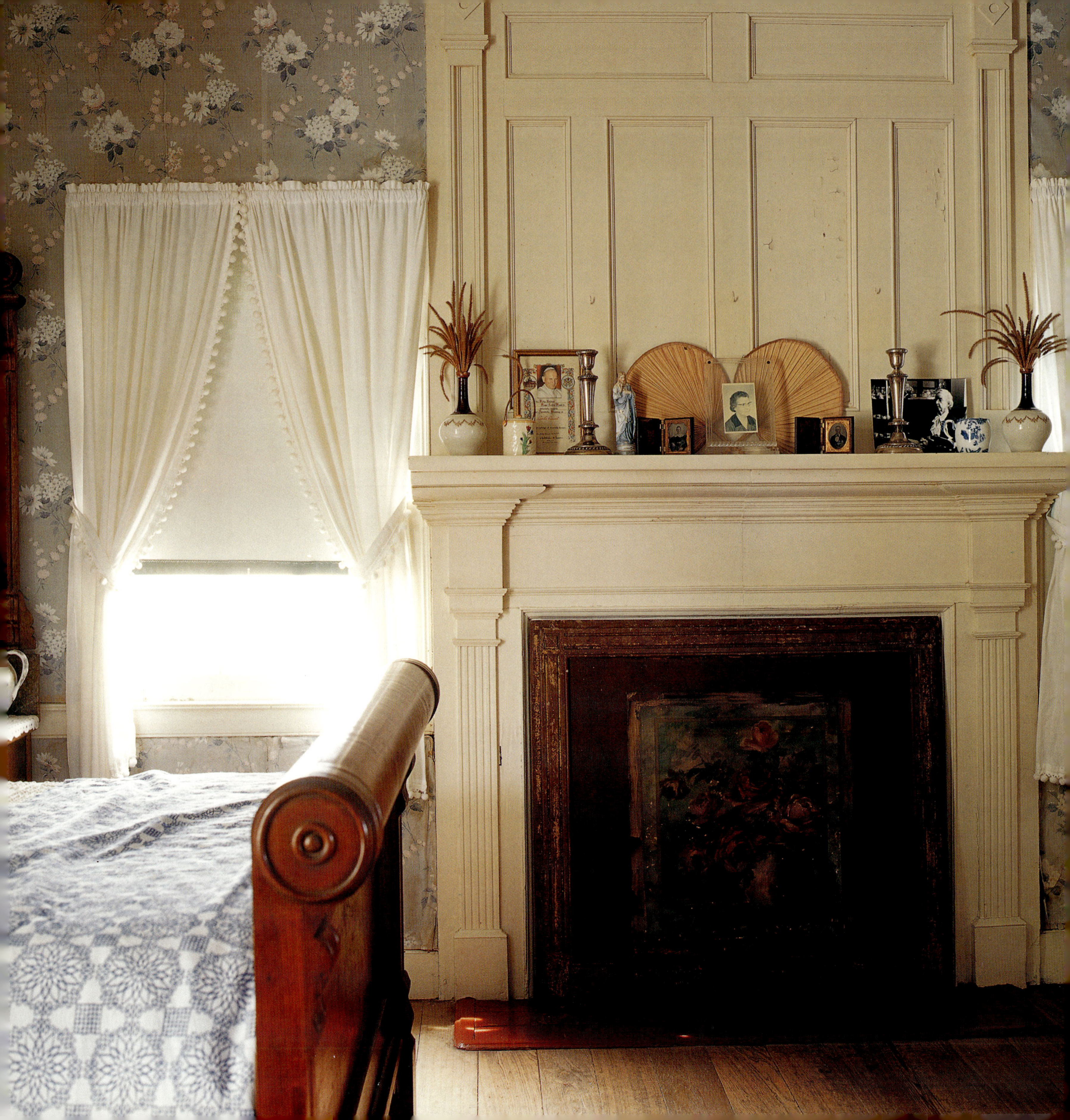

OPPOSITE
The mantelpiece in Lucille Couret's bedroom displays family photographs and a pair of palmetto leaf fans, which Creoles used to circulate the sometimes still air of southern Louisiana. The improvised fire screen, a metal-framed floral canvas, was found in the attic.

RIGHT
This was Miss Lucille's bedroom from 1910 until 2003, and its furnishings and decor scarcely changed over that span. A huge Victorian-era bed stands upon cypress floors, which are covered by handmade rag rugs. One of Miss Lucille's own diplomas hangs to the right of the bed. The room exemplifies Couret Plantation's unfussy, traditional design.

TOP LEFT
The spare bedroom showcases Louisiana crafts of a rustic character, including a trio of locally made cowhide-bottom chairs. Standing by the hearth, straw brooms are ready to sweep ash back into the fireplace. In the corner, a wooden rack holds vintage cotton coverlets, locally woven. The traditional Acadian craft lives on in this part of Louisiana, although the number of weavers is dwindling.

BOTTOM LEFT
A fan of woven palmetto leaves and a kerosene hurricane lamp perch on the mantel. Essential in the past, they still come in handy in an area where the weather can be sultry and hurricanes (and their accompanying power outages) visit regularly.

OPPOSITE
French doors lead from Miss Lucille's room to the spare bedroom. The floors are raw cypress everywhere but the parlor, where the wood was varnished; Creoles often reserved costly adornments for rooms used by guests.

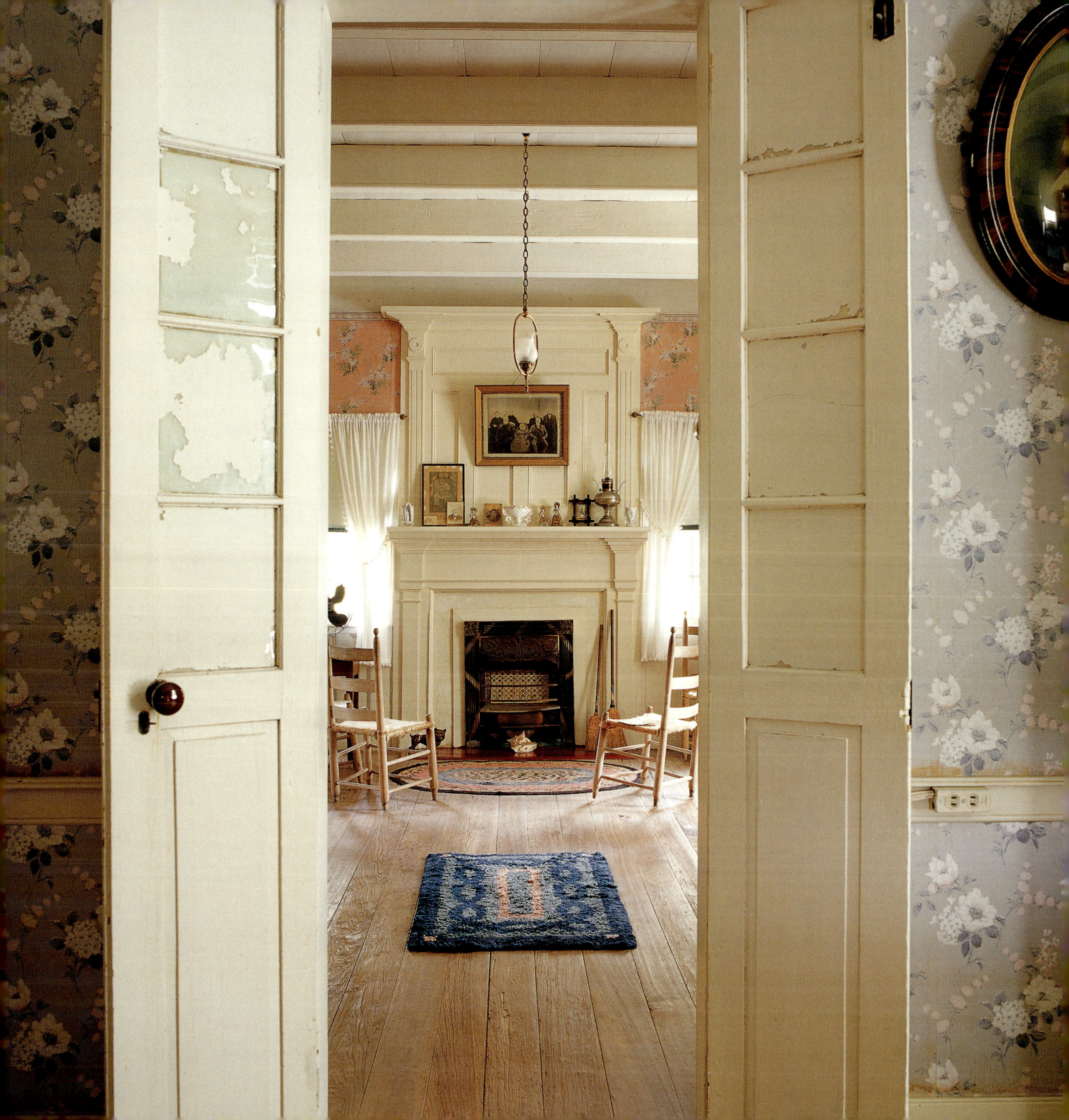

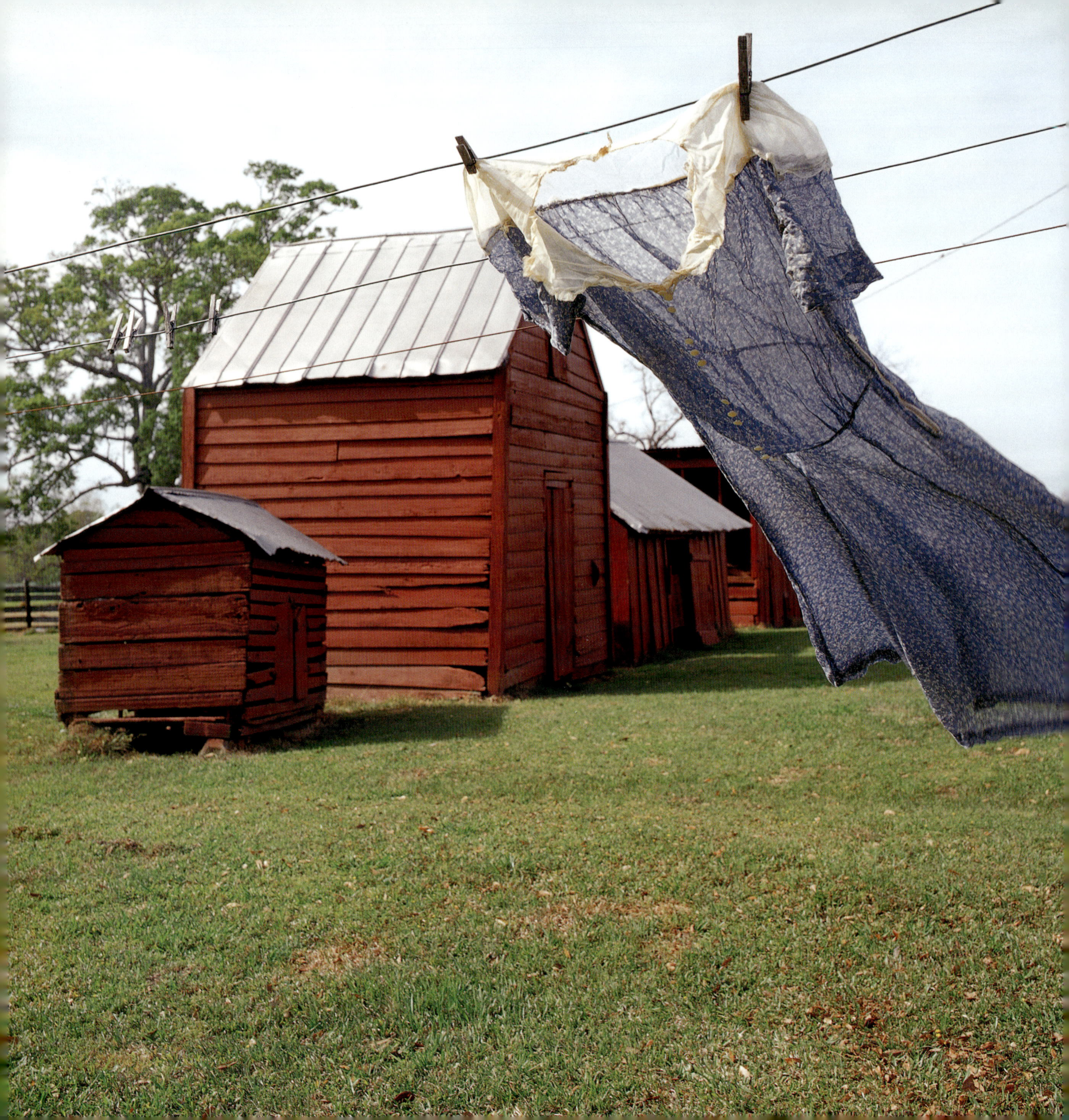

OPPOSITE
One of Lucille Couret's cotton dresses flutters on the clothesline, set against a backdrop of outbuildings.

RIGHT
Acadian textiles and a brace of feather pillows get a good airing out on Couret's gallery railing. The deep galleries extended the living space in temperate and warm weather, and lightweight furniture was moved in and out accordingly. For shade and privacy, cloth panels were suspended from iron rods hung between the columns.

Acadian Village

The Acadians who migrated to Louisiana in the late 1800s made new lives in the bayou country, where they resourcefully lived off the land. For generations they kept largely to themselves in close-knit communities, maintaining their own traditions, a unique French patois, and—unsurprisingly, for people exiled for their faith—a devout Catholicism.

Acadian life in these rustic locales gave birth to a distinctive Cajun culture that may be best known for its robust fare and lively music. Festivals and dances counterbalanced long days of hard work. The community gathered for the Saturday-night fais-dodo, waltzing and two-stepping to fiddles and accordions. Making fine instruments was an Acadian specialty, as were spinning, weaving, and boat building.

Their modest homes employed a form that was, like Creole houses, derived from French traditions: the one- or two-room cottage with timber framing and *bousillage* infill. They emulated Creole adaptations to the environment by adding a front gallery and raising the house on piers, but retained their native land's high-pitched gabled roof and the use of the attic it created as a sleeping loft for boys. (Creoles deemed attics too hot and otherwise unsuitable for living.)

None of the original Acadian enclaves survives intact, but a number of vintage structures have been salvaged and assembled at historic re-creations like Lafayette's Acadian Village. There, eight early-nineteenth-century houses were relocated along a bayou setting with replicas of a general store, blacksmith shop, and chapel. Together they illuminate Louisiana's Acadian heritage and help preserve its architectural traditions.

One of the buildings is outfitted as a schoolhouse; others contain exhibits on weaving and the development of Cajun music. The homes, furnished with local pieces, convey the simple but rich life of the Acadians, through whose resilience Cajun culture has not merely survived through the centuries but flourished.

ABOVE
The Aurelie Bernard House, an Acadian cottage built about 1800 in Saint Martinsville and enlarged about 1840, is the oldest structure in the Acadian Village. The steep staircase rising from the front gallery is typical of such modest dwellings; it led to the attic sleeping loft. Also typical is its *bousillage* construction of mud and moss—abundant, inexpensive materials that provided durable insulation. Early buildings like the two pictured here had solid wooden shutters, a style that eventually gave way to louvered ones.

OPPOSITE
The Dorsene Castille House (about 1860), like most Louisiana Creole buildings, was constructed of old-growth cypress; its lumber was naturally resistant to insects and rot. Once abundant in the lower Mississippi Valley and coastal marshes along the Gulf of Mexico, it is now rare, and the lumber industry that thrived here is much diminished. This Acadian cottage (with the typical inset porch and gabled roof) came from Breaux Bridge, about ten miles from its present site.

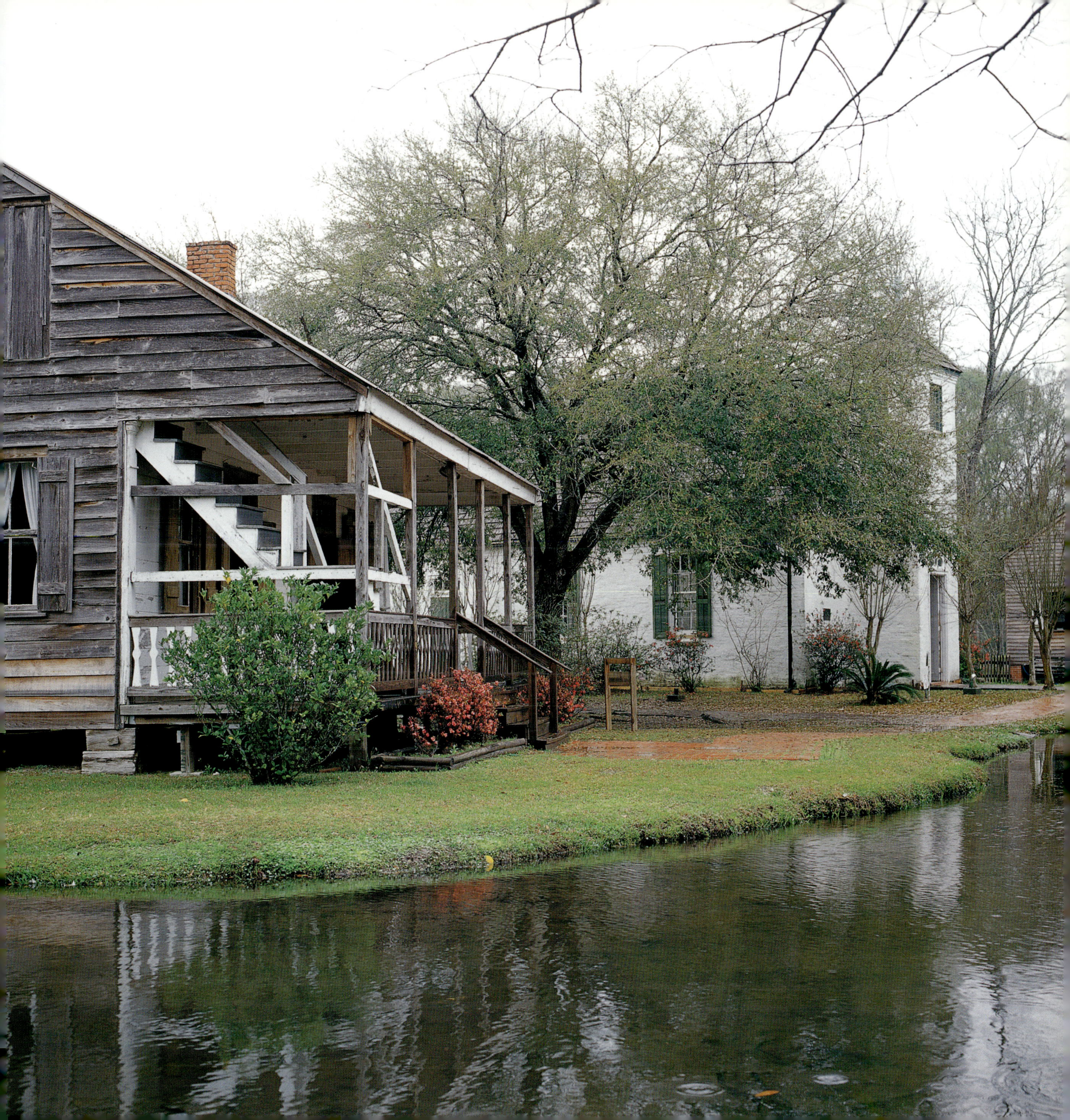

LEFT

The New Hope Chapel at Acadian Village, a 1976 replica of an 1850 church, is a simple structure—just a sanctuary covered by a steeply pitched roof, with a square bell tower forming the entrance. Catholicism has been central to the Acadian and Creole cultures for centuries, and churches like this one dotted the southern Louisiana countryside. A local carpenter modeled these pews after a 150-year-old example. The altar's original home was Saint Anne's in Youngsville.

OPPOSITE

Dorsene Castille House's bedroom furnishings, including the ornately carved bed, reflect the Victorian taste of the mid- to late nineteenth century. However, the smooth *bousillage* walls, board ceiling with exposed beams, and unfinished cypress flooring belong to a timeless Creole aesthetic.

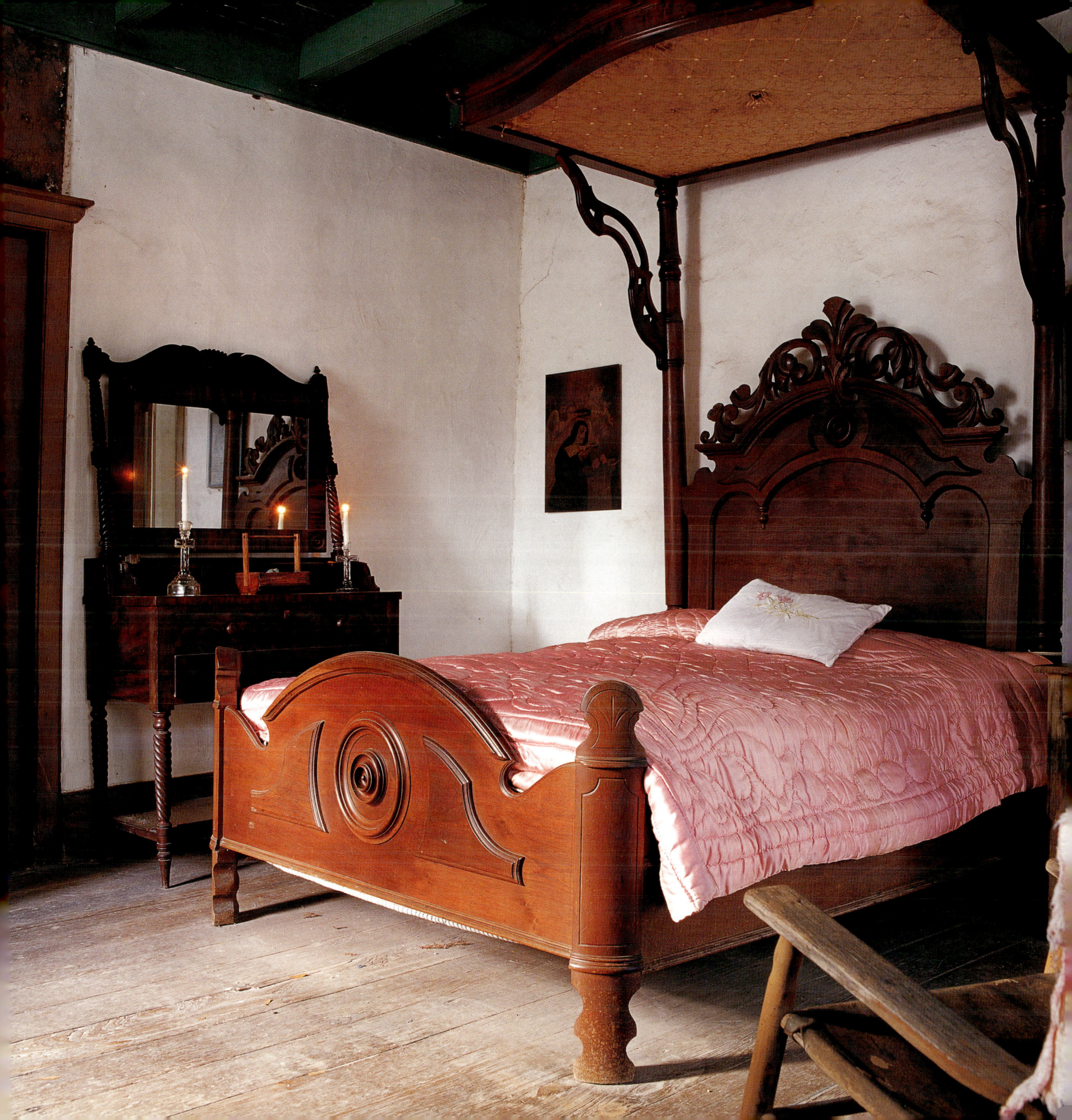

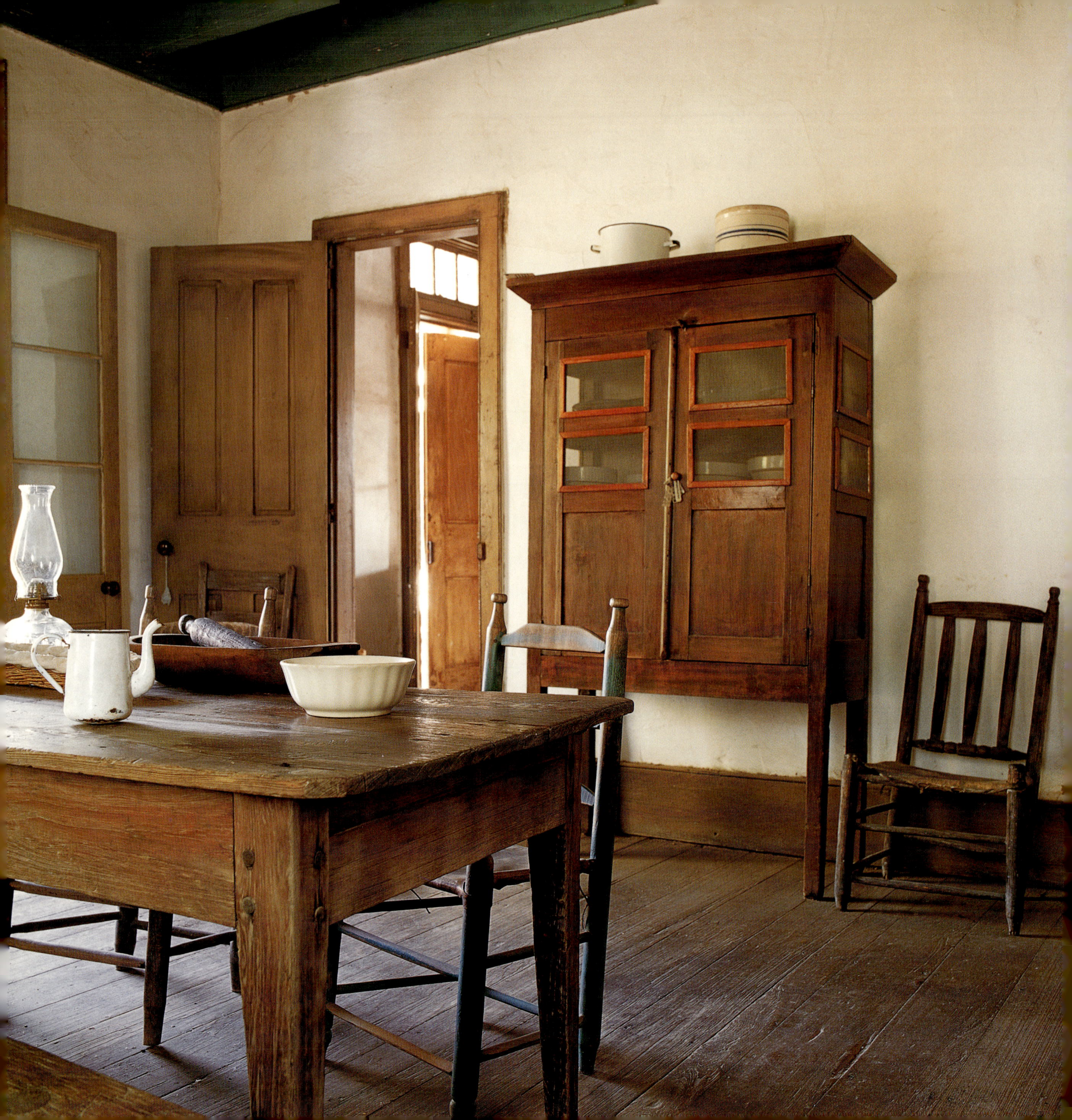

OPPOSITE
This room in the Dorsene Castille House, outfitted as a kitchen, contains a cypress worktable and a garde-manger, each bearing traces of the *gros rouge* finish so popular in the region. Also typical are the unfinished cypress floors, worn smooth by years of use. A few chairs with hide seats complete the arrangement.

RIGHT
This mantel with an elaborately carved central medallion is a focal point of this room at Dorsene Castille House. All the house's mantels have a similar decoration, which represents two fish surrounding a rosette and is said to symbolize a prosperous family.

Hilaire Lancon House

The 1848 Hilaire Lancon House, originally on Bayou Cypremort, was nearly razed in the 1990s to increase acreage for growing sugarcane. Fortunately, it was instead given to Steve and Suzanne Stirling, ardent preservationists who relished the challenge of salvaging a vernacular gem that been much damaged by the flooding and winds of countless hurricanes. They saw in the house, with its efficient floor plan and well-proportioned, high-ceilinged rooms, a fine home for themselves and their three children. In 1992 they relocated it twenty-three miles north to Franklin, on the bank of Bayou Teche, Acadian Louisiana's principal waterway.

Steve Stirling had accumulated old lumber, bricks, hardware, and other essentials in anticipation of a fine restoration and was ready to begin work on the house, constructed of joined and pegged cypress. Every piece of hardware is either original to the building or to the period. After five years of meticulous work, the family moved in.

The original occupants were members of the Weeks family, who were prominent in the area. It was not their main house but a simple refuge some distance from it, used when work on the property's canal or in the outlying fields necessitated a night away. The house's namesake, Hilaire Lancon, acquired the property in 1877 and lived there until his death, in 1913.

Today the house is set among other historic buildings and reconstructions in a landscape of live oaks, cypress trees, and nonnative species popular in southwestern Louisiana during the nineteenth century: citrus, sweet olive, fig, crepe myrtle, and magnolia. Its overall form is that of an Acadian-style cottage, with exterior chimneys set at the gabled ends. Downstairs four rooms flank a large central space (used as dining room, office, and foyer) that extends from front to back. A steep staircase on one side (a

ABOVE
Icons of faith fill the house, as was common in Catholic French Louisiana. Two are opposite the stairs: a print of the Sacred Heart of Jesus, in its original cypress frame, which once hung in Dimiceli's grocery, a local landmark; and a chalkware statue of Our Lady of Fatima from the Catholic Daughters meetinghouse in uptown New Orleans. The cypress-peg coat rack to the left is a fixture of Louisiana country houses.

OPPOSITE
Hilaire Lancon House faces Bayou Teche, much as it once faced Bayou Cypremort. The current site was previously occupied by the Camperdown Plantation sugar mill, which ceased operations in the 1920s. Molasses barrels were loaded onto steamers from the slip on the bayou that marks one of the property's borders. The mill rollers' brick foundations remain in the front yard.

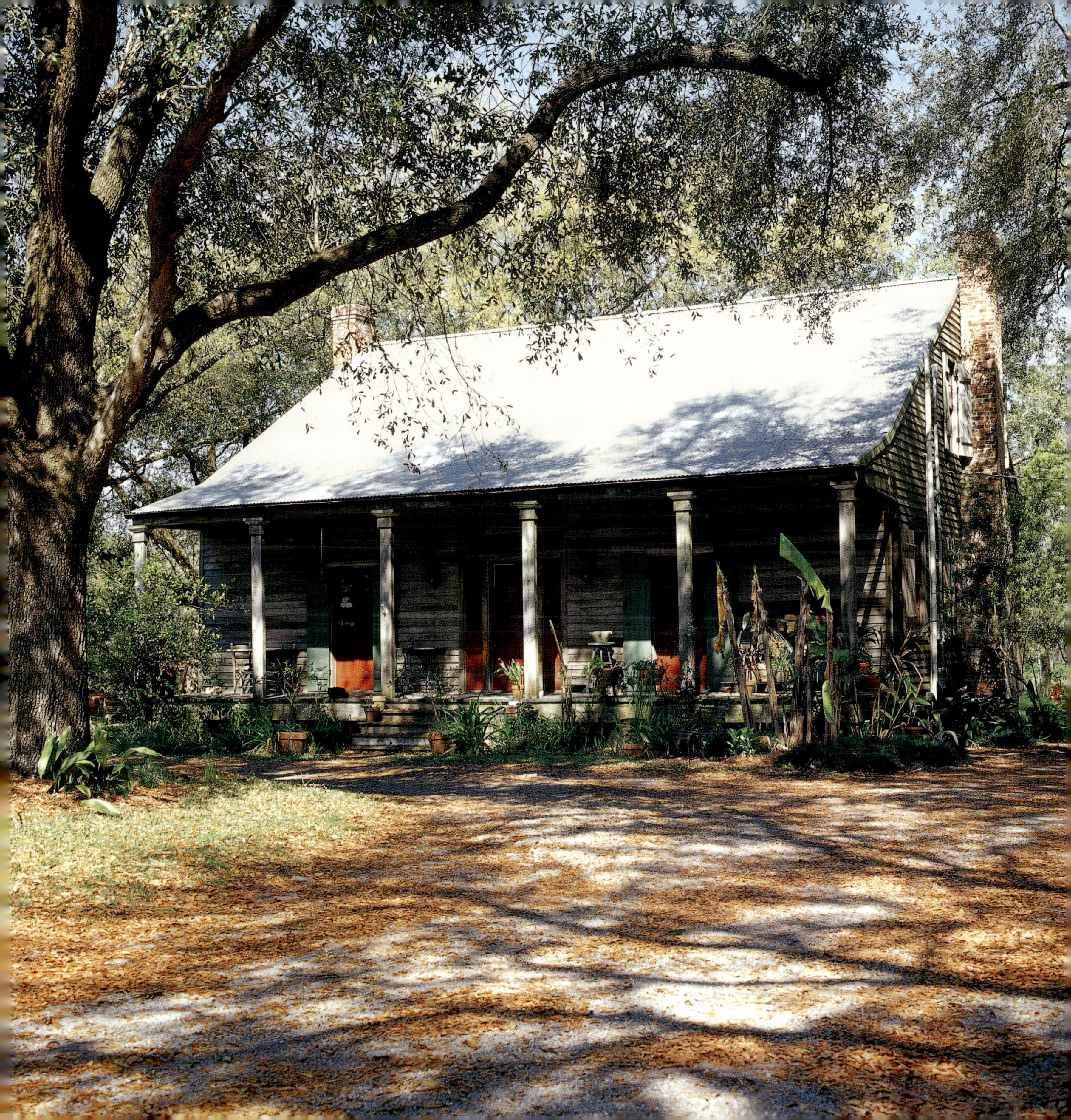

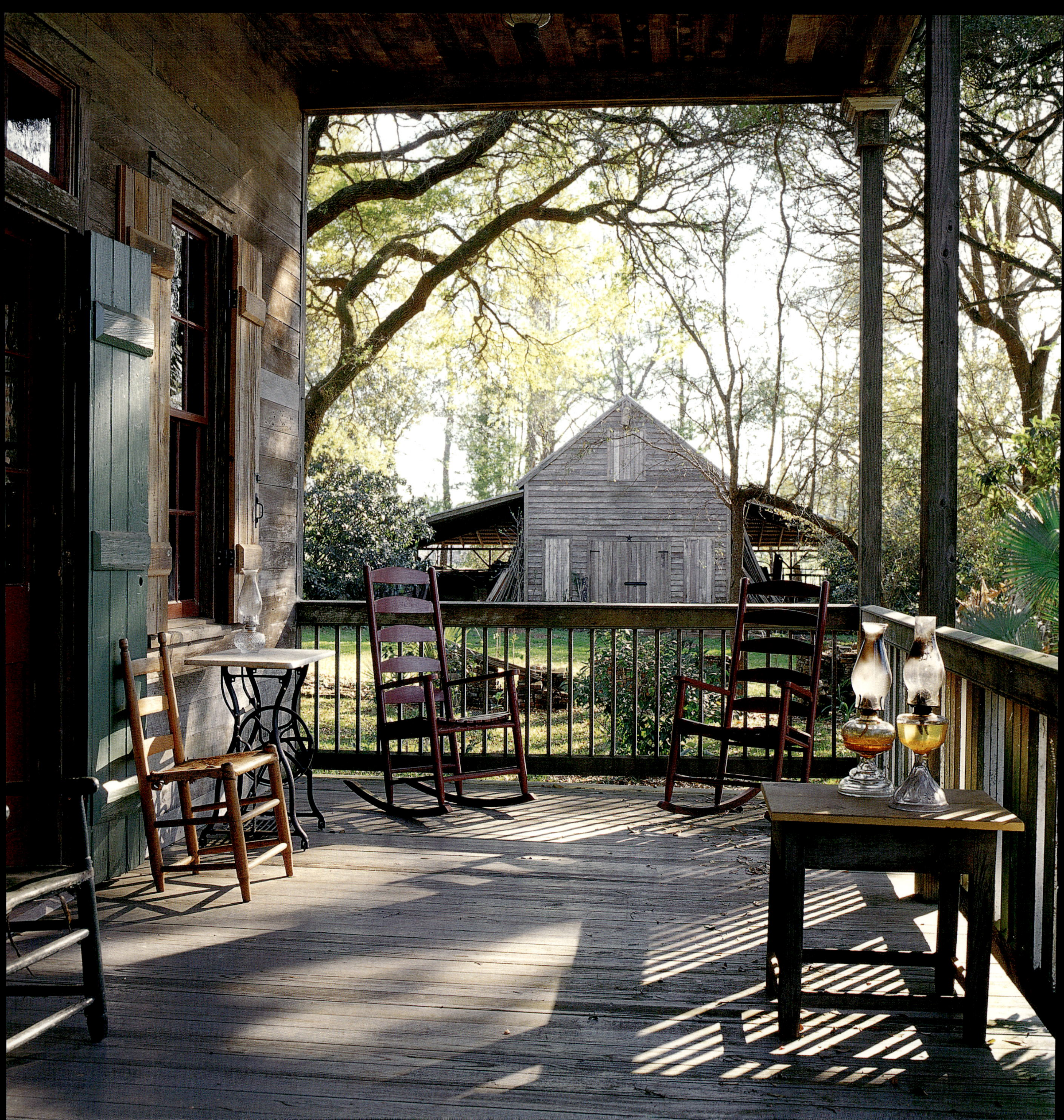

OPPOSITE
Lancon House's deep porch is a favorite place to dine, with hurricane lamps glowing in the evening light. Two such lamps sit on an early cypress side table; another is set upon a table made of a sewing machine base topped with marble. The barn in the distance, recently built of old lumber, is Steve's woodworking shop. It is filled with materials for future restoration projects.

RIGHT
The Stirlings moved this *garçonnière* (young men's quarters) here to save it from demolition and will use it as a guesthouse. The iron syrup kettle pays tribute to the property's former use as a sugar mill; many of the kettles were reduced to scrap iron during World War II. Nearly all of the plants here were "pass-alongs" from friends, not often available at nurseries but plentiful in old gardens and around old house sites.

later addition) leads up to two bedrooms and a bath. Porches stretch across the full width of the house, some forty-two feet.

With great care and a balanced, conscientious approach, the Stirlings bestowed new life upon a damaged and vulnerable work of historic architecture. Their effort garnered a National Register designation for Lancon House in 2001. Beyond that, they proved that such a building, after generations of neglect, could be made to serve as well as—or perhaps even better than—it originally had.

TOP LEFT
On the desk by the porch door are several contemporary art objects, including a Chitimacha basket woven by one of the few people who still practice the ancient craft. The milk glass lamp was a gift from Steve Stirling's grandmother, who shaped his love of history and antiques. Above the desk hangs an 1802 print of Napoléon made in London.

BOTTOM LEFT
When the Stirlings occupied the house in 1997, they gave it its first-ever coat of paint, using historically appropriate colors. Thanks to its construction of old-growth cypress—an extremely durable wood—the house had withstood 150 years without that protective layer. In the background, the living room mantel is bedecked with nineteenth-century French items, including an Empire clock. A whitewashed cypress tool chest serves as coffee table. On the cypress floor is a sisal rug, typical of nineteenth-century Southern houses.

OPPOSITE
The eight-foot-wide center hall serves as foyer, passageway, and dining room, with a French chandelier and French and American side chairs surrounding a mahogany Federal-style table. The unpainted cypress ceiling is an original surface rarely encountered in houses of this age—most were painted, especially in a home's public areas. The paintings, copies of works by Marie Adrien Persac, show plantation homes from the area. Persac's meticulously detailed paintings from the 1850s and 1860s provided Steve a guide for landscaping Lancon House.

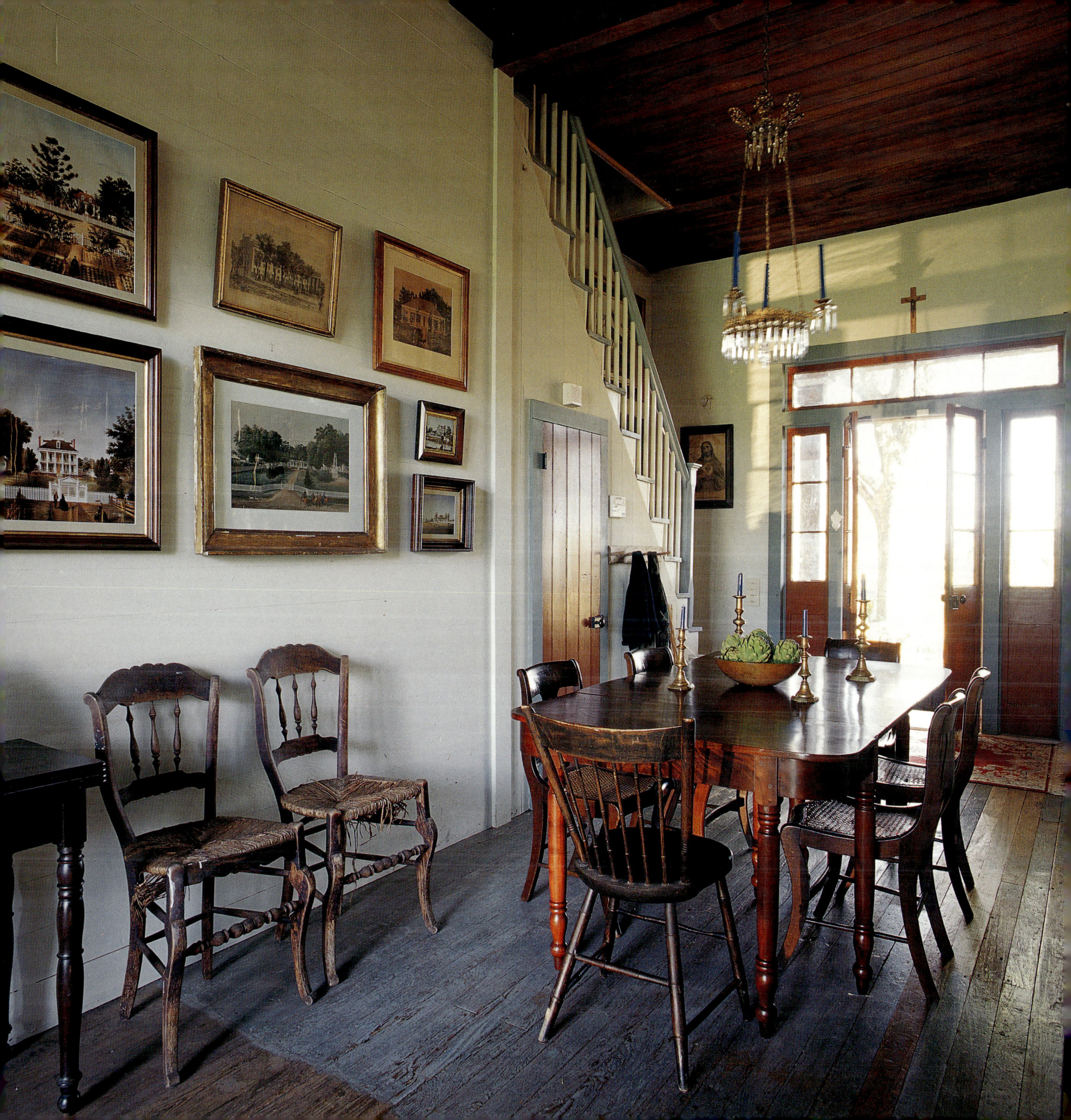

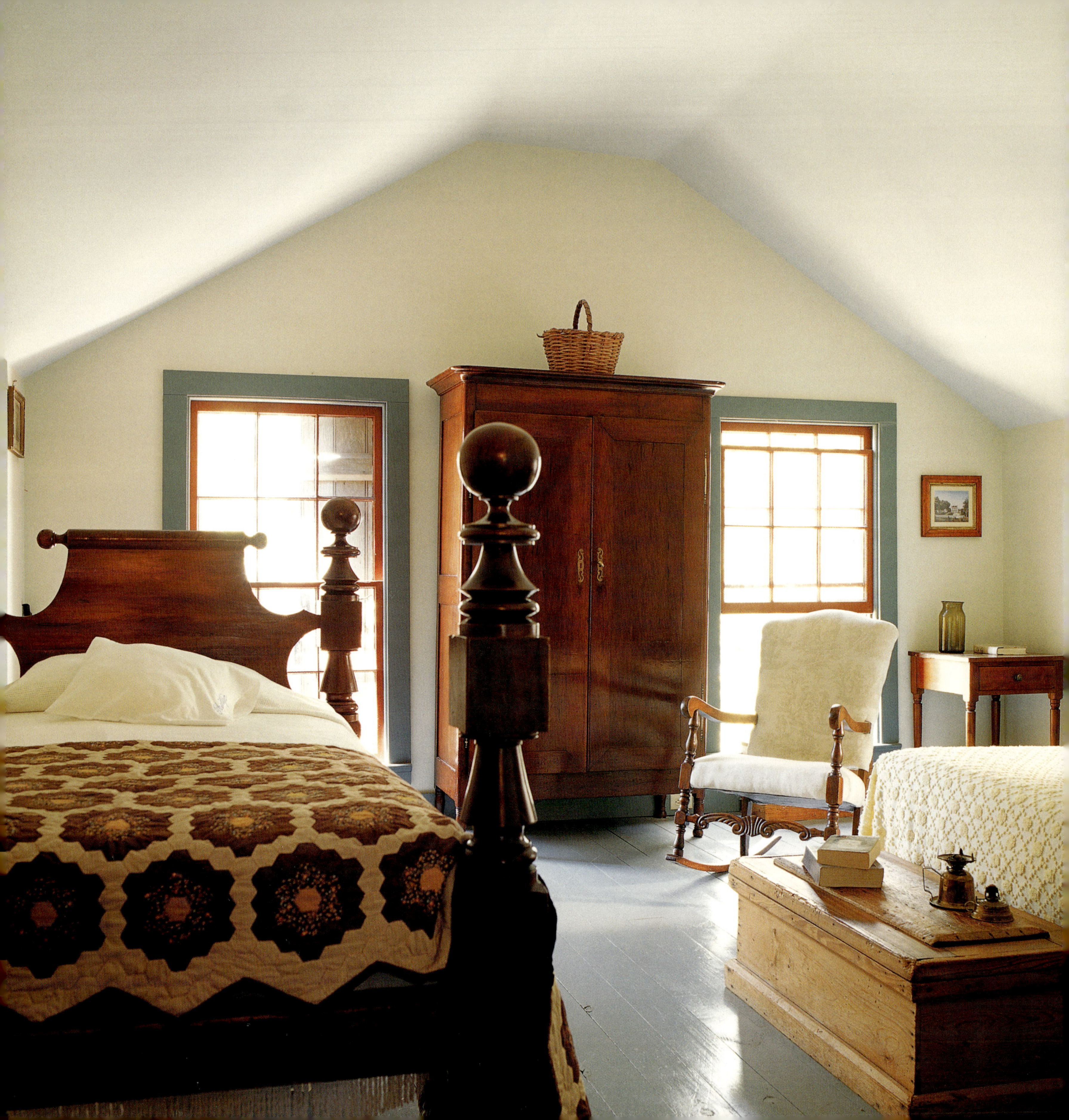

OPPOSITE

The quilt on the American twin bed in this upstairs children's room was made by Steve Stirling's maternal grandmother, an award-winning quilter. At the foot of the other bed stands a cypress trunk, found locally. Perched on top of the Louisiana cherry armoire is a split-oak egg basket that belonged to Suzanne Stirling's great-grandmother. The windows extend nearly to the floor, seeming to bring the treetops inside; the five acres of shady property ensure privacy while rendering curtains unnecessary.

RIGHT

The walnut high-post bed in the downstairs bedroom is covered with a 1940s patchwork quilt made from feed sacks. The engravings depict local episodes from the Civil War: the sinking of the gunboat *Cotton* and the Battle of Irish Bend, which took place in the nearby cane fields. On the other side of the door is a photograph of Alexander Ruffin Stirling (Steve's great-great grandfather), a sugar planter who enlisted as a private in that war. The Louisiana ladder-back armchair, with its original hide seat and green paint, was rescued from a local dump.

Dumesnil House

Over the course of almost two centuries, Dumesnil House has been taken apart repeatedly—by a series of owners as well as by forces of nature, especially 1992's Hurricane Andrew. Its most important features have been altered, removed, and restored, and its use has evolved. Once the principal house on a working sugar plantation, it now serves primarily an escape from the city. Surrounded by live oaks, it is thoroughly and appealingly rustic.

Dumesnil is situated in Saint Mary, a parish on the bayou country's southeastern coast. The house rests on a former Spanish land grant and was probably constructed during the first quarter of the nineteenth century. It is still owned by descendants of the original builders.

It has the steeply pitched gabled roof and deep front porch typical of an Acadian raised cottage, with its chimney placed at one of the gabled ends, not at the center. Some other characteristically Acadian features are no longer extant: For example, the steep staircase from the porch to the attic sleeping loft was relocated to the interior long ago.

Other elements of the house point to an architectural lineage that is Creole in equal measure: It has exposed, beaded ceiling beams, and it originally had cabinets projecting from the rear. Dumesnil's construction of timber framing with *bousillage* infill is typical of both Acadian and Creole houses.

The furnishings suggest a countrified Creole sensibility. Sophisticated tastes infuse this rural dwelling, as can be seen in an exquisitely crafted cherry "rolling pin" bed and the simple elegance of a Directoire-style side table.

Although Dumesnil House has been modified extensively to serve generations of residents' changing needs, it has retained its utility and architectural integrity. In this, it again implies a dual heritage, exhibiting typical Acadian resourcefulness and an adaptability that is quintessentially Creole.

ABOVE
During an expansion in the late nineteenth century, the entire house was clad in weatherboard siding that was narrower than the original boards, and the latter were recycled as interior wall paneling. Some of the solid cypress shutters are original; others are replacements made of old lumber. The roof is now corrugated metal, but the original construction would have used cypress shakes.

OPPOSITE
Set amid a grove of live oak trees and surrounded by a sugarcane field, Dumesnil (also known by its original name, California Plantation at Aston) exhibits typical features of an Acadian cottage: It is raised a couple of feet above the ground on brick piers, with a steeply pitched gabled roof and a gallery extending across its full width. Clapboards protect the exterior walls that are fully exposed to the elements.

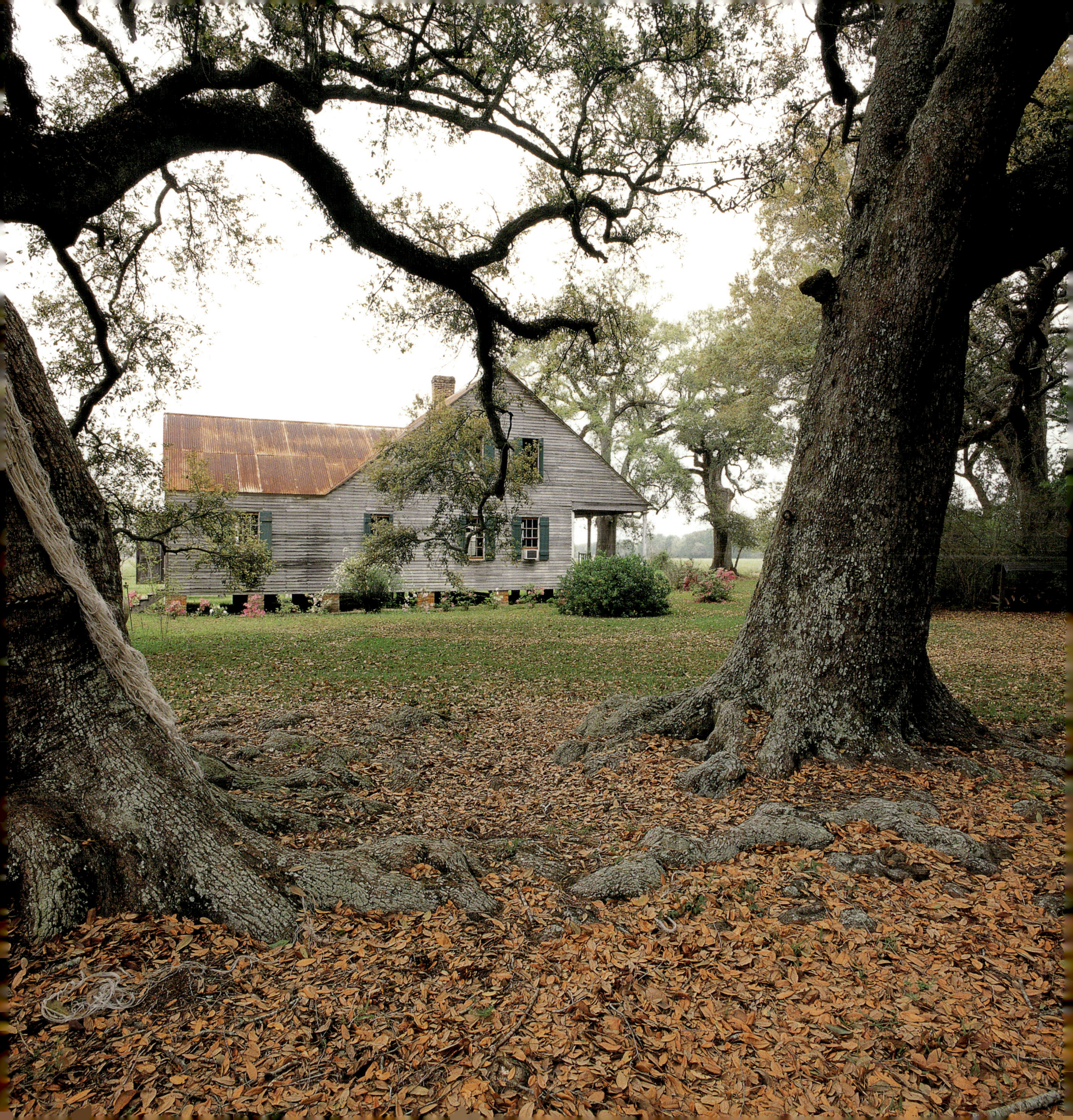

TOP LEFT

The garde-manger, or food safe, dating from about 1900, now displays photographs and other keepsakes in the family room. It retains its original side-panel screens, but the screened doors on the upper half have been removed. It is one of Dumesnil's few furnishings that survived the ravages of 1992's Hurricane Andrew. The chair rail around the room is original; during restoration, the *bousillage* underneath it was found to be unwhitewashed, evidence that it had been installed before the interior was painted.

BOTTOM LEFT

The family room is also used for dining, with a French refectory table and ladder-back chairs dating from the mid-1800s. Suspended above are a coal-oil lamp and yellow-painted punkah from the nearby home of a great-grandfather. Other family pieces include the rocking chair and cypress sofa. The simple cloth across the door permits air to circulate but blocks the sun's glare.

OPPOSITE

The kitchen has been fashioned from one of two bedrooms added in the late 1800s. The walls are made from the house's original nine-inch-wide cypress weatherboards. The worktable and the soapstone sink (probably a garden sink originally) are French and date from the nineteenth century. The cypress garde-manger by the sink dates from the early twentieth century. The New Orleans–made cypress cabinet to its right is a bit later. The refrigerator is a 1940s Frigidaire. All the floors in the house are cypress.

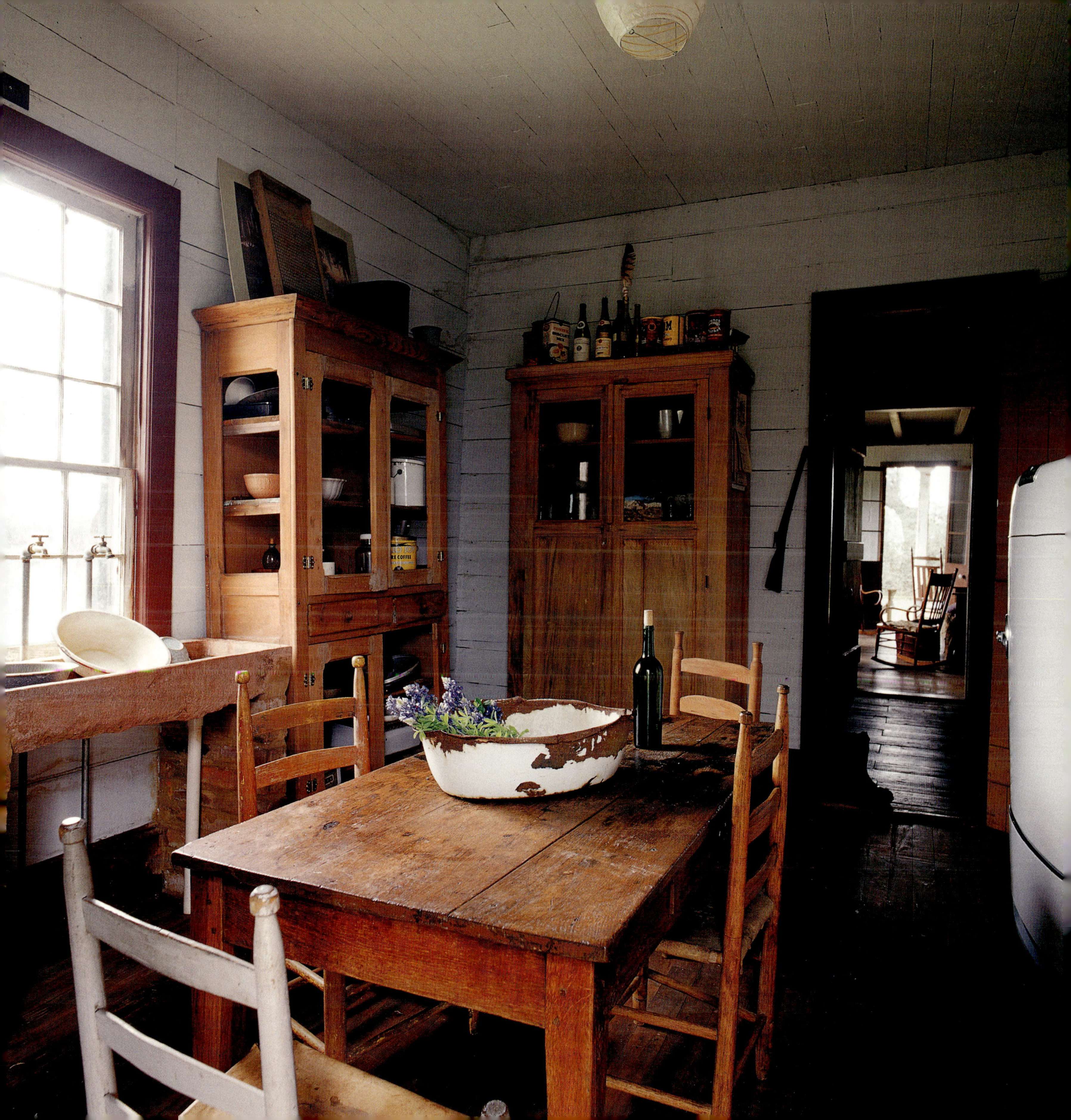

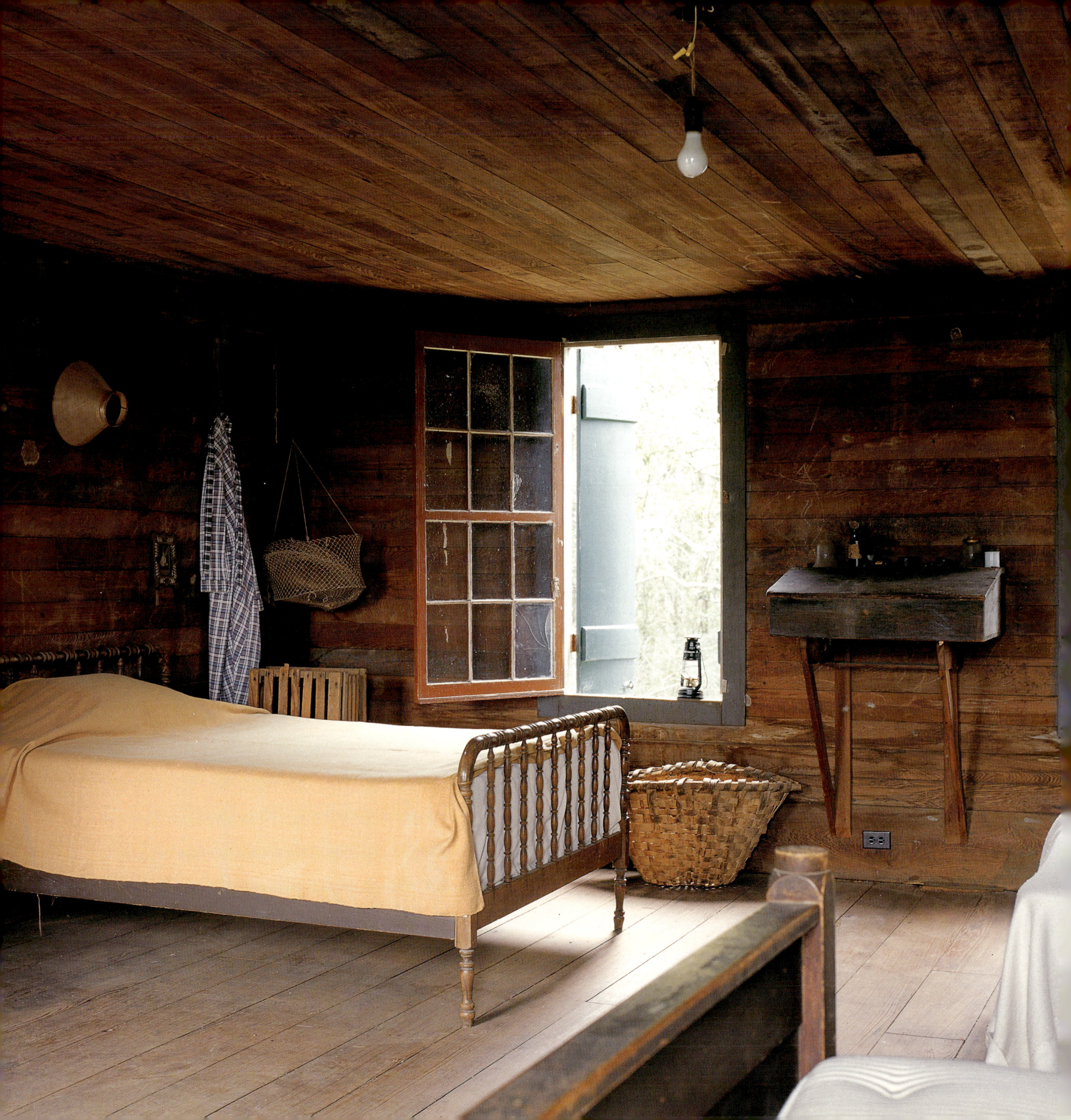

OPPOSITE

The attic sleeping loft had only screens and solid cypress shutters until a restoration in the 1990s; this casement is the first window it has ever had. The homespun heavy cotton blanket on the spool bed comes from an ancestral home in Broussard. The slant-top wall-hung desk contains nearly two hundred years of receipts for the plantation's cane, which was hauled to nearby mills for grinding. The woven cane basket and the crab trap in the corner were found in the barn.

RIGHT

This bedroom is one of two added in the late 1800s. Its walls were wooden, rather than *bousillage*, and later covered with drywall to improve insulation; the stenciling, a typically Victorian fashion, was added at the same time. The high-post bed is an early-nineteenth-century piece made in Louisiana of cherry with a "rolling pin" headboard. The striped bed covering was woven by a family member a century ago. The small side table is French, and the side chair came from a plantation near Baton Rouge.

Natchitoches and Cane River

Louisiana's oldest city is not New Orleans (established by the French in 1718) but Natchitoches, settled under the French flag in 1714. The settlement and its fort were critical to France's claim to western parts of the Louisiana Territory. Natchitoches (pronounced Nak-uh-tish and named for the native people who once lived there) lay at the intersection of French and Spanish lands in the New World. Their borders, and later those of the United States, were often vague, making this frontier area a crossroads for cultural exchange, trade, informal alliances, and occasional military saber-rattling. The settlers also traded actively with the Native Americans, with whom relations were generally amicable and intermarriage was common.

Natchitoches, in the north-central part of the state, about 240 miles northwest of New Orleans, was set along the mighty Red River, which joins the Mississippi and the Atchafalaya Rivers to the south. It was an important and prosperous trading port until about 1840, when the Red shifted its course. That change simultaneously diminished Natchitoches's role in commerce (until the arrival, fifty years later, of the Texas & Pacific Railroad) and created an oxbow lake called Cane River. Cane River Lake extends some thirty miles from downtown Natchitoches through the countryside, where cotton, sugar, indigo, and tobacco plantations thrived on the fertile, alluvial soil.

The planters built expansive homes on their farmland and also maintained elegant town houses in the city, where they conducted their business and social affairs. Today Natchitoches's landmark district contains more than fifty historic buildings, including Creole town houses with ironwork balconies. The outlying Cane River Heritage Area remains a bucolic setting for numerous Creole plantations and farmsteads. But Creole heritage is more than a history lesson here. Many residents trace their roots in the area to the eighteenth century, including the descendants of Marie Therese Coincoin, a freed slave. She eventually purchased her enslaved offspring's freedom, established a successful plantation, Melrose, in 1794, and founded a large, tight-knit, and still flourishing community of Creoles of color. Among such longtime locals, the old traditions remain a vibrant, vital part of daily life.

Nineteenth-century buildings line Front Street, in Natchitoches's historic district on the Cane River.

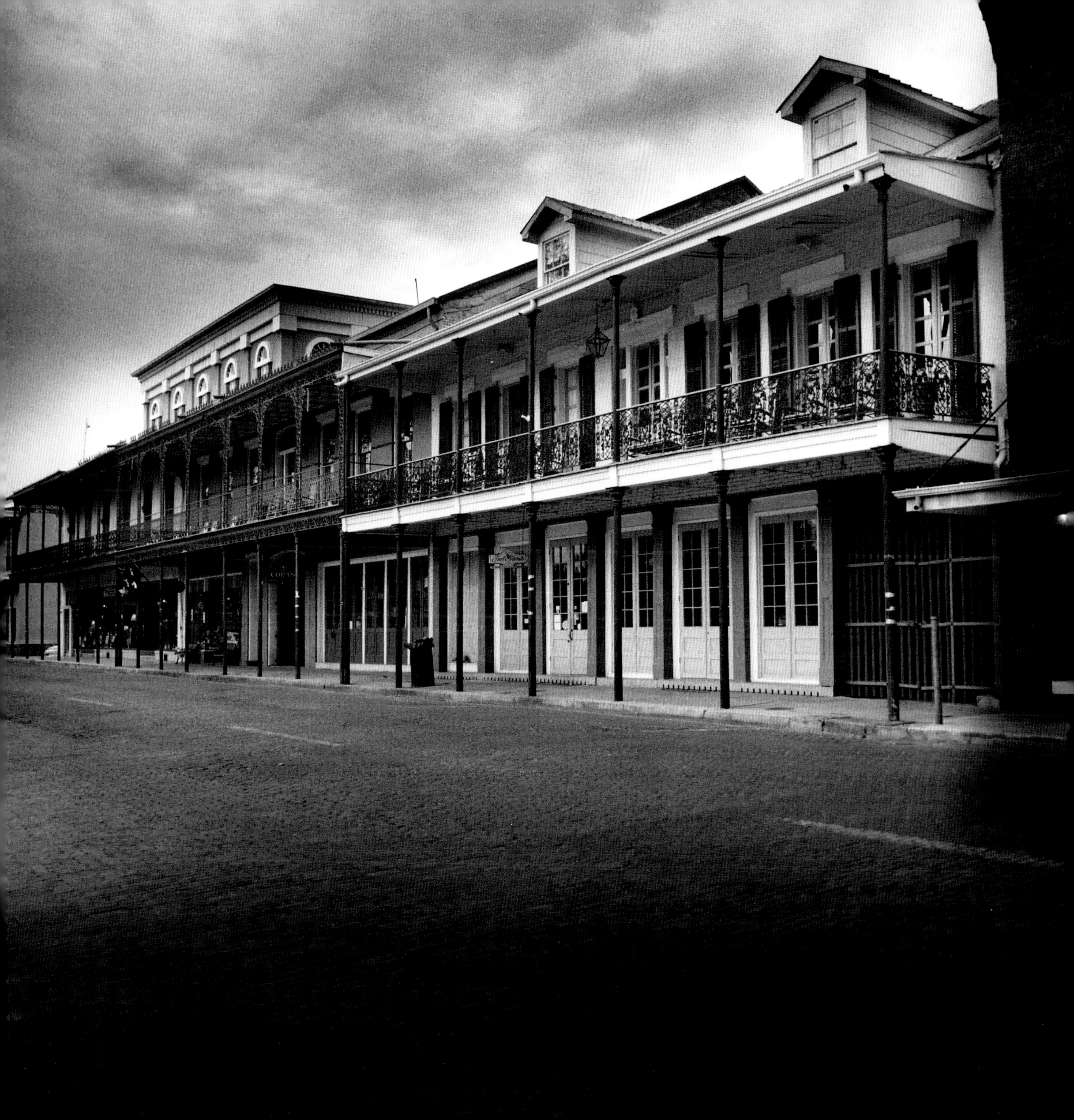

Tante Huppé House

The very name "Tante Huppé" conjures visions of a genteel Creole woman sipping a demitasse of strong chicory coffee with her breakfast of calas, traditional rice pancakes sprinkled with powdered sugar. Though Tante Huppé departed this world in 1862, her gracious spirit lives on in the brick house she built. It stands in the historic section of Natchitoches, fronting the Cane River.

The house was constructed between 1827 and 1830. Though it bears many characteristics of earlier Creole architecture, such as a galleried front and doors that open from each room to the outdoors, it also has American attributes, including a plan with a center hall and details inspired by the Greek Revival style. Many of the furnishings were selected and used by Tante Huppé herself.

She was born Suzette Prudhomme in 1799 of a prominent Creole family, but social advantage could not protect her from sorrowful loss. By the time she was thirty-six she had been widowed three times—her third marriage, to Dr. Jean Baptiste Huppé, was in 1829—and her only child had died. Resiliently, she transformed most of the rooms in her house into bedrooms, so that she could invite her friends and relatives to stay with her in town. She thus surrounded herself with an adoring extended family, whose name for her—Tante (Aunt) Huppé—endures to this day.

Another relative now owns and cherishes the house, Bobby DeBlieux, the former mayor of Natchitoches, who is an ardent preservationist and history lover. The national Natchitoches Historic District was created in 1974 from an application he authored, and the Historic District Ordinance was enacted during his tenure as mayor in 1976–80. His Tante Huppé would undoubtedly be pleased.

ABOVE
This room at the rear of the house was used as a secondary dining area. Above a small dining table, the punkah, its paddle covered in patterned paper, remains in its original location. The interior staircase leads to the second-floor dormered rooms. The piano beneath it has entertained many generations of music lovers here.

OPPOSITE
The raised cottage is constructed of brick and has a deep front gallery. The wing that extends from the back of the house was originally the quarters for household slaves.

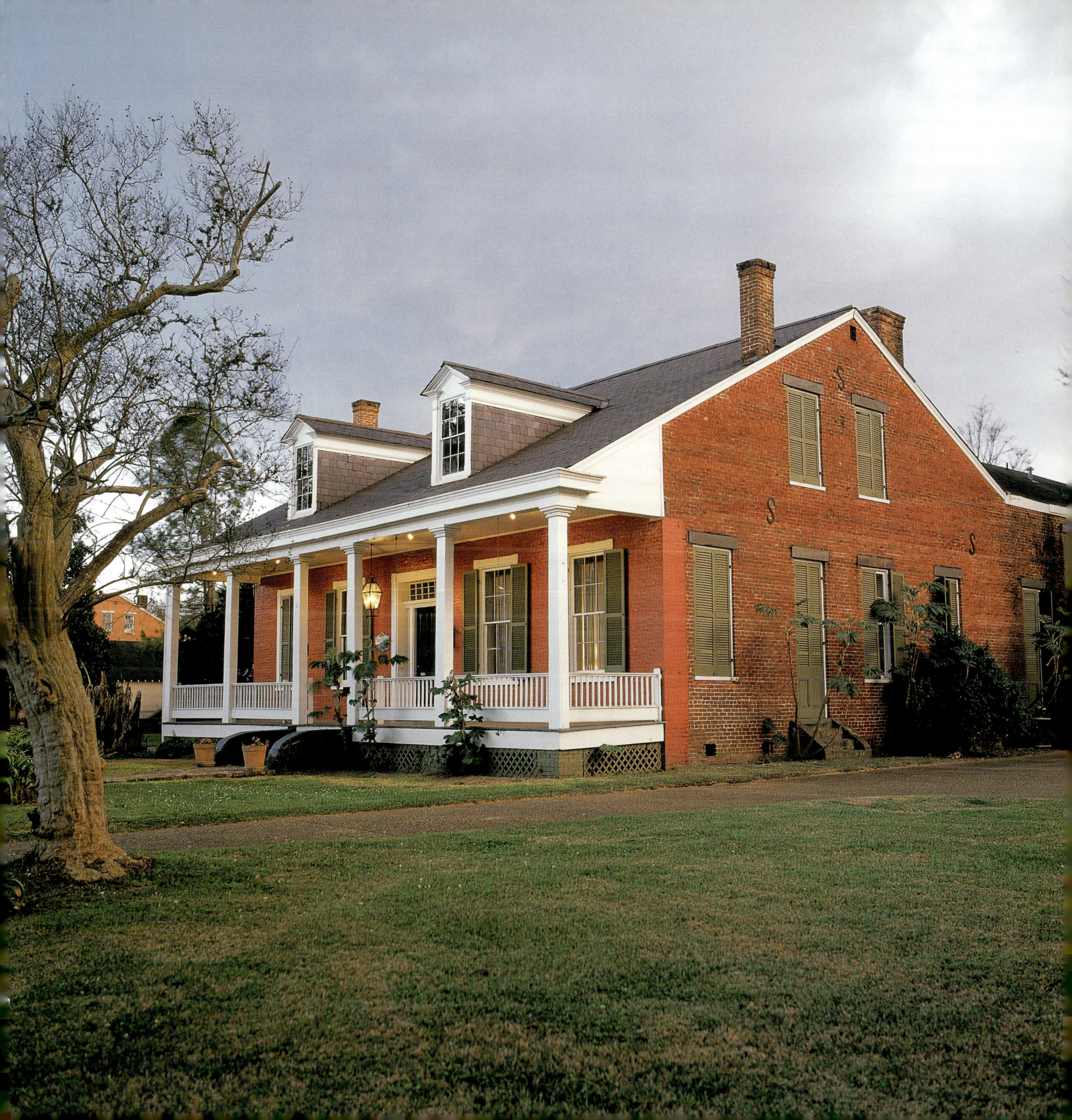

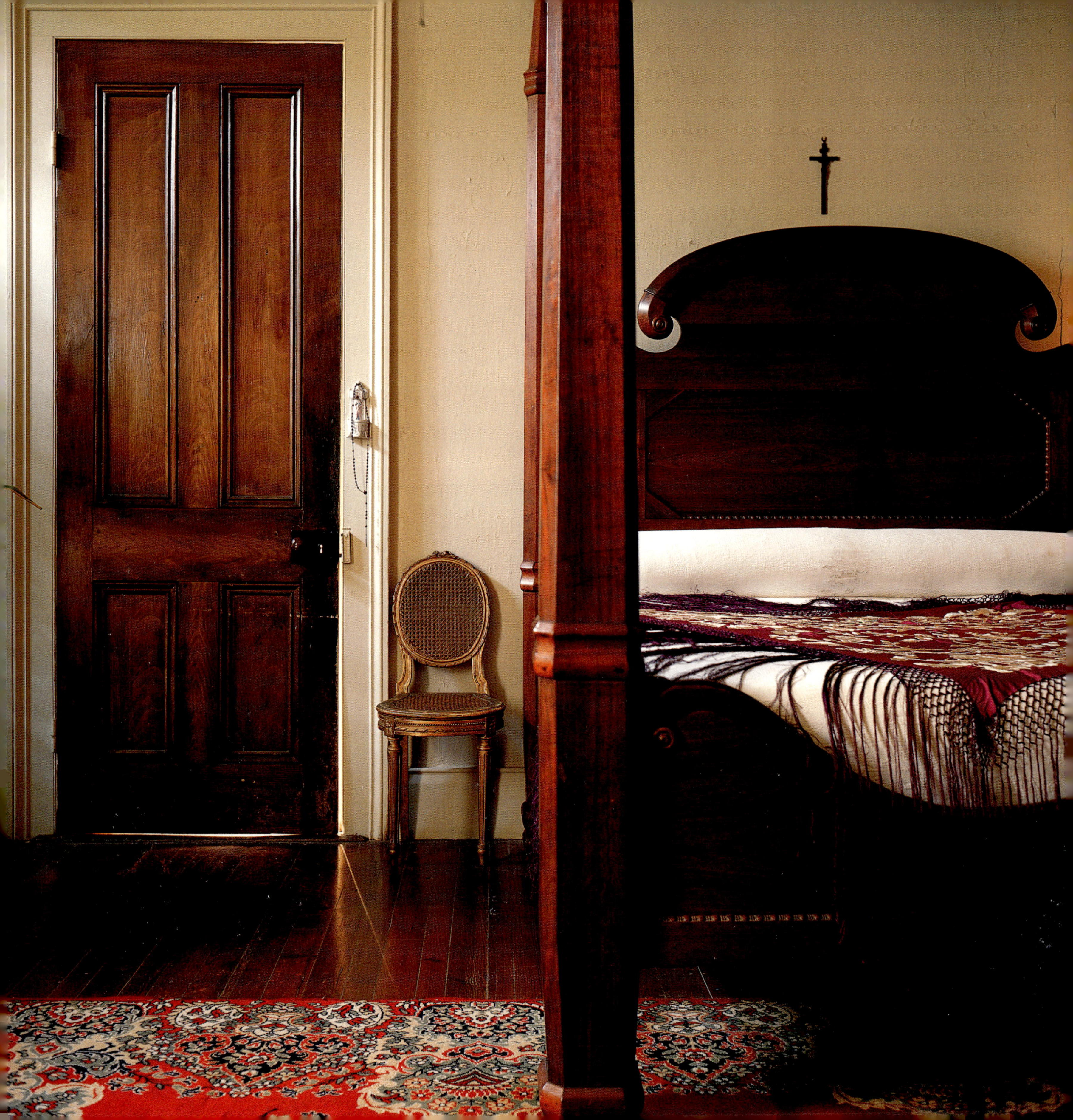

OPPOSITE

In Tante Huppé's bedroom, an enormous four-poster walnut bed contrasts with a diminutive Venetian giltwood chair. On the bed is a shawl one of Tante Huppé's relatives brought back from India in the 1880s. The holy water font and crucifix were de rigueur in Catholic Creole bedrooms. Doors throughout are either varnished cypress or, as seen here, have a faux bois treatment resembling oak.

RIGHT

The dining room chairs belonged to the house's original owner, Tante Huppé. She brought the chandelier with her from her family's nearby plantation; it still uses only candles. The table is set with family silver. Sprays of ginger from the garden fill the pair of Old Paris vases on the mantel.

LEFT
The library has expanded with each generation and contains works published as early as 1718. The books reflect a French Creole taste: With subject matter ranging from geography to philosophy, literature, and gardening, they were written in French. The shelving includes an armoire whose doors have been removed. Bound volumes of nineteenth-century sheet music are piled on the library table.

OPPOSITE
Above the library's roll-top desk is an 1830 map of the United States by John Mitchell. Tante Huppé's nephew Lestan Prudhomme Jr. purchased it in Philadelphia in 1835, and it has occupied that wall ever since. The simple Greek Revival mantel holds a pair of Old Paris vases (about 1850), gifts to Suzette Prudhomme from her second husband's family. The photograph above it is of present owner Bobby DeBlieux's two daughters.

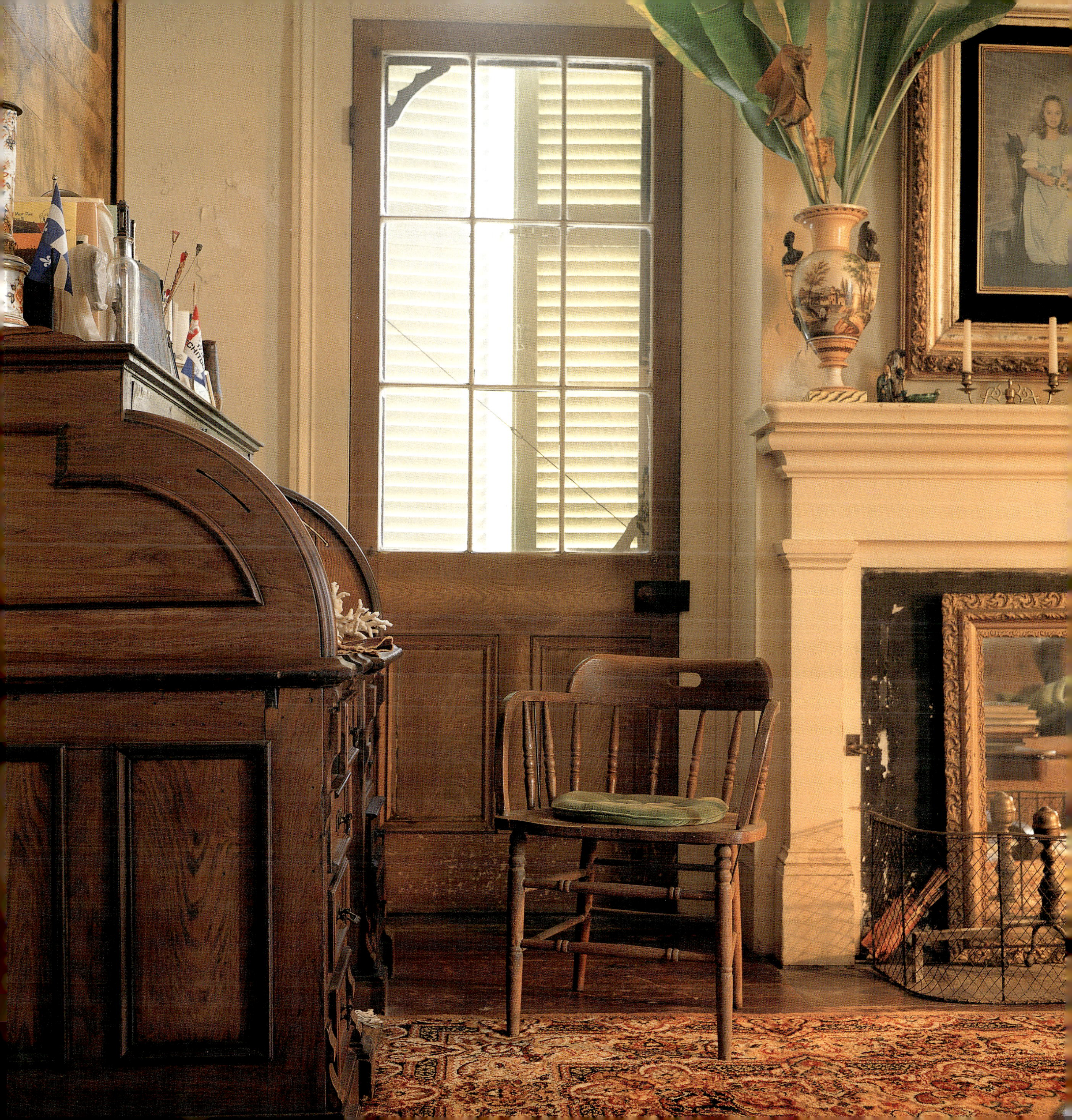

Wells House

The same year that thirteen colonies on the eastern seaboard of North America declared their independence from the British crown, Gabriel Buard of Natchitoches, then part of the Spanish colony of Louisiana, built a two-room dwelling with a central fireplace, a covered gallery on all four sides, and a hipped roof. It still stands on the east bank of the Cane River, one of the oldest houses in the Mississippi Valley. In its early years it was used as a trading post.

The house passed to Buard's daughter, Mrs. Edward Murphy, and it remained in the Murphy and related Tauzin families for more than a hundred years. In 1914 the property was purchased by Dr. Richard Williams, who sold it to Dr. and Mrs. Thomas Wells in 1965. Remarkably, the house both survived the areawide destruction during the Civil War's Red River campaign and escaped demolition for the commercial development that predated the 1974 establishment of downtown Natchitoches's historic district.

The galleries began to be enclosed in 1791; eventually, all of them except the front gallery were enclosed to provide additional living space. Gables added to the ends of the house in 1914 produced the current roofline. But the Wells House still reflects a colonial Creole past in its *bousillage* construction, hall-free floor plan, and French doors protected by solid wooden shutters. Despite the changes to the building over more than two centuries, it maintains a balance and grace, attesting to the adaptability of early Creole structures.

The current resident, Carol Wells, an educator and historian, began restoring the house in the 1960s with her late husband. She has steadfastly and carefully removed layers of modernization to reveal the simplicity of this nationally landmarked building.

ABOVE
Hanging by the fireplace in the living and dining area are iron tools for both cooking and tending the fire—also, a curiously shaped piece of driftwood. The mantel shelf and surround of beaded board echo the simple plank wall, original to the house. Plank walls were among the earliest types of interior partitions, but few have escaped demolition or modernization. A trio of brass pitchers and an eighteenth-century French faience plate adorn the mantel.

OPPOSITE
Wells House's original structure, from 1776, comprises the central chimney and one room to either side. The rough-hewn posts supporting the roof are replacements that used old timbers, which were fitted into tenons of the top plate and pegged in place like the originals. The front yard is dotted with wildflowers, shrubs, flowering bulbs, and other plants. "At first I wanted only native plants in the yard," Carol Wells said. "But people kept giving me things from their garden, and I abandoned my original plan."

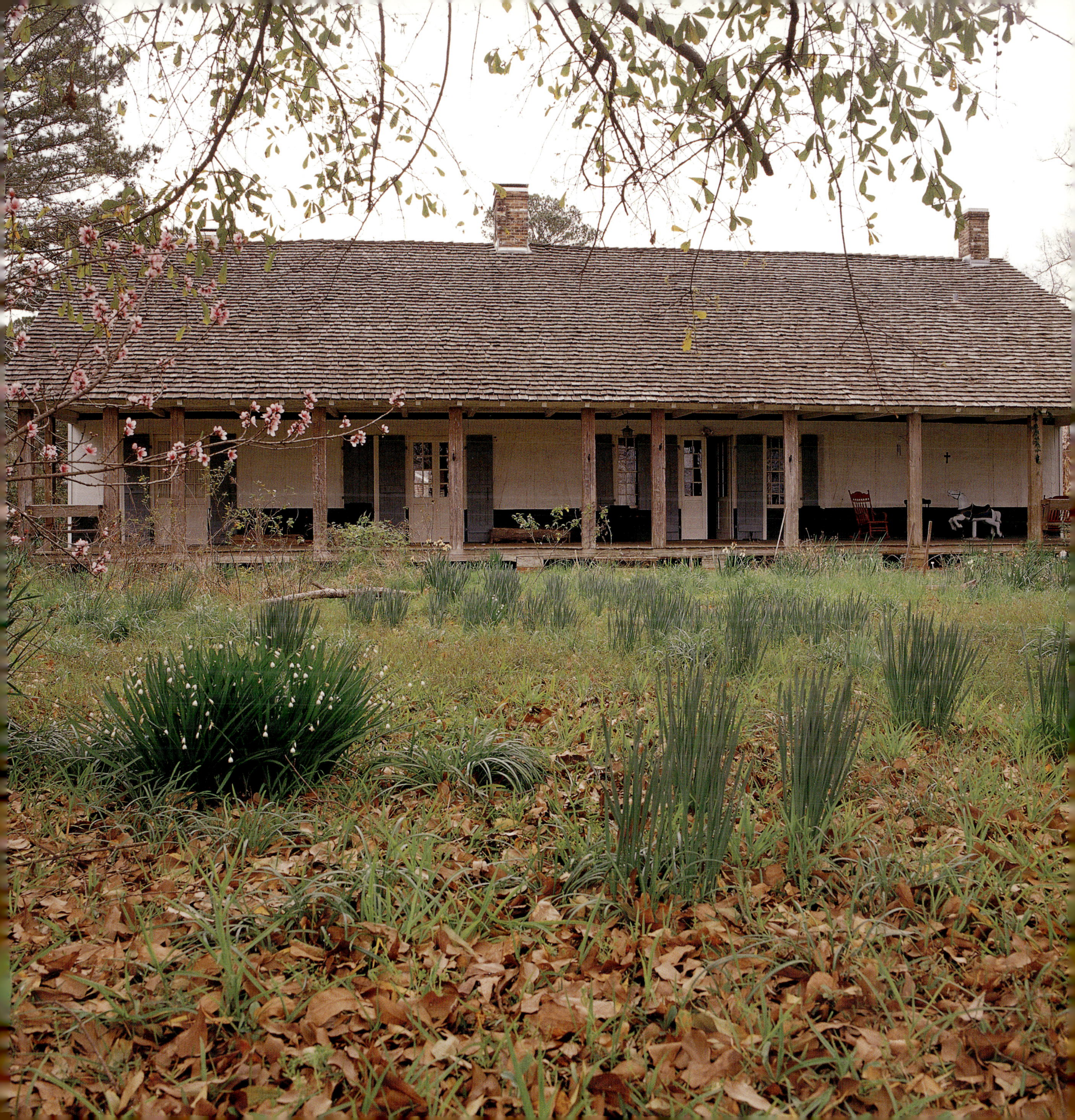

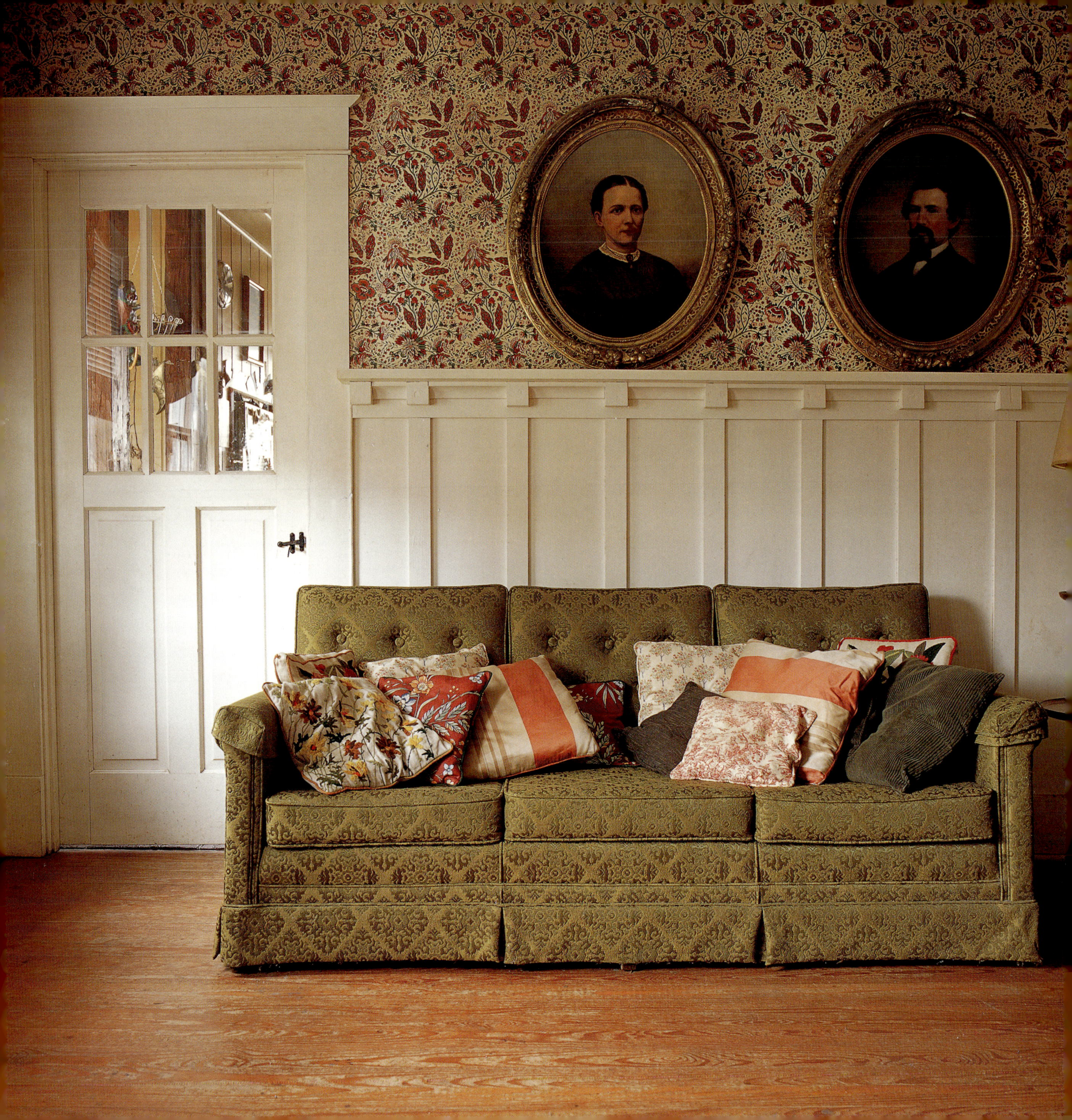

OPPOSITE

This room, now used as a sitting area, was created by enclosing part of the rear gallery. The portraits are of the owner's ancestors, Mr. and Mrs. Charles Henry Pray Lower of Pennsylvania.

TOP RIGHT

The fireplace in one of the two original rooms was probably used for cooking as well as heat. The paint scheme is the same inside and outside the house, with whitewashed walls set off by dark gray borders at the ceiling and wainscot. Furnishings include a French table and benches in walnut and an early armoire from Natchitoches.

BOTTOM RIGHT

Carol Wells has furnished her home with many family heirlooms from the mid-Atlantic and New England, including this eighteenth-century blue-painted Pennsylvania chest. Her mother used the smaller trunk to hold doll clothes.

TOP LEFT
An iris and books represent Carol Wells's two passions—gardening and history. The fireplace in the background was part of the original construction. It shares the central chimney with a firebox that serves the adjacent room.

BOTTOM LEFT
The original bedroom fireplace was discovered beneath two subsequent additions. To the left is an armoire from an Episcopal church in Natchitoches. The cherry desk in the foreground belonged to a Mr. Davenport of Grand Écore, who was the business partner of Edward Murphy, an early owner of the house.

OPPOSITE
The pencil-post bed from Maine dates from the late eighteenth century. It occupies the second of the building's two original rooms, where its strong verticality echoes the timber framing of the whitewashed walls. The table to the left is from Parlange Plantation in Pointe Coupée Parish. The painted table to the right was found in the nearby town of Coushatta.

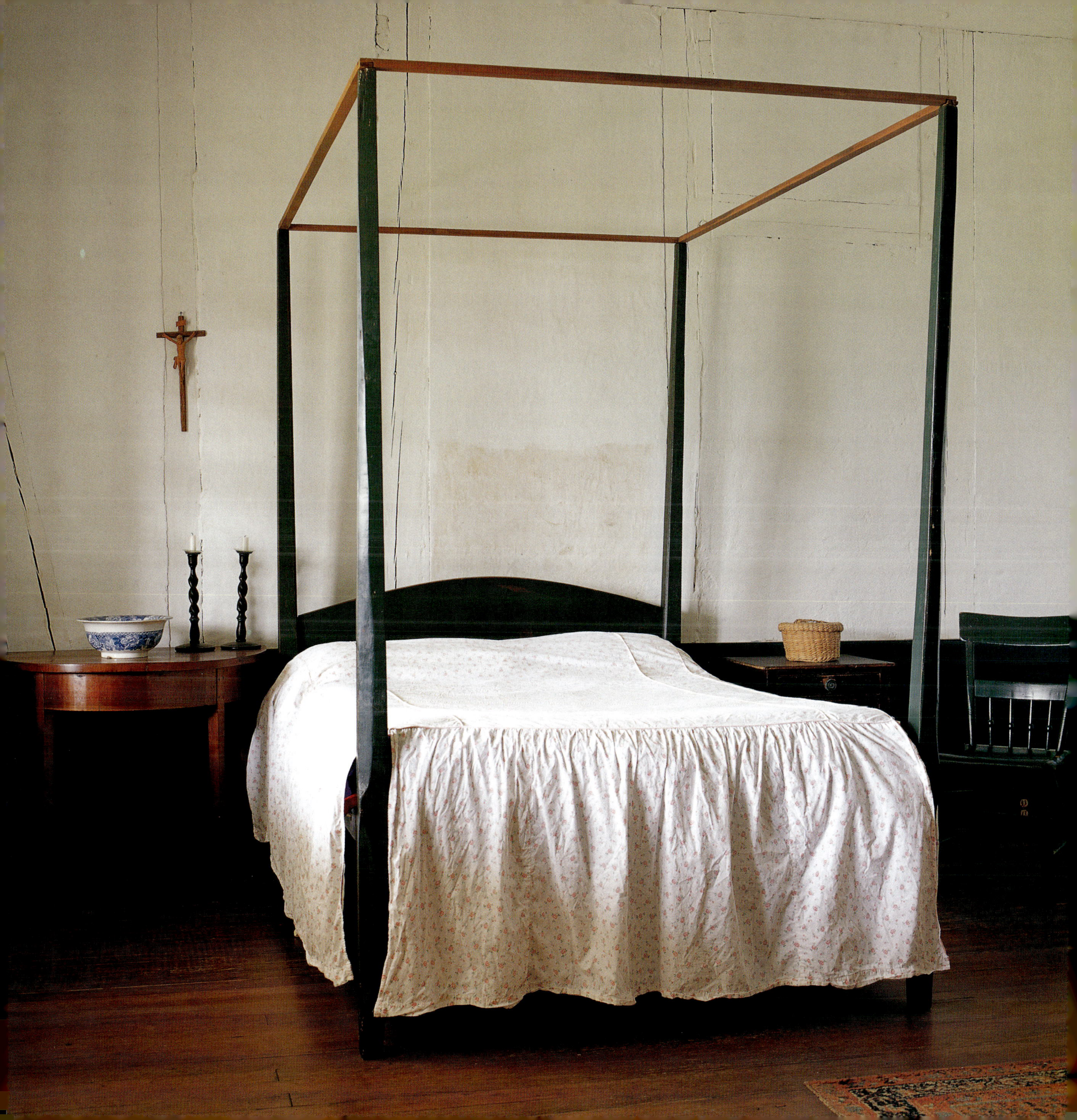

Cherokee Plantation

Some of Louisiana's best farmland is in the Cane River vicinity, where cotton has long been grown. Cherokee Plantation (whose name comes from the Cherokee roses blooming there) still cultivates cotton, so its landscape changes year-round. In spring the fields are plowed for planting, revealing the ruddiness of the bare earth. Once the cotton is planted, its foliage covers the fields in green. In the fall the fields are white with the crop, ready for harvesting. A more picturesque setting is hard to imagine. A double row of mature live oaks defines the approach to the house, maintained in tip-top condition by the owner, Theodosia Nolan.

Cherokee was constructed about 1839, demonstrating that Creole-style architecture still endured a generation after Louisiana joined the Union, in 1812. The wealthy planters who built it, Clarisse Prudhomme and her husband, Charles Sompayrac, may have modeled it on Clarisse's parents' nearby home, Beaufort Plantation, which likely was constructed at the turn of the nineteenth century.

Cherokee is a raised plantation house on brick piers, with walls of *bousillage* construction protected on the exterior by cypress weatherboards. Inside, the timber framing and whitewashed *bousillage* are visible. Many of the furnishings are original to the house and remain placed as they have been for generations

Cherokee once had galleries on all four sides, but the north gallery (along the building's right side when viewed from the front) was enclosed some time ago. Also on the property are three very old cypress barns, one of log cabin–style construction, and a slave cabin with its original fireplace—the last survivors from a large collection of outbuildings. In recognition of its significance, Cherokee was placed on the National Register of Historic Places in 1973.

ABOVE
The deep, covered gallery makes for a comfortable outdoor living space, sheltering rocking chairs and benches that afford views of the grounds. The chamfered posts of solid cypress at the roof's edge have held it aloft for almost 175 years. In the distance is one of the old cypress barns, which is constructed of solid squared timbers in the Creole *pièce-sur-pièce* technique, inspired by a French Canadian form of log construction.

OPPOSITE
Cherokee, framed here by branches of live oaks, has a restful solidity, emphasized by its massive umbrella roof. The roof is finished in wooden shingles, as it was originally. The enclosure of the side gallery, which created two bedrooms and a kitchen, can be seen at right.

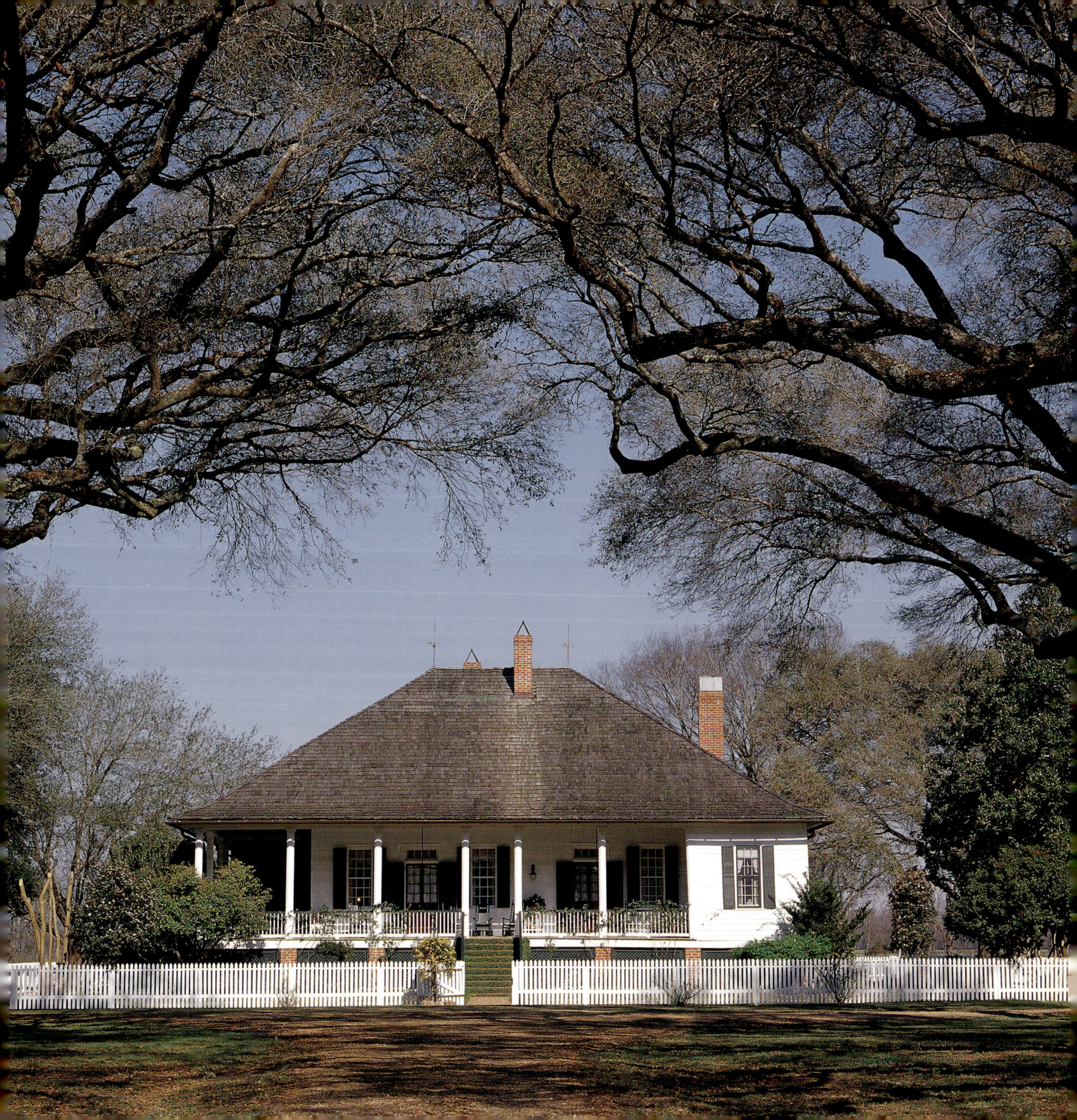

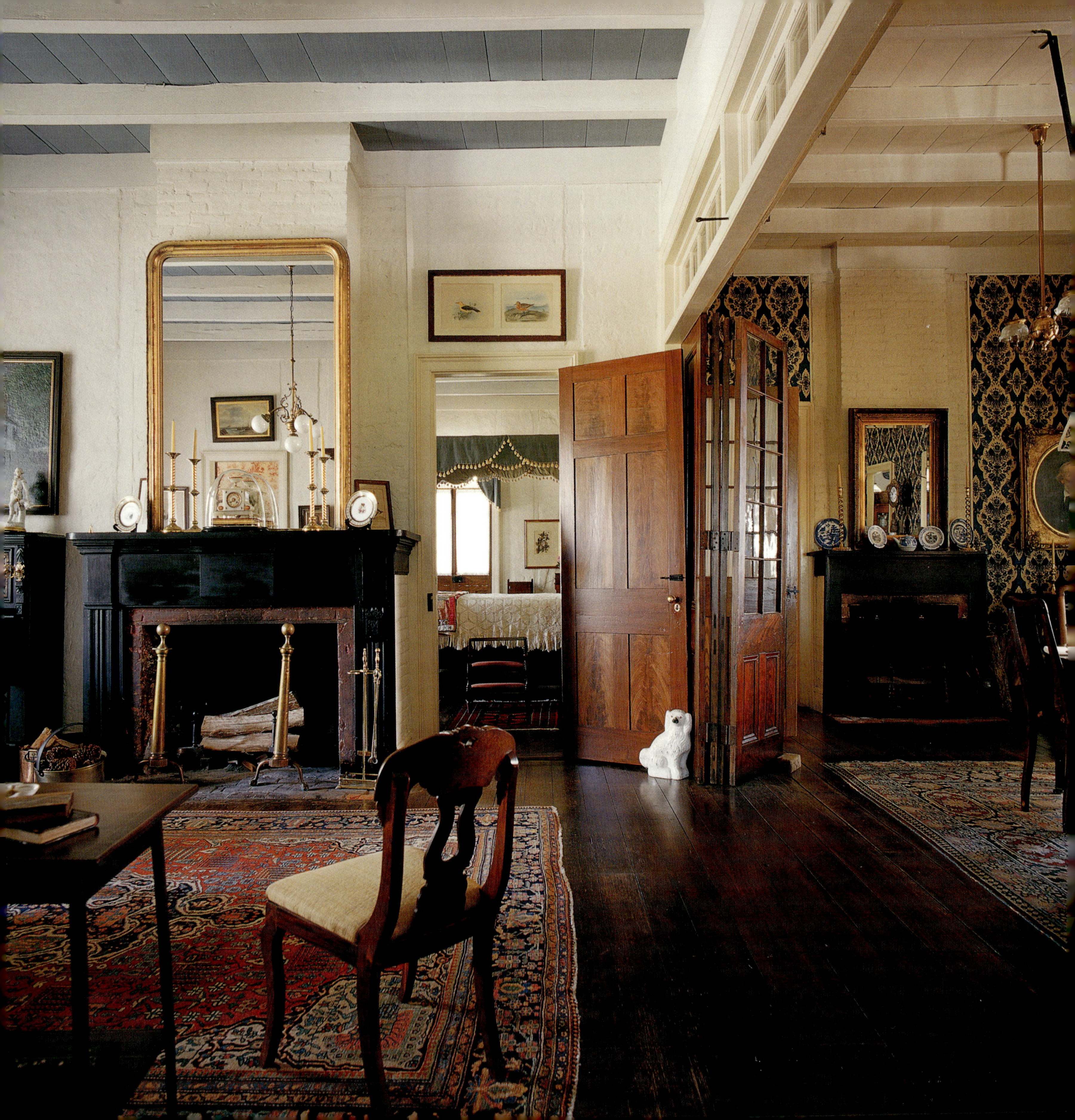

OPPOSITE
The *salle principale,* or main parlor, occupies that room's traditional position at the center of the primary living level. To the right is the dining room, which can be closed off by a set of folding doors. Creole taste is exhibited in the black box mantels and the placement of mirrors above them. French clocks, like the one on the parlor mantel, were traditional wedding gifts. The six-paneled door to the bedroom still wears its original faux bois finish.

RIGHT
A boldly patterned silk fabric covers the dining room walls and the paddle of a massive punkah. The wallcovering is a historic reproduction. The mantel and fireplace surround are much simpler in their ornamentation than those in the adjoining parlor.

TOP LEFT
In Creole fashion, rooms served multiple purposes. A bedroom might be used as a breakfast room, office, or sitting room throughout the day. In this bedroom, a secretary is positioned to take advantage of the light streaming in from the windows and doors opening onto the gallery. The fireplace provides winter warmth, and family keepsakes are displayed on its mantel shelf and chimney in a jumbled arrangement that is typically Creole.

BOTTOM LEFT
A family portrait, with its rich jewel colors, stands out against a whitewashed wall of *bousillage*. It is of Annette Sompayrac and was painted by Theodore Sidney Moïse (1808–1885), one of New Orleans's leading portraitists. A piano attests to the Creole love of music and dancing; the instrument was a household fixture.

OPPOSITE
The kitchen was created by the enclosure of the gallery adjacent to the dining room; originally, meals were prepared in a separate kitchen building. A traditional Creole white enameled drip coffeepot sits on the table; baskets and gourd dippers recall the food gathering and meal preparations of an earlier time. The pie safe holds china as well as sassafras twigs, bay leaves, and scuppernong jam

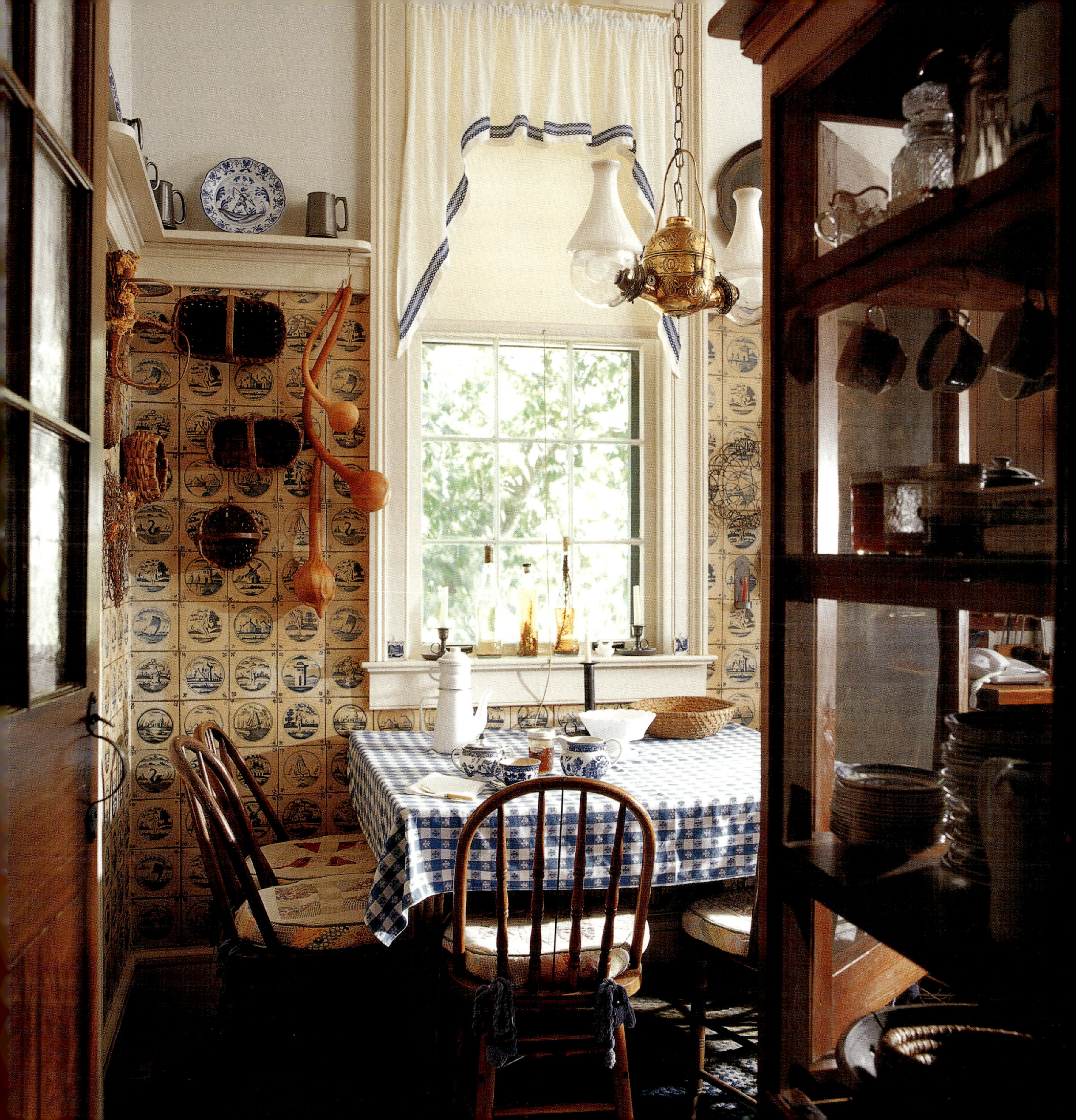

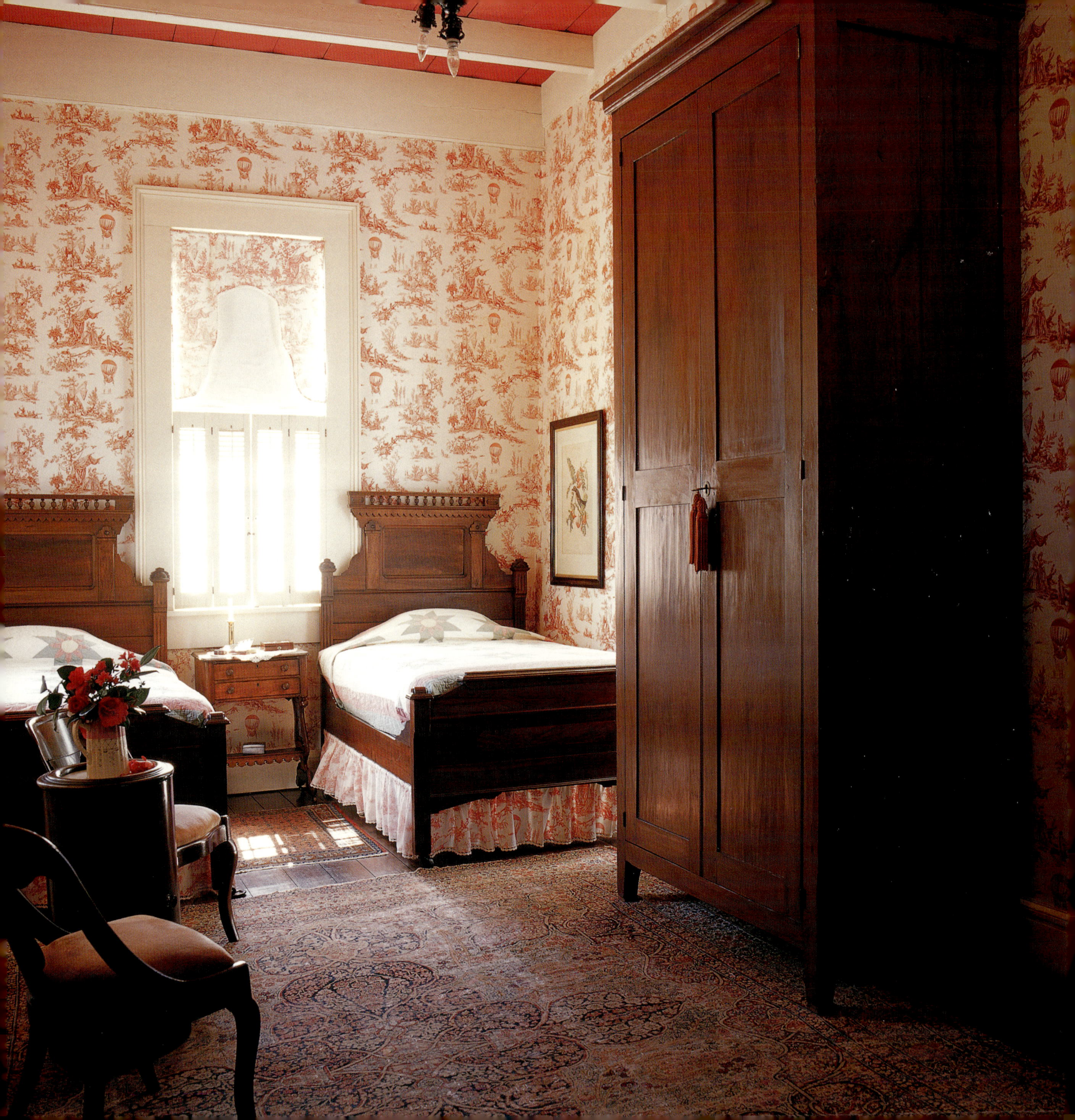

OPPOSITE

A massive cypress armoire, fabricated before the Civil War by slaves at Cherokee, dominates one of the bedrooms that were created by the enclosure of a side gallery. The light raking across the doors' flat panels reveals the long strokes of the hand plane that smoothed them. This room, at the front of the house, was known as the Traveler's Room. If a light was on in its window, wayfarers were welcome to spend the night.

TOP RIGHT

A marble-topped dresser is set against wallpaper reproduced from a nineteenth-century toile pattern of hot-air balloons. In the early 1800s wallpapers were imported to New Orleans by the barrel, and many styles were available to those who could afford them. Though notable examples of papered rooms exist in Creole plantation homes, the overall preference tended toward simpler painted surfaces. The simple batten door exuberantly exemplifies faux bois decoration.

BOTTOM RIGHT

The parlor's whitewashed wall exhibits the house's *bousillage*-between-posts construction, here with vertical timbers that were spaced unusually close. Artwork is displayed above the door opening, a common Creole practice, as well as on either side.

Suggested Reading

Bannon, Lois Elmer, Martha Yancey Carr, and Gwen Anders Edwards. *Magnolia Mound: A Louisiana River Plantation.* Gretna, La.: Pelican Publishing Company, 1984.

Brasseaux, Carl A. *French, Cajun, Creole, Houma: A Primer on Francophone Louisiana.* Baton Rouge: Louisiana State University Press, 2005.

Christovich, Mary Louise, Sally Kittredge Evans, and Roulhac Toledano. *The Esplanade Ridge.* Gretna, La.: Pelican Publishing Company, 1977.

Christovich, Mary Louise, and Roulhac Toledano. *Faubourg Tremé and the Bayou Road.* New Orleans: Pelican Publishing Company, 1980.

Edwards, Jay Dearborn, and Nicolas Kariouk. *A Creole Lexicon: Architecture, Landscape, People.* Baton Rouge: Louisiana State University Press, 2004.

Farnsworth, Jean M., and Ann M. Masson, eds. *Architecture of Colonial Louisiana: Collected Essays of Samuel Wilson, Jr., FAIA.* Lafayette, La.: Center for Louisiana Studies, University of Southwestern Louisiana, 1987.

Fricker, Jonathan, Donna Fricker, and Patricia L. Duncan. *Louisiana Architecture: A Handbook on Styles.* Lafayette, La.: Center for Louisiana Studies, University of Southwestern Louisiana, 1998.

Heard, Malcolm. *French Quarter Manual.* New Orleans: Tulane School of Architecture, 1997.

Kingsley, Karen. *Buildings of Louisiana.* New York: Oxford University Press, 2003.

Logan, William Bryant, and Vance Muse. *The Smithsonian Guide to Historic America: The Deep South.* New York: Stewart, Tabori & Chang, 1989.

Poesch, Jessie, and Barbara SoRelle Bacot, eds. *Louisiana Buildings 1720–1940: Historic American Buildings Survey.* Baton Rouge: Louisiana State University Press, 1997.

Toledano, Roulhac, Sally Kittredge Evans, and Mary Louise Christovich. *The Creole Faubourgs.* Gretna, La.: Pelican Publishing Company, 1974.

Wilson, Samuel, Jr. *The Pitot House on Bayou St. John.* New Orleans: Louisiana Landmarks Society, 1992.

Saint Francisville's Oakley Plantation, shaded by live oaks and crepe myrtle trees, dates from 1806–15.

LEFT
After Hurricane Katrina's floodwaters receded, this old rosebush on Bayou Saint John rebounded in full bloom.

Editor: Nancy E. Cohen
Designer: Robert McKee
Assistant Designer: E.Y. Lee
Production Manager: Jacquie Poirier

Library of Congress Cataloging-in-Publication Data
Gross, Steve.
Creole houses: traditional homes of Old Louisiana / photographs by Steve Gross and Sue Daley; commentary by John H. Lawrence; foreword by James Conaway.
    p. cm.
ISBN 10: 0–8109–5495–8 (hardcover with jacket)
ISBN 13: 978–0–8109–5495–3
1. Architecture, Domestic—Louisiana—Pictorial works.
2. Vernacular architecture—Louisiana—Pictorial works.
3. Creoles—Dwellings—Louisiana—Pictorial works.
I. Daley, Susan, 1953– II. Lawrence, John H. III. Title.

NA7235.L8G76 2007
728.09763—dc22
                    2006025833

Text copyright © 2007 John H. Lawrence
Photographs copyright © 2007 Steve Gross and Sue Daley

Published in 2007 by Abrams, an imprint of Harry N. Abrams, Inc. All rights reserved. No portion of this book may be reproduced, stored in a retrieval system, or transmitted in any form or by any means, mechanical, electronic, photocopying, recording, or otherwise, without written permission from the publisher.

Printed and bound in Singapore
10 9 8 7 6 5 4 3 2 1

HNA
harry n. abrams, inc.
a subsidiary of La Martinière Groupe

115 West 18th Street
New York, NY 10011
www.hnabooks.com

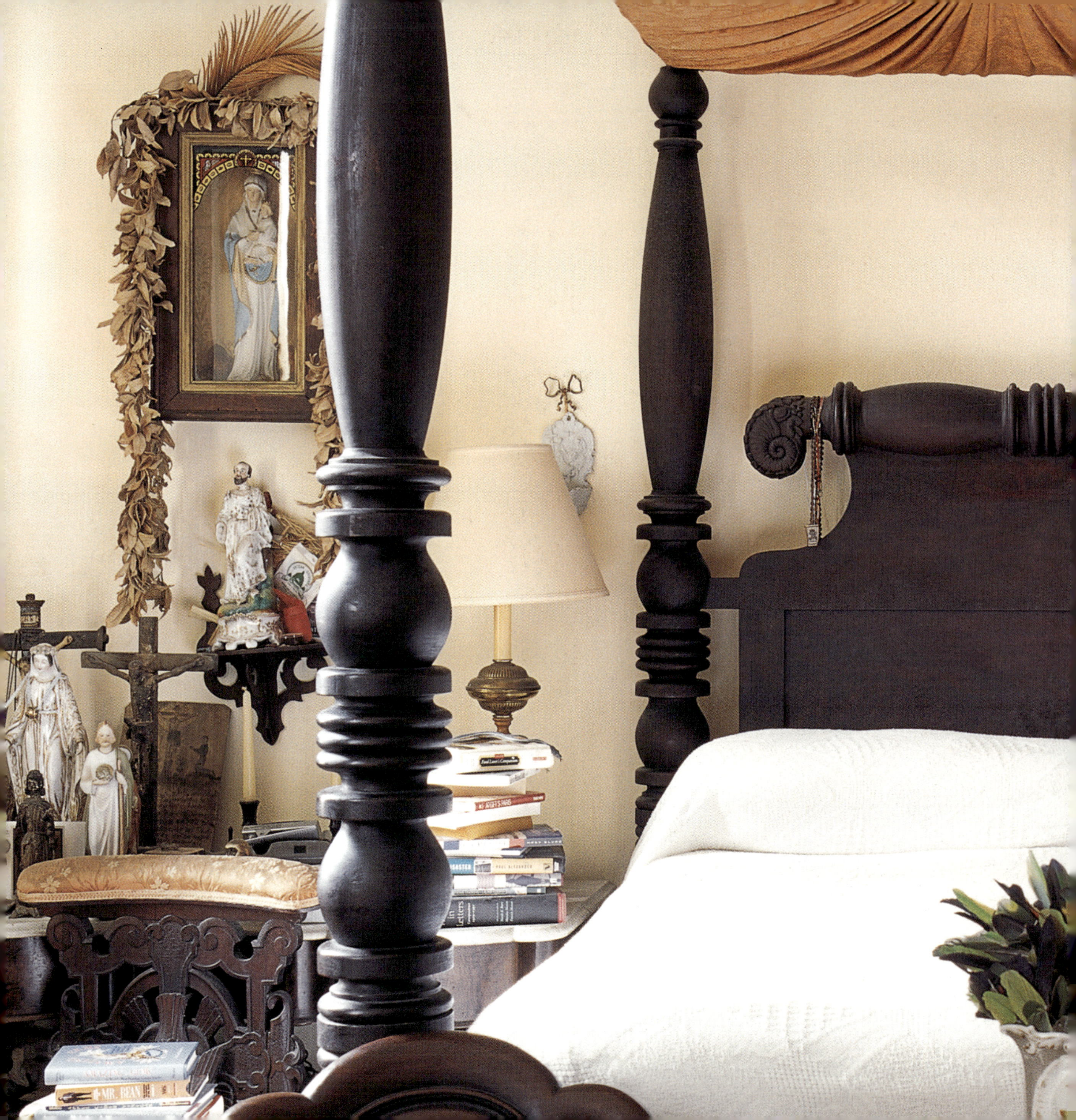
in Letters
MR. BEAN